LATIN AMERICA
IN WORLD POLITICS

OF INTEREST TO HISTORIANS

BY THE SAME AUTHOR

THE UNITED STATES AND MEXICO

―――――

BY COUNT MAX MONTGELAS

BRITISH FOREIGN POLICY
UNDER SIR EDWARD GREY

BY ALFRED FABRE-LUCE

LOCARNO: THE REALITY

BY HERMANN ONCKEN

NAPOLEON III AND THE RHINE

BY HERMAN STEGEMAN

THE MIRAGE OF VERSAILLES

LATIN AMERICA IN WORLD POLITICS

AN OUTLINE SURVEY

BY J. FRED RIPPY, A.M., Ph.D.

PROFESSOR OF HISTORY IN DUKE UNIVERSITY
ASSOCIATE MANAGING EDITOR OF "THE HISPANIC
AMERICAN HISTORICAL REVIEW"

NEW YORK · ALFRED · A · KNOPF
MCMXXVIII

327.8
R593L

TO

HERBERT E. BOLTON

AND

WILLIAM E. DODD

TEACHERS, SCHOLARS, UNFAILING

FRIENDS OF YOUNG MEN

FOREWORD

For some time students of Latin-American diplomacy have felt the need for a general survey of the relations of the southern nations of the Western Hemisphere with the leading Powers of the world. More recently this need has been emphasized in the United States by growing suspicions and antipathies which have developed along with our rapidly increasing economic and strategic interests in Latin America.

One of the most important problems confronting the United States at present is the proper ordering of its intercourse with its southern neighbors. A flood of literature bears witness to the fact that we are rapidly coming to a realization of the situation, but much that hitherto has been published is somewhat provincial, and inadequately grounded in the past relations of Hispanic America with all the great nations. In fact, researches in the field have not yet reached the point where an exhaustive work may be written on the subject of Latin-American diplomacy in its broader sense. It is now possible, however, to trace the general outlines of the story, to reveal something of the international rivalries and the crosscurrents of sentiment, and to furnish the historical setting for a fairly adequate understanding of the contemporary con.plex situation.

For four hundred years Latin America has been a not unimportant arena for the contests of world politics. It has possessed many elements of attraction for the European nations and Japan—gold, silver, diamonds, tin, copper, nitrates, iron, petroleum, rubber, superb timbers, tropical luxuries, fertile soils, succulent grasses for stock, as well as backward natives to Christianize, civilize, and exploit. At certain periods—from 1580 to 1763, from 1808 to 1867, and from 1896 to the present—the region has received much consideration and not infrequently has become almost a storm-center. During most of the time its rôle has been mainly passive, but more recently its governments and diplomats have revealed a tendency toward active participation in world affairs.

The theme, therefore, is one of large proportions, and I offer this outline survey not without some anxiety. I have emphasized the modern period and the phases which have seemed to me most

FOREWORD

important, but I know full well that there will be differences of opinion and probably just reasons for complaint regarding questions of inclusion and exclusion. I have examined the sources bearing upon many of the topics treated, but in some sections, notably in the first three chapters, I have relied largely upon the labors of others. I venture to hope that the work as now presented will not only throw some light upon current inter-American perplexities, but will also point the way and stimulate further investigation in this virgin field.

I have neither the desire nor the space to discuss fine points of terminology. "Latin America" and "Hispanic America" have seemed sufficiently similar in meaning to justify their use as synonyms. I have employed the term "world politics" in a rather free manner, but I see no good reason why it should be applied to certain international phenomena of the nineteenth and twentieth centuries and denied application to the same or analogous phenomena in the sixteenth, seventeenth, and eighteenth centuries.

In the preparation of this volume I have had the generous assistance of my graduate students as well as of the library staffs of Chicago University, Duke University, the Pan-American Union, and the Library of Congress. During the later stages of the research a Guggenheim subsidy enabled me to examine materials which otherwise might not have been available. It is a pleasure also to acknowledge the helpful suggestions of Dr. P. H. Box (Bedfordshire, England) and Professor W. W. Pierson, and the patient encouragement of my wife. But I feel most deeply indebted to the two men to whom it is my privilege to dedicate this book.

J. FRED RIPPY.

CONTENTS

MAPS

LATIN AMERICA
IN WORLD POLITICS

CHAPTER I

THE PARTITION OF THE NEW WORLD (1493–1763)

THE expansion of European culture, commerce, and dominion has been one of the most striking developments of modern history. At the close of the eleventh century the Europeans, save a few notable individuals, were superstitious, disorderly, backward, provincial peoples, who knew little of the non-European world and were even ignorant of Europe itself. But the next three hundred years, thanks to the operation of economic, intellectual, and spiritual forces even now not thoroughly understood, witnessed a marvelous transformation. By 1450 the European leaders were ready to begin a career of expansion destined to be the most remarkable in world history. The descendants of the eleventh-century Europeans soon proved themselves superior to all other peoples in bold energy, self-reliance, inventiveness, and organizing skill. They had no inferiority complex. They felt that theirs was the only religion and culture, that they were God's anointed, and that the earth was made for them.

Although these energetic peoples first directed their efforts toward the East, America was the first region of major proportions to be conquered and divided among them. In fact, the first partition took place while the New World was still unsubdued and little known. By 1494 Papal Bulls and the Treaty of Tordesillas had divided most of the Western Hemisphere and certain portions of the remainder of the earth between Portugal and Spain, the pioneers of this great expansionist movement. But this distribution was not permitted to stand. Many subsequent readjustments had to be made, and other European states came in for a share. In fact, the final partition did not occur until 1763, and certain new arrangements among the Europeans were effected even after this date.

Nevertheless, it remains a fact that before the states of Europe marked out spheres of influence in the Near and Far East, before they seized Australia, divided up the Pacific Islands, or partitioned Africa, and even before they subjected the larger part of India to their rule, they had parcelled out the Americas. Thus the New World was the first to be seized and Europeanized, the first great battleground whereon European nations fought for the privilege of gathering in resources and of civilizing, Christianizing, exploiting, and sometimes even exterminating the native peoples.

Nor did this rivalry cease with the achievement of American political independence. It has continued to the present day in Latin America, only it has been somewhat more pacific and has been participated in, and in a measure controlled by, the United States, perhaps the most European of the American nations; and it explains, in part, the hostile criticisms of our recent Latin-American policy which have appeared in the newspapers and magazines of the leading nations of Europe. Present attitudes are to some extent based upon past rivalries and animosities.

We must also turn back to former decades to understand the sensation aroused throughout Latin America by Admiral Latimer's procedure in Nicaragua. Behind this procedure and the reaction to it is a whole series of events and reactions which stretch back to the opening of last century; and the events have been interpreted and the reactions in a measure stimulated by European propaganda hostile to the United States.

The Rivalries of Spain and Portugal in South America

Christopher Columbus, while returning from the historic voyage that was destined to open the New World to European enterprise, was forced by a storm to land at the mouth of the river Tagus. Soon afterwards the great discoverer had an interview with the Portuguese monarch, who "showed that he felt disgusted and grieved because he believed . . . this discovery was made within the seas and bounds" of Portuguese claims, and "likewise because the Admiral [Columbus] . . . in the account of his affairs always went beyond the bounds of truth." Thus Columbus's discoveries threatened to provoke an international difficulty even before he returned to Spain from his first voyage. It was at this early date that America, in a passive way, entered the realm of world politics.

When the Spanish sovereigns, Ferdinand and Isabella, learned of Columbus's achievement and of Portugal's attitude, they at once appealed to the Pope, the highest international authority at that time, to confirm their rights to the new discoveries. This exalted official, who happened to be a Spaniard and a personal friend of Ferdinand, issued bulls (1493) in favor of the Catholic Majesties of Spain, to whom were forthwith assigned all of the lands, discovered and to be discovered, to the west and south of a meridian one hundred leagues to the west and the south of the Azores and the Cape Verde

Islands. The rulers and subjects of all other states were forbidden to frequent these lands and waters for trade, or for any other purpose, without the special permission of the Spanish monarchs.

The Portuguese king, thoroughly dissatisfied with this partition, is said to have planned to send a fleet across the Atlantic to make good his pretensions; but the Spanish government, in a conciliatory mood, suggested a conference for the purpose of discussing conflicting claims. Out of this suggestion grew the Treaty of Tordesillas (1494), which fixed the dividing line 370 leagues west of the Cape Verde Islands. Spain and Portugal agreed to ask the Pope to confirm this pact and the pontifical sanction was given in 1506.

Thus the first partition of America. But neither beneficiary was satisfied; the line of demarcation was never run. The whole of the New World and a part of the Old had been given to them by papal decree, yet they were not content with their portions. A few decades later the nationals of the two countries began a struggle in South America which was to last almost three centuries and lead to no definite and decisive settlement. Along all the tributaries of the Amazon and all the eastern tributaries of the La Plata, in the very heart of the South American jungle, Spanish soldiers, padres, and converted Indians engaged Portuguese miners, prospectors, and slave-hunters in an unending, bloody combat; and the independent nations of South America inherited the dispute. In general the Portuguese were victorious, but their successes were not followed by definitive treaties and the establishment of boundary monuments. This work was left to complicate the later relations between Brazil and its Spanish-American neighbors. When it was finished Brazil was several times larger than it would have been under a strict application of the treaty of 1494.

The Iberian Monopoly

While the Iberian nations were thus disputing over the partition of South America, they attempted to shut out all other Powers from the New World. A rigid monopoly was the Hispanic ideal. "Under penalty of excommunication . . . we strictly forbid all persons of whatever rank . . . , estate, degree, order, or condition to dare, without your special permit or that of your . . . heirs and successors, to go for the purpose of trade or any other reason" to the areas granted to His Catholic Majesties. In this fashion spoke the Pope near the end of the fifteenth century, and his words were supposed to have great weight. He had already issued a similar decree regarding the regions claimed by Portugal. In both instances he was only expressing the aspirations of the nations concerned. The New World was to be developed and exploited under the monopolistic principle.

The monopoly to which both Spain and Portugal aspired was threefold: navigation of the seas, trade with the natives, occupation of the land. It was destined to be maintained for a century and more, was asserted for a much longer period, and was not entirely abandoned until the colonies were lost in revolt.

Portugal began to develop its share of the New World (Brazil) in 1531. By 1600 settlements extended along the coast from Natal to São Paulo, and the civilized population had probably reached 80,000. The native tribes had been reduced to serfdom or slavery, and in many instances driven back into the interior and exterminated, the harshness of civil policy having been relieved only by the sacrificing labors and constant protests of the Jesuit missionaries. The crown had decreed from the start that trade with Brazil should be confined to Portuguese subjects and had reserved for itself the monopoly of spices and brazil-wood, as well as a share of all the minerals and precious stones which should be discovered and the right to impose duties on exports. The next two centuries witnessed a more rapid expansion and development. Settlers spread southwestward from São Paulo, northwestward from Natal, and westward into the interior of the continent. Indians continued to be exterminated and negro slaves were introduced for labor in the gold mines discovered in 1693 and in the diamond fields discovered in 1721. More than five hundred tons of pure gold and some twenty million dollars' worth of diamonds had been extracted at the close of the colonial era (1821). By this time the population had reached almost four million, half negroes, a sixth mulattoes, and the rest white and civilized Indians, while the imports and exports amounted to more than $21,000,000 annually.

The Spanish monopoly extended over a larger area of the New World and was organized with greater care. By 1600 Spain had planted colonies in the most important of the West Indies and on the mainland from New Mexico and Florida to the Rio de la Plata and Chile, while Spanish explorers had carried their national flag along the principal river systems and all the coast lines of the Americas as far north as Oregon and Nova Scotia. Shortly before this time the civilized population of Spanish America was estimated at a little less than six million, of which about five million were subdued Indians, two hundred thousand Spaniards, and the rest negro slaves and mixed breeds. Soon afterwards the value of the minerals annually extracted from the mines of Mexico and Peru amounted to some $15,000,000. Millions more had been plundered from the treasures of the native semi-civilized races. Add to these sums the precious stones, hides, sugar, forest products, and other commodities produced in abundance; take into account the American market for finished products, and you have a fairly accurate conception of the treasure house which Spain possessed in the New World at the opening of the seventeenth century. Before 1800 the total annual trade of Spanish America had reached $140,000,000, and the civilized population—Indian, mixed, white, and black—amounted to about 16,000,000.

With reference to these vast treasures and markets Spain had adopted from the outset the policy of a closed door. Commercial relations with the New World were subjected to strict supervision. Inside of the Spanish peninsula, the only ports qualified for the trade were Cádiz and Seville, and outside, only the Canary Islands. In general only Spaniards were permitted to engage in this commerce: a rigid system of registration was set up in order to eliminate foreigners, and emigration to America was subjected to careful scrutiny. The difficult task of applying this restrictive policy was assigned to the House of Trade, which "saw to the execution of all the laws and ordinances relating to trade and navigation with America," and to the navy, which was employed to protect Spanish commerce from pirates and to seize and punish all interlopers.

The Breakdown of the Monopoly

Such were the possessions of Spain and Portugal and such their exclusive ideals with reference to them. According to their view, only the north Atlantic was open to the explorers, merchants, conquerors, and colonizers of the remainder of Europe. That this pretension could be enforced indefinitely, was hardly to be expected; that it was effectively upheld for almost a century, was due to the terrors of unfamiliar seas, the lingering influence of the Pope, and the prestige of the Iberian nations. The monopoly was eventually broken by the combined assaults of France, England, and the Dutch Netherlands. Sometimes the blows were delivered by private enterprise acting either independently or else in secret coöperation with the governments of these states; sometimes they came directly from the governments themselves.

To complete the breakdown in all of its phases almost two hundred years were required. First the navigation, then the trade, and finally the territorial monopoly was wrested from the hands of Spain and Portugal. The first was shattered before 1600, the second and third by 1682. French corsairs, British seadogs—such as Hawkins and Drake—, and Dutch fighting sailors broke the naval strength of Spain by 1588; and this meant that of Portugal as well, for the two Powers were then united under a single crown. Many of these bold seamen combined the pursuits of piracy and smuggling, making great inroads upon Spanish trade. After the destruction of the Armada this illicit traffic could proceed with greater freedom. Its profits corrupted revenue and port officials of mother-countries and colonies alike. The crushing of Spanish naval power likewise made it possible for the rival nations to begin territorial occupations.

The successful colonization of England, France, and the Dutch Netherlands in the New World began soon after 1600. With the exception of Dutch and French assaults upon Brazil and the seizure of Jamaica by the British (1655), these rival Powers confined their seizures during most of the seventeenth century to remote and unoccupied areas. By 1660 the Dutch had established themselves in northern Brazil, Guiana, the Lesser Antilles, and along the Hudson River. Four years later they lost all of their New World possessions save Guiana and a few small islands in the West Indies. The decline of the Dutch republic was almost as sudden as its rise. It quickly descended to the status of a third-rate Power. Meanwhile the English were taking possession of the Bermudas, a number of the West Indies, the Atlantic coast from Maine to the Carolinas, and the Hudson Bay region, and were planting a few settlements in Guiana and Central America (Belize); and the French, having established themselves in Acadia, the Lesser Antilles, the St. Lawrence valley, and Guiana, were preparing to seize a portion of the island of Haiti and to take permanent possession of the Great Lakes region and the Mississippi valley.

Thus Spain's territorial and navigation pretensions had given way before the onslaught, but Brazil still remained intact. In like manner the trade monopoly of both powers crumbled. Between 1641 and 1669 Portugal signed treaties with the rival Powers, ceding the privilege of trading with Brazil through the mother-country. This shielded the colony from violence, but it meant the end of the closed door. According to an English estimate of about the year 1700, "half of the Brazil trade" was "in English hands, the remainder being carried on by France and Holland." Spain, however, was more stubborn. In 1648 she acknowledged the right of the Dutch Netherlands to sail to and acquire territory in the West Indies, but not the right to trade with the Spanish possessions there. Similar concessions were made to England and France a few years later, but the pretension to commercial monopoly was cherished until the close of the colonial era.

To be thus persistent was but to invite destruction. Perhaps it were better to have legalized by treaty what could not have been prevented by sheer force. In this fashion the Spanish coasts might have been spared the bloody and destructive raids of the Buccaneers, and the corruption of the officials who had been appointed to administer the commercial system might have been avoided. In the end the monopoly had to go. The fleet which arrived at Cádiz from America in 1682 brought 22,809,000 pesos (dollars), of which thirteen millions went to England, France, Holland, and Genoa. And this does not include the direct trade with the ports of Spanish America carried on by smugglers! Spain probably was not supplying more than a tenth of the commodities consumed by her American colonies. The Iberian trade monopoly had collapsed.

The Great Struggle for Commerce and Empire

If the European rivals of Spain and Portugal had confined their efforts in America until near the close of the seventeenth century mainly to the acquisition of trade and the seizure of regions not yet occupied by a Christian nation, they exercised no such moderation during subsequent decades. The eighteenth century was to witness direct attacks upon settled areas and a struggle for the redistribution of the commerce and territory of the Americas. The nations which had carried on the long attack against Spain and Portugal proceeded, once they had established colonies of their own, to apply similar systems of exclusion. If they had not done so, if all of the colonizing Powers had agreed upon a policy approximating free trade, the history of the Western Hemisphere might have been very different. But monopolistic ideas are too deeply imbedded in human nature, and were too widely accepted by the pseudo-statesmen of the time, to permit of such a change. Hence the opening years of the eighteenth century found these Powers dissatisfied with their domains and eager for a larger share of American commerce. Every European dispute was looked upon as an occasion for the modification of transatlantic holdings. Each European war had profound reverberations overseas.

Portugal and the Protestant Netherlands did not play an important rôle in this era. England, France, and Spain were the leading rivals in the great contest. Whenever the Portuguese and the Dutch participated, they usually did so as the satellites of Great Britain. This advantage enjoyed by Britain was in a measure balanced by the growing harmony between France and Spain. In its later phases the struggle virtually became one between England and the two branches of the Bourbon family for the possession of the New World.

The bounds set for this chapter prevent a narration of the details of this long struggle. The fact can only be noted here that it continued intermittently for nearly seventy-five years (1689–1763), was bloody and cruel, involved at one time and another a war zone which extended from Hudson's Bay to the basin of the La Plata, ended in deep humiliation for the Bourbons—especially those of France—, and to all appearances brought great advantages to England.

Except for certain fishing rights on the Newfoundland banks and two islands off the northeastern coast, a few of the small islands of the West Indies group, and a portion of Guiana, France was expelled from the Americas and they were left in the hands of Spain, Portugal, and England. Barring Russian acquisitions during the next few decades in the Aleutian Islands and in Alaska, and the small gains to be made by England on the Pacific slope, in Central America, and south of the Orinoco, the partition of the Americas, so far as the European Powers were concerned, was now about complete.

But in 1763 these Powers little realized the finality of the partition stipulated by the terms of the Treaty of Paris. France and Spain were particularly grieved and they were to give ample evidence of their dissatisfaction in the near future. England, on the other hand, was triumphant. She now confronted Spain along the Mississippi River from mouth to source (except the Isle of Orleans). Beyond the Great Lakes she reigned supreme and hardy pioneers were advancing the British flag toward the Pacific. Moreover, Great Britain held an enviable position in American commerce. "Shortly before 1740 the English alone are said to have had as much share in the Spanish colonial trade in ways prohibited as the Spaniards themselves had in authorized ways." A report laid before Pitt about 1760 estimated that England's portion of a total Spanish-American export trade, amounting to the value of 3,320,000 pounds sterling, was some 1,090,000 pounds. But in less than twenty years Britain's triumph was to be changed into deep humiliation.[1]

---

[1] This introductory survey is based mainly on the following works:

Frances Davenport, *European Treaties bearing on the History of the United States* . . . (1917).

E. G. Bourne, *Spain in America* (1907).

C. H. Haring, *Trade and Navigation between Spain and the Indies* . . . (1918). *Buccaneers in the West Indies* . . . (1916).

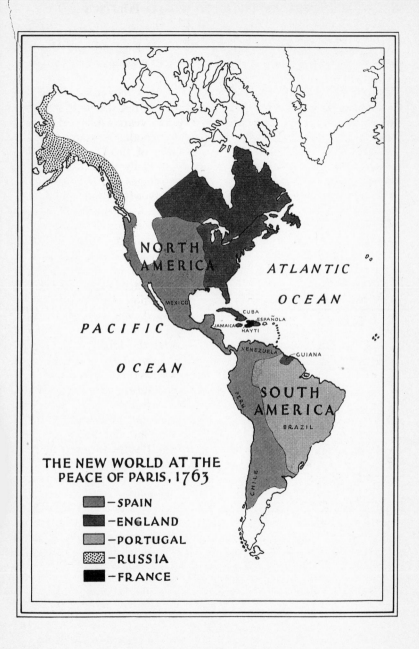

NORTH
AMERICA

ATLANTIC

OCEAN

PACIFIC

OCEAN

MEXICO

CUBA
ESPAÑOLA
JAMAICA
HAYTI

VENEZUELA
GUIANA

SOUTH
AMERICA

PERU

BRAZIL

CHILE

**THE NEW WORLD AT THE
PEACE OF PARIS, 1763**

—SPAIN

—ENGLAND

—PORTUGAL

—RUSSIA

—FRANCE

A. G. Keller, *Colonization* (1908).

Herbert E. Bolton and Thomas M. Marshall, *The Colonization of North America* (1921).

H. G. James, *Brazil after a Century of Independence* (1925).

Wilhelm Roscher, *The Spanish Colonial System* (H. E. Bourne, ed.).

William Wood, *Elizabethan Sea-Dogs* (1921).

CHAPTER II

THE BIRTH OF A NEW RIVAL: THE CONTEST FOR THE MISSISSIPPI BASIN AND THE FLORIDAS

It is but a commonplace to assert that the revolt of the Thirteen Colonies of England was the first successful colonial revolution in American history and one of the few completely successful colonial uprisings of modern times. Its outcome, as is well known, was determined largely by the assistance of France and Spain, granted mainly because of the fears and ancient grudges which they harbored with reference to England.

The British did not look upon the gains of 1763, great as they were, as final. Political, military, and economic successes of previous decades spoke promisingly of rewards to be obtained by further effort. Every English settlement in America was a center of expanding activity; every English settler dreamed of a step beyond. During the next decade British claims were extended into the Far Northwest, around Honduras Bay, and in Mosquitia and the Falkland Islands. British merchants continued to insist upon introducing their commodities into Spanish-American markets in violation of treaty stipulations.

The Spanish monarch, in spite of preoccupation with ambitions of conquering Portugal, regaining Gibraltar, and consolidating the Iberian Peninsula under his single rule, undertook a reorganization of his American empire. He sent to America his ablest administrators, tightened up his commercial regulations, and pushed his claims into California and Oregon in order to forestall the British and Russians on the Pacific slope.[1]

Frenchmen nursed their wounds, pined over their colonial misfortunes, dreamed of revenge and the recovery of their lost rôle in Europe, and awaited their opportunity. Their influence in Spain was never stronger. Perhaps it could be used to regain their ancient position in the Old World and recoup their losses in the New.

[1] Vera L. Brown, "Anglo-Spanish Relations . . . (1763-1774)," in *The Hisp. Amer. Historical Rev.*, V (1922), 474.

English America's Need, France and Spain's Opportunity

While France and Spain were thus brooding over former injuries and planning for the future, the rebellion of the Thirteen Colonies broke out. The insurgent movement aroused great interest in both nations. Perhaps here was an opportunity for France to weaken England, save the remnant of her colonies in America, regain Canada and Louisiana, and recover her lost position on the Continent. At any rate some of these ends might be accomplished. Perhaps here, too, was a chance for Spain to enfeeble a lusty rival, regain the Floridas, seize the eastern half of the great Mississippi basin, and secure a frontier which would serve at once as a bulwark against Anglo-Saxon expansion and as a base for the enforcement of trade regulations and the domination of the Gulf of Mexico. To both Powers it was an inviting prospect, but the situation was not without its perplexities.

Would the revolting colonies appeal for aid? Experiences of the previous seventy-five years had not impressed them with the advantages of a European connection. For all this time they had borne something of the brunt of England's struggle for commerce and empire in America, and their rewards had not been important. During the war which closed in 1748 the men of New England had participated in the capture of Porto Bello and died of disease under the walls of Cartagena. They had also taken a brilliant part in the siege of Louisburg. "Here they had landed cannon on a lea shore when the great waves pounded to pieces their boats and when men wading breast high were crushed by the weight of iron. Harnessed two and three hundred to a gun, they had dragged the pieces one after the other over the rocks and through bog and slime, and had then served them in the open under the fire of the enemy. . . . The graves of nearly a thousand of them lay on the bleak point outside the wall." [2] They had not been pleased with the treatment the mother country had accorded them. There had been murmurings before the gates of Cartagena and there was resentment at the return of Louisburg to the French at the close of the war. "A spirit of discontent went abroad and, after this sacrifice of colonial interests, never wholly died out." The colonies had played an even larger rôle in the war which preceded the treaty of 1763 and during its course they had been offended by British snobbery and impressed by their own prowess. And now the British government, struggling under the weight of an enormous debt in-

[2] George M. Wrong, *The Conquest of New France* (1921), p. 94.

curred by these long colonial struggles, decided to shift a portion of this debt, as well as a part of the expenses of future defense, to the colonies. This determination and the method of carrying it out furnished the immediate cause of the American Revolution.

The experience of the Colonies therefore was not one which counseled the continuation of old connections or the establishment of new ones, and the insurgent leaders moved with great caution. Arms, money, and supplies were to be asked of the European rivals of England, but nothing more than commercial concessions was to be offered in return. No alliances were to be made. It was not until the situation of the colonists became desperate, not until they had been frightened by the prospect of England's obtaining European assistance to quell them, that they finally overcame their scruples against the formation of connections with France and Spain. They acted with great hesitation and abandoned their first resolution under duress.[3]

The Reluctant Support of France and Spain

Nor was it easy for the French and Spanish governments to reach a decision to support a revolt in England's colonies. Envious of England and eager to secure colonial and international advantages for themselves, they officiated at the birth and administered to the infancy of the new nation; but they had their apprehensions. They half-suspected that the child might belong to a giant race and might some day turn upon its sponsors. In 1775 the French Foreign Minister predicted that the Americans would "immediately set about forming a great marine" and ere long would have such fleets "as would be an overmatch for the whole naval power of Europe could it be united against them. . . . In the end they would not leave a foot of that hemisphere in the possession of any European power." Three years later he pointed out the danger that the United States, once independent, would be seized with a desire to conquer the Floridas, Louisiana, and Mexico, in order to dominate all the approaches to the sea. Such fears were general in France and they were also felt in Spain. In 1777 a member of the Spanish Royal Council contended that Spain should be "the last country in all Europe to recognize *any* sovereign and independent state in North America." Spain must not be left alone to confront a warlike Power "formidable on account of the size of its population and the ratio of increase thereof" and unrestrained by any balance of power. He

[3] *Cf.* J. Fred Rippy and Angie Debo, *The Historical Background of the American Policy of Isolation* (1924).

predicted, moreover, that the breach between England and her former colonies would one day be closed; "the English and the American powers would still be of one nation, one character, and one religion, and would so form their treaties and compacts as to obtain the objects they both desire." Confronted with such a combination, Mexico would surely be lost. Another high official of Spain expressed anxiety respecting the possible influence of the example of American independence upon the Spanish colonies, and Count Aranda predicted (1783) that the American pigmy would become a giant and, forgetting the benefits received from France and Spain, would think only of self-aggrandizement at their expense.[4]

These apprehensions led to the discussion of policies by no means friendly to the struggling colonies. First the suggestion was made that it would be in the interest of the Bourbon kingdoms to prolong the struggle until both belligerents had been exhausted. Later it was advised that seeds of jealousy should be sown between the two branches of the Anglo-Saxon family; that Great Britain should be allowed to retain Canada and Nova Scotia; that the United States should be hemmed in between the Atlantic and the Alleghenies, and the West turned into a buffer state.

It was the knowledge that such views as these were being harbored that led the commissioners of the United States to break the American pledge to France and attempt to negotiate a separate treaty with England. When they turned to the British diplomats they found them quite willing to cede to the United States the area between the Mississippi River and the eastern mountains. European jealousies had thus conferred double benefits upon the new nation.

Inklings of Manifest Destiny

Nor can one read the forebodings of French and Spanish statesmen without being impressed with their prophetic ring. The United States was indeed quickly to become a menace to the European Powers in America. The people of the new nation soon developed a magnificent notion of their future career. In fact an inkling of this may be found in the *Works* of John Adams as early as 1755, when he predicted that "the great seat of empire" might some day be transferred "into America." "If we can remove the turbulent Gallics [French]," he went on to say, "our people, according to exactest computations, will in another century become more numerous than

---

[4] E. S. Corwin, *French Policy and the American Alliance* (1916), pp. 67-68, *passim*.

England itself. Should this be the case, since we have . . . all the
naval stores of the nation in our hands, it will be easy to obtain
the mastery of the seas; and then the united force of Europe will
not be able to subdue us." [5] In the darkest of the Revolutionary
days Benjamin Franklin declared that Britain should cede the
provinces and colonies of "Quebec, St. Johns, Nova Scotia, Ber-
muda, East and West Florida, and the Bahama Islands, with all
their adjoining and intermediate territories now claimed by her . . .
It is absolutely necessary for us to have them for our own security." [6]
On January 25, 1786, Thomas Jefferson wrote from Paris to his
Virginia neighbor: "Our confederacy must be viewed as the nest
from which all America, north and south, is to be peopled. We
should take care . . . not to think it for the interests of that great
continent to press too soon on the Spaniards. Those countries cannot be in better hands. My fear is that they are too feeble to hold
them till our population can be sufficiently advanced to gain it
from them piece by piece." [7]

Thus early appeared the first glimmerings of manifest destiny.
Its dawn was to be hastened by the gathering momentum of the
westward movement and the irritating intrigues of European agents
in the great Mississippi valley. Before long it was to hurl the
American frontiersmen against Spain, despoiling her of an empire,
and send them out with less success to confront the British in
Canada and Oregon. Moreover, the nation which the European
diplomatists, in a fit of self-seeking and envy, had helped to bring
into existence was soon to adopt a policy of exclusion that more
and more interdicted their participation in the political affairs of
the New World and even aroused anxiety regarding the safety of
their commerce.

Continuation of the Rivalries in the Mississippi Valley and the Floridas, 1783-1819

The treaty of 1783 was followed by four decades of rivalry, in
which the United States participated, for the control of the Mississippi valley and the north coast of the Gulf of Mexico. Although
this agreement had left these areas in the hands of the United States
and Spain, none of the Powers considered the settlement final.

Whether viewed from the standpoint of strategy, or of naviga-

[5] As quoted in *ibid.,* pp. 218, note, 219, note.
[6] *Writings* (Smythe ed.) VI, 352–353.
[7] *Works* (National ed.), VI, 75.

bility, or of the fertility of the region it drains, the Mississippi is one of the world's greatest river systems. The importance of the location and natural resources of the Floridas requires no comment. Both regions were prizes well worth a contest.

The policies of the rivals were characterized by differing degrees of vigor. That of Spain was for the most part defensive, or aggressive-defensive. If at times the Spanish government sought to control the region between the left bank of the Mississippi and the Alleghenies, it did so mainly from fear of the impact of the frontiersmen of the United States upon its territory and commercial monopoly. The French government, moved, on the other hand, by an anxiety to recover its lost colonies, was consistently aggressive in intent until 1803, and remained a factor to be reckoned with throughout the period. Due to the proximity of the areas in dispute and the vigor of its frontier population, the United States was almost from the outset to put forth a formidable effort. For the same reason Britain and British subjects were to play an important part in the contest, although officially Great Britain was perhaps not as ambitious to acquire the regions as were the others.

That the United States finally emerged victorious was due more to the exigencies of European politics than to the superior prowess of American citizens and diplomats. Throughout this epoch, as in 1775–1783, the official circles of Europe appeared to agree in the conviction that the struggling young nation across the Atlantic constituted a menace to their colonial possessions and even to the European system of government itself. Their consistent impulse was to limit its growth and confine its energies. But once more, as during the Revolution, the shifting currents of international politics forced them to consider measures which tended to augment the strength of the very nation whose power they feared.

If the three European Powers, or even France and England, could have reached an understanding, particularly in the early years when the federal government of the United States was in the experimental stage, they might have succeeded in permanently fettering the growth of the new nation; for, once firmly established in the great basin of the Mississippi and in the Floridas, they could have defied all American attempts to dislodge them and forced the United States to enter the European concerts. But they were unable to do so, and discords extending through these early critical years thus saved the Americas from the later fate of Asia and Africa and insured their independent and somewhat isolated development.

Except for a few settlements in Kentucky and Tennessee, the vast region extending from the Alleghenies to the Mississippi and from the Great Lakes to Florida was in the possession of powerful Indian confederacies in 1783. During the next decade thousands of Anglo-Americans were to pour through the mountain passes, but only a few had found their way into the West when the United States first entered upon its independent career. Moreover, England and Spain were resolved to control the native races and either to prevent the frontiersmen of the United States from settling in this large area or else to steal away their loyalty when they came. The Frenchmen, still repining over the loss of Louisiana and Canada, were closely watching developments.

When George Washington took charge of the new government, in 1789, the international position of the republic which he had helped to found was far from satisfactory. "On either flank were powerful Indian confederacies, controlled respectively by England and Spain, threatening our advance." France was eager for an opportunity to recover her former possessions. The United States had been "unable to obtain for the inhabitants of the Mississippi Valley the navigation of their great river, and it continually opposed their attempts to make war on the Indians . . . These conditions constituted a grave menace to the future control of the interior of the Union. . . . In these early days an independent confederacy [in the West] under the protection of some European flag was entirely within the realm of possibility. . . ."[8]

Europe's Turmoils, America's Opportunity

Just at this critical juncture, however, disturbances occurred in Europe which were destined in a few years to throw the Mississippi basin into America's lap and to render the acquisition of the Floridas relatively easy. A few months after Washington became the chief executive of the new national government in the United States, the French Revolution broke out. The French monarch, in desperate need of funds partly because of expenditures occasioned by aid given the American revolt, had convened the Estates General for the first time in almost two centuries. Inspired by America's democratic example and exasperated by ancient grievances, the leaders in this assembly took the reins in their hands. Four years later the king and queen were executed and the French nation entered upon a career of radicalism and aggression which kept Europe in turmoil for more than twenty years.

These disturbances brought first perils and then benefits to the

[8] F. J. Turner, "The Diplomatic Contest for the Mississippi Valley," in *Atlantic Monthly*, XCIII (1904), 680.

United States. In the beginning there was danger that the United States would be involved on the one side or the other. The Nootka Sound crisis (1790) between Spain and England threatened to draw the United States into the maelstrom. France tried to persuade her recent ally to come to her support against the European coalition which was formed against her, but the United States managed to keep out of the contest. Soon afterwards European rivalries played directly into America's hands. In 1794 Britain agreed to a treaty which pledged her to abandon the posts illegally held south of the Great Lakes and greatly raised the prestige of the United States. The European situation had been responsible for this conciliatory step. The British government "stood confronted with all the dangers of a revival of the old Armed Neutrality" of the Baltic States "at a time when the First Coalition" against France "was giving indications of collapse." Further antagonism in the Northwest was unwise. News of this settlement between England and the United States had great influence upon negotiations then in progress with Spain. In July, 1795, the Spanish Prime Minister, Godoy, had signed a peace with France which was expected to bring down upon Spain the wrath of England. This was followed immediately by negotiations looking toward a Franco-Spanish alliance. France demanded, among other things, the cession of Santo Domingo and Louisiana. Godoy yielded the former but was reluctant to give up the latter. "Threatened thus with isolation, and confronted by the prospect of war with England, he was disposed to conciliate the United States, lest she join England and take Louisiana by force." For some time the United States had been trying in vain to reach an agreement with Spain regarding the West, but now Godoy was found eager to meet the American terms. The right to navigate the Mississippi and deposit goods at New Orleans was granted, and the Florida posts north of the thirty-first parallel were ceded.[9]

These treaties raised the prestige of the United States in all sections and particularly in the West. Their general tendency was to develop the loyalty of the western settlers and render them immune from European intrigue. Impressive evidence of this fact was given two years later in the failure of the Blount Conspiracy, which might have placed Louisiana and Florida in the hands of England. Loyal frontiersmen came forward to expose the plot and it ended in a miserable fiasco. Europe's difficulties had proved America's salvation.

But other dangers lay just ahead. For the next decade the struggle

[9] Samuel F. Bemis, *The Jay Treaty* (1923), pp. 221–229;—*Pinckney's Treaty*, (1926).

for the control of the Mississippi basin and the Floridas narrowed down mainly to a contest between the United States and the Franco-Spanish alliance, formed in spite of Spain's refusal to retrocede her share of Louisiana, with Spain swinging more and more into the orbit of France. French motives continued to be a desire to find means of injuring England, to mend their colonial fortunes, and to limit the growth of the United States and render it more subservient to French policy.

All this is made clear by official correspondence of 1796 and 1798. Instructions given to the agent of the French Directorate sent to Madrid in the spring of 1796 referred to the Anglo-Saxon peril in America. They pointed out that American frontiersmen were pouring rapidly into Kentucky and Tennessee and that the United States, acting in concert with Britain, "would soon give the reins to those fierce inhabitants of the West." This would mean the invasion of Louisiana and ultimately the conquest of Mexico and of all North America. Only France, in possession of Louisiana and in alliance with Spain, could oppose a counterpoise to this menace. France could hold the province "beyond insult by Great Britain," and its possession would furnish a base for intrigue with the western settlers and a means of forcing the United States into "the line of duty by fear of the dismemberment which we can bring about." In 1798 the notorious Talleyrand advanced a similar argument in the hope of persuading Spain to cede both Louisiana and the Floridas. "There are no other means," wrote Talleyrand in his instructions to the French minister in Spain, "of putting an end to the ambitions of the Americans than that of shutting them up within the limits which nature seems to have traced for them [namely, the Atlantic and the Alleghenies]; but Spain is not in a condition to do this work alone . . . Let the court of Madrid cede these districts to France, and from that moment the power of America is bounded by the limits which may suit the interests and the tranquillity of France and Spain to assign her. The French republic, mistress of these two provinces, will be a wall of brass forever impenetrable to the combined efforts of England and America."[10]

When Napoleon eventually succeeded in wringing Louisiana, but not the Floridas, from the reluctant hands of Spain (1800), he was merely proceeding along the lines traced by his predecessors. The American threat of an English alliance, European complications too familiar to narrate at this point, and unanticipated difficulties

[10] *Cf.* Turner, "The Policy of France toward the Mississippi Valley . . . ," in *The Amer. Historical Review*, X (January, 1905), 268 ff.

in Haiti, caused a sudden change in his policy. He sold the entire province to the United States.

This acquisition, like the treaties of 1794 and 1795, added much to the prestige of the United States. "From that cession," says Professor Turner, "dates the emancipation of North America from the state systems of Europe, and the rise of the United States into a world power, the arbiter of America." [11]

Against this important extension of territory the British diplomats raised no objection. They were so glad to see it taken from the hands of France that they had no mind to protest. The expulsion of France from North America now seemed final. There would be no return to French dreams of the last century. His Britannic Majesty received the intelligence "with pleasure." This did not mean, however, that Britain would continue to approve the expansion of the United States.

The Acquisition of the Floridas

The United States perhaps had not been familiar with every detail of the numerous intrigues which for two decades had kept the frontier in ferment and threatened the very security of the nation, but enough had been known to arouse apprehension with reference to Europe and European ambitions in America. The most obvious way to remove the danger would be to eliminate Europe from the Gulf Coast and the entire basin of the Mississippi. Moreover, the diplomatic victories of 1794–1795 and 1803—though Americans could justly claim very little credit for them—increased the pride and aggressiveness of American diplomats and frontiersmen alike.[12] Accordingly, during the next sixteen years both are found working, albeit hardly in collusion, for the acquisition of the Floridas and the maximum limits of Louisiana to the west.

The story of the diplomatic bickerings and bargainings need not be related in detail. It will be sufficient to note that Spain, after a futile protest against the occupation of the main centers of the province of Louisiana, attempted to reduce it to the smallest possible area, and that the United States, taking the position—with little his-

[11] Turner, "The Diplomatic Contest for the Mississippi Valley," *loc. cit.,* p. 817.

[12] Ample support for the assertions contained in the paragraph to this point may be gleaned from the notes to Turner, "The Policy of France toward the Mississippi Valley . . .;" from Marshall, *The Western Boundary of the Louisiana Purchase* (1914), pp. 9 ff.; and from Cox, *The West Florida Controversy* (1918), Chs. I–III.

torical evidence to support it [13]—that the region extended from the
Perdido on the east to the Rio Grande on the west, approached both
Spain and her ally, France, in a vain endeavor to secure the coveted
districts. At the beginning of the Napoleonic régime in Spain negotiations were dropped, not to be resumed until after Waterloo.

Meanwhile the American frontiersmen had become consciously
or unconsciously the agents of a more or less pacific penetration the
effectiveness of which Jefferson had foreseen but had done little
to promote. Indeed promotion was unnecessary. The westward-
moving emigrant obeyed an uncontrollable impulse. Bribery of his
reputed leaders to induce them to hold him in check proved unavail-
ing. Unfriendly declamations of Spanish officials could not "stay his
course. Time and the river currents were all in his favor. The hostile
savage, secretly abetted by a few scattered Spanish garrisons, could
not terrorize him. Virgin soil . . . had for him an irresistible attraction." [14] Hatred for the Spaniard, who often interfered with the
transportation of his tobacco, timber, wheat, and other commodities
to profitable markets and sometimes set the Indians to burn his
home and kill his family, soon became as natural as hatred for the
Indian himself. "Against Indians and Spaniards the western settler
held loose notions of law; his settled purpose was to drive both
races from the country and to take their lands." [15]

American traders and adventurers soon made their way into Texas
and New Mexico, where they aroused alarm and hostility and sometimes participated in the incipient revolutionary movements against
the royal authority of Spain; but the time for effective work in this
region had not yet arrived.[16] It was in the Floridas that their efforts
came to the earliest fruition. At Bayou Sara and Baton Rouge,
where they constituted nine-tenths of the population, they initiated
a "movement for self-government" in the summer of 1810. At first
they declared their loyalty to Ferdinand VII and their undying hostility to Napoleon, but by the latter part of September they had
defied Spanish authority and proclaimed the independence of West
Florida. They then appealed to the government at Washington to
annex the province to the American Union. In December Governor
Clairborne of Mississippi Territory, following out instructions from

---

[13] For the eastern boundary of Spanish Texas, see Bolton, *Texas in the Middle Eighteenth Century* (1915). Henry Adams, though in error with reference to
the western boundary of Louisiana, gives a good discussion of its eastern boundary (*History of the United States* [1889], II, 5 ff.). See also Cox, *op. cit.,* Ch. I.

[14] Cox, *op. cit.,* pp. 665–666.

[15] Henry Adams, *op. cit.,* I, 339.

[16] See Marshall, *op. cit.,* Chs. I–II and authorities cited.

President Madison, occupied the region between the Mississippi and the Pearl Rivers. American settlers and filibusters soon afterwards attempted to repeat the procedure in the vicinity of Mobile and in East Florida. The effort failed at Mobile, but American operations in East Florida would have been crowned with success had it not been for the interference of Madison and the United States Congress. By April, 1813, however, the whole of West Florida had been occupied and placed under the civil and military jurisdiction of the United States, the aggressiveness of the federal government having been due in large measure to the demands of the western members of Congress and the fear that Great Britain, now the ally of Spain and the common enemy of frontiersmen and Easterners alike, would take possession of the region. Five years later General Andrew Jackson, a product of the frontier and with an army made up mainly of frontiersmen, invaded and took possession of East Florida. Thereupon the Spanish government, perceiving that further resistance would prove futile and already greatly alarmed regarding the security of New Spain and other Spanish possessions now in revolt, sacrificed the Floridas and the claims north of the forty-second parallel in order to hold the Americans at the Sabine.[17] The western settler had demonstrated his power in a fashion not soon to be forgotten by Spain and the Spanish Americans.

Britain's Reaction

Nor did Great Britain view the acquisition of this north coast of the Gulf with friendly complacency. The British minister at Washington had protested against the seizures of the United States in 1810 and 1811.[18] Castlereagh had pronounced an irritated warning in 1816, when, after having declared that his government did not covet the region, he went on to exhort: "Do you only observe the same moderation. If we shall find you hereafter pursuing a system of encroachment upon your neighbors, what we might do *defensively* is another consideration." [19] The movements of Englishmen on Amelia Island and in Florida may have been in part an expression of this jealousy of the expansion of the United States and of the hope that their operations might win the approval of the British government.

[17] Cox, *op. cit., passim;* Fuller, *The Purchase of Florida* (1910); Platt, *Expansionists of 1812* (1924).

[18] Cox, *op. cit.,* p. 523, *passim.*

[19] Conversation with J. Q. Adams, as reported by Adams to Monroe in despatch of Feb. 8, 1816. Adams, *Writings,* V, 502.

The resentment of the British at the final acquisition of Florida by their American kinsmen is demonstrated by a leading article in the London *Times*. Having expressed the view that all Christian nations should desire the termination of the struggle between Spain and her colonies, the writer continued as follows:

"It cannot be said that America [the United States] has not an interest in the conclusion of these fatal troubles; at least she has shown that she has been able to sack no small advantage from their continuance and that to our great and lasting detriment. Old Spain having rejected arbitration may carry on the contest more feebly and more feebly still, till at last she may concede all her trans-Atlantic possessions to America, one after another, simply because she herself is unable to reduce them, and because America finds their occupation necessary for the tranquillity of her contiguous provinces.

". . . Are we to stand by and suffer a procedure which in its sinister effect upon us will have all the consequences of collusion between Old Spain and the United States? Are we to refrain from intercourse with the insurgent provinces of South America (simply because the Spanish Government at home calls itself at war with them) till they drop at last exhausted into the hands of our great commercial rival? The court of Madrid will be pleased to observe that America has been paid for her forbearance. If she has hitherto abstained from acknowledging the trans-Atlantic states, she has had her price for it, in the cession by Old Spain of certain wealthy provinces. Far indeed from Great Britain be such conduct as this! Far removed from us be the baseness of extorting a bribe from the impotence of the old government in order to induce us to disown the rising liberties of the new ones! No; let us remember that we are England still; that we have an established name for honor and integrity, as well as for valor and enterprise, among the nations of the world; and that, if we have hitherto abstained from interfering in the sanguinary troubles which desolate the fields and towns of New Spain, it has been from dignity and moderation, not from the sordid hope of gain. We have not hovered like the vulture over the contending armies till we could seize a breathless carcass for our prey.

". . . We believe it is some time since America proposed to us to acknowledge the government of Buenos Aires. This is an important fact; and so far the conduct of America appeared to be candid and friendly to England. We know not whether her secret objects might be to quicken Spain in her bargain about the Floridas.

However, the result is such as we have seen. America has *not* acknowledged any of the insurrectionary states as she proposed to us; and she has accepted a valuable cession from the court of Madrid. Hence, therefore, commences a fresh epoch in the war. Shall we suffer this or any similar traffic to succeed? We do not use the language of menace; there is no occasion to go to war; but shall we allow America to reap first the advantage of many valuable possessions from Old Spain as the price of withholding her acknowledgment of the patriot governments; and then shall we suffer her to insure the gratitude of those patriot governments by being still the first to treat with them as independent. America cannot deny this fact—she is at present leagued with Old Spain against the colonies. She has accepted the Floridas as the price of that union; for we know that she did propose to us to acknowledge the new states; that she has *not* acknowledged them; and that she has, without the slightest pretext of justice, accepted the Floridas from Old Spain. She has, in familiar language, been, for a while at least, bought off. Our course is now, therefore, not one of our own choosing, it is imposed on us by the necessity of things; we cannot, without madness, desist from acknowledging the independence of Buenos Aires and the other Spanish provinces. The court of Madrid must have looked to this as a result, when it gained the forbearance of the United States by consigning to them the Floridas in our detriment; and we should be sunk into a very abject condition, indeed, if we allowed Spain to think it of more importance, even to purchase the neutrality of America than to retain ours as a boon, or as the natural consequence of our disinterestedness." [20]

Such was the feeling of some Englishmen, at least, with reference to the Florida acquisition. The *Times* has been quoted at length because its pronouncement clearly reveals British motives and marks the beginning of a strong sentiment in favor of counteracting the influence of the United States in the Western Hemisphere. In this article commercial and political factors appear intricately related. The writer was alarmed at the prospect of the United States' securing a predominance in the councils as well as in the markets of Hispanic America, the influence of the United States in either sphere having been considered a possible detriment to British interests. Such a view was destined to lead to interesting developments in the near future.

[20] Issue of April 19, 1819, as quoted by J. B. Lockey, *Pan-Americanism: its Beginnings* (1920), pp. 196–199.

CHAPTER III

THE WESTERN POWERS AND THE INDEPENDENCE MOVEMENT IN LATIN AMERICA

SEVERAL years before France and Spain sought to humble England by supporting a revolt in the English colonies of America the idea of revolutionizing Spanish America had been suggested to the governments of Britain and France, Spain's chief rivals after the decline of the Dutch Netherlands. Nor is there any reason to doubt that the insurgent movement which began south of the Rio Grande in 1808 was due in some measure to British and French intrigue and propaganda, official and unofficial.

The motives which led to this support of insurgency were mixed. A leaning toward liberalism was doubtless influential in the case of some leaders in both nations; and it is equally certain that rivalries and jealousies played their part. Both England and France perceived the growing impotency of Spain and each feared that the other might gain some advantage therefrom. Each would have preferred that the Spanish colonies should achieve independence rather than that they should fall into the hands of its rival, and each expected the successful revolt of these colonies to be attended with some advantage to itself, whether in the form of commerce, territory, new domain for an allied House, or a modification of the balance of power. The Portuguese colony of Brazil did not cause great concern.

Early Schemes

One of the earliest suggestions for instigating and supporting a revolution in Spanish America was that of Stephen Deveros in 1741. In a memorial of that year this British subject, with experience gained from years spent in the West Indies, deprecated the fact that many Britons favored the conquest of Spanish America. He declared that maintaining possession of this vast region, once the initial conquest had been made, would prove very expensive and troublesome. The envy of the other Powers would be aroused and a formidable coalition would be provoked against England. He therefore contended that the wisest policy would be for Great Britain to form an alliance with the Spanish Americans "as with free people" and help them to throw off the Spanish yoke. "It well becomes a free people," said Deveros, "to place others in the same condition with themselves. To deliver so many nations from Tyranny will be truer Glory than Alexander gained by all his Victories . . . We shall thereby greatly increase our own Riches w [hi] ch is the end of all conquests: and we shall do it without raising the just envy of our neighbors, w[hi]ch is likely to make our happiness the more lasting." [1]

In December, 1776, an actual plan for annihilating "universally the Spanish dominions in America" was laid before the British government. This plan, which had been drawn up by a certain Captain Kaye, suggested that the attack should start from the Mosquito Shore and that England should furnish some fifteen thousand troops and a fleet. The government of the Incas of Peru was to be restored and the inhabitants of other sections were to be permitted to set up the governments of their choice. England was to be reimbursed and rewarded by the revenues of Spanish America while the war of liberation continued, by the confiscation of certain properties, by "free and exclusive trade and commerce," and, lastly, by the possession of all the seacoasts of Spanish America. This project was to be undertaken, apparently, only in case of war with Spain. In carrying it out the ready coöperation of the natives was expected. "What of all things most merits attention," wrote Kaye, "is a predilection which the Natives of Spanish America have in favor of this Expedition, arising from a Prophecy of Old Date, Universally believed and carefully handed down from one Generation to Another; 'That a far distant Nation, Commanding the Sea, Shall Come in Ships to their deliverance, and, freeing them from the Yoke and Oppression of the Spaniards, shall Restore them to the possession of their Liberty and Country.' This may be used to the best advantage both in composing the Manifestos and in publishing them among the people." [2] Kaye had served on the coasts of Spanish America and must have known something of the inner thoughts and ambitions of the people. One wonders whether the tradition to which he referred may not have been instilled by generations of Englishmen who had been carrying on contraband trade in these regions. Or was it due to English exploitation of the Aztec legend of the Fair God?

It was only natural that these schemes for detaching the Spanish colonies from the mother country should have multiplied during and after the revolt of the English colonies. Between 1779, when Spain

[1] Robertson, *Francisco de Miranda* (1907), pp. 197-198.
[2] As quoted in *ibid.*, p. 199.

entered the war on the side of the United States, and the close of the Revolution, numerous projects were presented, some of which appear to have been examined by the British government. Moreover, by 1783 the Spanish Americans had become accustomed to look to Britain for support in their plans for the achievement of independence.[3]

The earliest French schemes for dismembering the Spanish empire seem to have had their origin in jealousy and fear of England. About 1773 a project for forming a republic out of the colonies which France had ceded to Spain in America was laid before the French government. "The author, who is unknown, described the great power and prestige of England, which he compared with that of Rome. Whether the discontented colonies in America remained under her control or not, he asserted, that nation would try to extend her dominions at the expense of Spain in America. Hence the American colonies ceded by France to Spain might be subjected to English invasion. Spain could not easily put these colonies in a condition to reimburse her for their immense expense. The dangerous proximity of the English would always cause trouble. The writer queried whether it would not be more advantageous to Spain and even to France that this immense domain become independent and thus form a formidable bulwark against England, 'the natural enemy of commercial nations.'"[4]

These early proposals are important merely as indicating the trend of the times. Their more serious consideration had to await the turmoil of the Revolutionary and Napoleonic era. Meanwhile the soil was being prepared in Spanish America by French radical philosophy and by both the political ideas and the example of the United States.

The Influence of French Radical Philosophy

"In defiance of the Inquisition the works of Montesquieu, Voltaire, and Rousseau had been smuggled into Spanish America and found thousands of readers. The famous *Encyclopédie,* of which Diderot was the chief editor, was a veritable arsenal from which the Creoles drew their weapons in their attacks on Spain's system of government."[5] A French traveler who visited Venezuela in 1783 relates how a physician of that country led him to a secluded part of his house where he showed him "with infinite satisfaction the

[3] Robertson, *Francisco de Miranda* (1907), pp. 198–210.
[4] *Ibid.,* p. 211.
[5] James and Martin, *The Republics of Latin America* (1925), pp. 81–82.

works of J. J. Rousseau and Raynal, which he kept concealed as his most precious treasure in a beam scooped out for that purpose." [6] In 1794 Antonio Nariño, of New Granada, printed a Spanish version of the Declaration of the Rights of Man at Bogotá and began its clandestine circulation in northern South America. At about the same time Manuel Morena published a translation of *The Social Contract* in the viceroyalty of La Plata. The close of the eighteenth century found the students and faculty at the University of Chuquisaca (Bolivia) discussing the "ideas of Rousseau and Montesquieu and of the French thinkers in general." [7] French revolutionary documents were found among the papers of the insurgent leader, Manuel Gual of Venezuela, in 1797; Miranda was steeped in French philosophy; Bolívar often perused *The Social Contract* and *The Spirit of Laws;* one charge brought by the Inquisition against the Mexican revolutionist, Miguel Hidalgo y Costillo, was that of reading French books. [8] The Spanish authorities soon became alarmed at the spread of these radical ideas and placed the works of the French revolutionary writers on the prohibited list. [9]

The Influence of the Political Ideas and Example of the United States

Officially the United States had little to do with the origin of the revolutionary movement in Hispanic America. There was no official propaganda worthy of mention and the government seldom departed from the path of strict neutrality. And yet the influence of the United States was powerful. Without substantial grounds for such a hope the Spanish Americans fully expected aid from their North American compatriots, and the character and liberal ideas of the Founding Fathers were ever a potent factor.

"The flame which was kindled in North America, as was foreseen, has made its way into the American dominions of Spain. The example of North America is the great subject of discourse and the grand object of emulation." At any rate this is what the *Political Herald and Review* (London) reported in 1785. [10] It would be difficult to say whether this was actually true at that date, but it would certainly describe the situation three decades later.

[6] Robertson, *op. cit.,* p. 223, quoting from Ségur.

[7] Raúl Orgaz, "A Synopsis of the History of Argentine Social Ideas," in *Inter-America*, VI (1921), 231; Robertson, *Francisco de Miranda*, pp. 223–225.

[8] Robertson, *op. et loc. cit.,* and see also his *Rise of the Spanish-American Republics* (1918).

[9] Pons, *Travels in South America* (London, 1807), I, 318–325.

[10] Chandler, *Inter-American Acquaintances* (1916), p. 8.

In 1791 a Jesuit Father, Juan Pablo Viscardo y Gúzman, a native Peruvian then in exile, challenged his compatriots by citing the illustrious example of the United States: "The valor with which the English colonists in America fought for the liberty they gloriously enjoy shames our indolence; we yield the palm to them as the first people in the New World who have been crowned in their independent sovereignty." Is not something of the state of mind in South America revealed by the fact that the Jesuit Father's letter was distributed at the time of Miranda's invasion of 1806 in Venezuela and circulated by the insurgent leaders of Buenos Aires in 1809?[11] Unless Miranda and these leaders mistook the psychology of the people there must have existed a disposition to listen to such propaganda.

While indulging in reminiscence in 1809 the Precursor recalled that he had conceived the idea of freeing his fatherland at the time when he was participating in the North American revolution. In 1783–1784 he visited the United States and met such prominent leaders as Alexander Hamilton, Henry Knox, Samuel Adams, Benjamin Franklin, Thomas Paine, and General Washington himself. For many years afterwards he appears to have expected the assistance of some of these leaders in his ambitious enterprise.[12]

In 1794 Antonio Nariño, a Colombian patriot, was tried for seditious practices. One of the charges brought against him was that of working in accordance with the Philadelphia constitution. He had in fact translated Tom Paine's *Rights of Man* and circulated it in his native vice-royalty in 1792; and during his trial he revealed familiarity with the state documents of the United States and expressed great admiration for the Franklins, the Washingtons, and the Adamses.[13]

In 1798 a certain agitator named Juan Picornell was accused of printing the Constitution of the United States for distribution in the Spanish colonies. During the same year the Jesuit Father to whom reference has already been made died in London. He left with the United States minister at the Court of St. James's a memorial urging the independence of Spanish America. Presumably through his correspondence Viscardo y Gúzman was in close touch with conditions there. With respect to his compatriots he remarked, in this memorial, that "the recent acquisition of independence by their neighbors in North America has made the deepest impression on them."[14]

[11] As quoted in Robertson, *Hispanic-American Relations of the United States*, pp. 61–62; Chandler, *op. cit.*, p. 15.

[12] Robertson, *op. cit.*, pp. 61–62.

[13] Chandler, *op. cit*, pp. 15–16.

[14] *Ibid.*, pp. 19–20.

That he was not entirely in error is perhaps indicated by the fact that as early as 1791 medals alluding to the achievement of the Thirteen Colonies had been struck off and circulated.[15]

For at least two reasons the ill-fated expedition launched by Miranda against Venezuela in 1806 must have increased the influence of the United States in the insurgent circles of Spanish America. It had been planned in the United States and numbered some two hundred Anglo-American enlistments. Several of them shared with the Spanish-American insurgents the pestilential dungeons of Venezuela.[16]

Nor should it be forgotten that Simón Bolívar visited the United States in 1806, when at the impressionable age of twenty-three. His itinerary included Boston, Lexington, Concord, New York, and Washington, and he met several of the celebrities of the country. Such an experience must have exerted some influence upon his later career.[17]

Another manner in which Anglo-American ideas may have been conveyed to the Spanish Americans was through commercial contacts. These began on the Caribbean and Atlantic coasts at a very early date and extended to the Pacific long before 1800. Pitkin, in his *Statistical View,* estimated the value of the trade between the United States and the Spanish colonies at more than three million dollars in 1795 and at more than twenty-one million in 1801.[18] One does not find it difficult to believe that the merchants introduced liberal ideas along with their commodities.

The loyalist ecclesiastic of Chile, Melchior Martínez, in a denunciation which may probably be taken as typical, makes the following charges: "The Boston republic [*sic* for the United States] . . . is making its greatest efforts to enlarge its boundaries and to extend its system, as the only method of providing for its stability and maintenance. To this end it puts into action all imaginable means, without hesitating at the most iniquitous and immoral, in order to attract the Spanish colonists to its depraved designs. The freedom of conscience and the freedom of the press assist it in publishing and spreading subversive and seditious principles and maxims, which always find reception with the majority of men, ruled by ignorance and malice. The clandestine trade and the permission to fish for whales introduce traders and adventurers from the United States into all the coast, ports, islands, and other Spanish possessions, giving them

[15] Chandler, *op. cit.,* p. 17.
[16] Robertson, *Francisco de Miranda,* p. 361 ff.
[17] Robertson, *Rise of the Spanish-American Republics,* p. 18.
[18] Robertson, *Francisco de Miranda,* pp. 228, 229, 252.

opportunity to persuade the Spanish colonists of the flourishing state and advantageous situation of their country, decrying the Spanish colonial government and subjection to the mother country in Europe as ignominious slavery. They magnify the riches and extent of these provinces; proclaim the injustice and tyranny with which the wealth is carried off to enrich Europe; describe the state of obscurity, abandonment, and civil nullity in which the colonists live; and offer with impudence all the aid of their great power to the people who may wish to shake off the yoke of legitimate and just government. Moreover, they have adopted and put into execution the most powerful means to undermine and destroy the political and religious edifice of the Spanish colonies, sending clandestinely to all and each one of these possessions subjects for the purpose of establishing themselves and becoming citizens, with the design of perverting and destroying allegiance to the mother country." [19]

These charges doubtless contained an element of truth. At any rate two incidents will serve to indicate the influence attributed to the ideas and example of the United States at the opening of the insurgent movement in Latin America: (1) the agents which Napoleon sent to Spanish America were instructed to hold up the United States as a model and to promise the natives of the country freedom and independence; [20] (2) the state papers and other writings of the North American leaders were known and used as propaganda in most of the early revolutionary centers of Spanish America.[21]

A consideration of the influence of French radical philosophy and of the political ideas and example of the United States has led us somewhat afield. It is time to return to the story of the official attitude and conduct of France and England toward the Spanish colonies.

Later Schemes

The year 1790 marks the beginning of serious discussion in European governing circles of the advisability of revolutionizing Hispanic America. It was at this time that the great English Prime Minister, William Pitt, apprehending a possible general war over the Nootka Sound dispute, examined attentively the plans of Francisco Miranda. Miranda's design was to form, with the assistance of Great Britain, a vast, independent, constitutional empire out of the American do-

[19] Bernard Moses, *The Intellectual Background of the Revolution in South America* (1926), pp. 39–41.

[20] Chandler, *op. cit.*, p. 55.

[21] Robertson, *Hispanic-American Relations of the United States,* p. 10, *passim.*

mains of Spain. "The projected state was to be bordered on the east by the coast line, the boundaries of Brazil and Guiana, and the Mississippi River. The northern boundary was to be a straight line, the parallel of 45 north latitude, drawn from the source of the Mississippi . . . to the Pacific Ocean. On the west the Pacific coast line was to form the boundary which was to extend as far south as the uttermost point of Cape Horn. The islands situated within ten degrees of the western coast were to be included within this imperial domain, but on the east Cuba alone was to be" embraced, for the reason that the port of Havana was considered the "key to the Gulf of Mexico." All the details of the scheme are not known, but it is probable that England's reward was to have been the remainder of the West Indies, the Floridas, and "great commercial advantages."

Pitt was evidently impressed by Miranda's project and more than once promised to take it up in the event of war. The outbreak of hostilities at this time would perhaps have given the signal for the dispatch of three British expeditions to Spanish America, two to the Atlantic and Gulf coasts, and one (from India) to the Pacific coast. New Orleans would doubtless have been attacked as a preliminary step in the overland march to Mexico. An attempt would also have been made to secure the coöperation of the United States.[22] But a general war was averted by opportune concessions on the part of the Spanish government, which found that revolutionary France was not disposed to stand by the family compact and feared the consequences of a break with England.[23]

Indeed, the French leaders were so far from accepting this Bourbon alliance that they actually contemplated an attack on the Spanish colonies. Early in 1792 the French minister of foreign affairs began to talk of a coalition between England, France, and the United States for the purpose of opening up the commerce of Spanish America and expelling Spain from the New World. With this idea in mind, Admiral Kersaint placed before the secretary an elaborate plan of attack. A quadruple alliance consisting of France, England, the United States, and Holland was to be formed. "England would be attracted to the plan by the immense commercial possibilities involved. In addition, she was to be promised the possession of Cuba. France was to get the Spanish part of Santo Domingo. Porto Rico was to be given to the United States. Trinity and other small islands along the coasts of Caracas and Louisiana were to be the reward of Holland. There

<hr>

[22] Robertson, *Francisco de Miranda*, pp. 266–287.
[23] Turner, "The Diplomatic Contest for the Mississippi Valley," *loc. cit.*, p. 684; Manning, *The Nootka Sound Controversy* (1912), pp. 454–456.

were to be four main attacks north of the equator and three south of that line. The attack on Louisiana was to be confided to the United States, aided by France. The attack on the kingdom of New Granada or the provinces of Caracas and Santa Marta was to be carried on by the Dutch, aided by the Prussians [provided they cared to join the alliance]. Cuba and Yucatan were to be attacked by the English and the French. The French, assisted by the English, were to operate against Santo Domingo and Mexico. It was also proposed that the English, reinforced by the French and the Dutch, proceed against Peru, Chile, and the Philippines. If Portugal would not remain neutral, her colonies were also to be attacked and to be declared independent." [24] Presumably independence was to be given to all of Spanish America except those portions which were considered as appropriate spoils for the conquering Powers.

The French government even went so far as to approach London with the view of carrying out this grandiose project, but Britain was discovered to be inevitably drifting into a coalition against France. The English government was too alarmed at the extravagances of the revolutionary leaders and the downfall of the French monarchy to enter into such a partnership. Until 1795 it remained loyal to the alliance with Spain.

Frenchmen nevertheless continued to consider various projects for revolutionizing Spanish America. One of the most important of these, though less extensive than that of Kersaint, involved the possible coöperation of the United States and probably contemplated the use of Miranda. Writing of the scheme on November 28, 1792, M. Brissot, who virtually dominated the foreign policies of France at the time, suggested that the Precursor be placed in charge of the French West Indies. "Miranda will soon quiet the miserable quarrels of the colonies," said Brissot; "he will soon bring to reason the whites who are so troublesome, and he will become the idol of the people of colour. And then with what ease will he not be able to revolutionize either the islands of the Spaniards or the American continent which they possess? At the head of twelve thousand troops of the line which are now at Santo Domingo and of ten to fifteen thousand brave mulattoes that our colonies will furnish him, with what facility will he not be able to invade the Spanish possessions, having besides a squadron under his orders, and the Spaniards having nothing to oppose him. The name of Miranda will be worth an army and his talents, his courage, his genius all promise success . . ." [25] Professor

[24] Robertson, *Francisco de Miranda*, pp. 289–290.
[25] As quoted in *ibid.*, p. 291.

Robertson thinks it "is entirely possible that the plans of the French were so all-embracing that at one time they contemplated sending Gênet to the United States and Miranda to Santo Domingo for the purpose of directing simultaneous operations against both the northern and the more southern part of Spanish America." [26] The ill-starred rôle played by Gênet in this vast scheme is well known. As for Miranda, he was not even given an opportunity to display his ability, but, falling into disfavor, was cast into prison in July, 1793.[27]

Passing over the French schemes of the next two years, which related mainly to Louisiana and the Floridas and to which brief reference has already been made in Chapter II, we shall merely note the influence that the detachment of Spain from the anti-French coalition in 1795 exerted upon British policy toward the Spanish-American colonies. For the next thirteen years, while Spain remained under the domination of Revolutionary and Napoleonic France, the instigation of a Spanish-American revolt became a topic of frequent meditation among British statesmen, for a good part of the time Miranda was pensioned and kept at the British government's right hand, and on several occasions preparations were made for launching English expeditions to carry out some such project. But the statesmen who controlled British policy usually took the stand that this step should be taken only in case it should prove necessary in order to prevent both Spain and her colonies from falling into the hands of France. As affairs never actually came to this pass England did not intervene, and after the Spaniards began a spirited resistance to Napoleonic domination (1808) these plans were abandoned.

Nevertheless British agents, acting during this period under instructions and sometimes contravening instructions, took steps which brought the day for a general revolt in the Spanish-American colonies appreciably nearer.

The propaganda of Thomas Picton from Trinidad furnishes a case in point. When this island was seized by a British fleet, early in 1797, Picton was appointed military governor. He was directed to declare the port of Trinidad free, to urge the Spanish Americans to continue their commercial and other communications with the island, and to assure them that if they cared to revolt they could depend upon British assistance. In June, 1797, Picton issued these various declarations in the form of a proclamation in the Spanish language which received a wide circulation in northern South America and did much to foster

[26] Robertson, *Francisco de Miranda,* p. 293.
[27] *Ibid.,* pp. 296–300.

the revolutionary spirit. This favorable beginning was followed by several years of persistent effort which apparently continued to be not without influence. At all events Picton was optimistic. In September, 1797, he felt that a revolution might be easily brought about by "generally arming the People." In 1798 he declared that if the British government would send an army to the coast of Venezuela and declare its intention of giving the South Americans independence and free trade, they would at once rise up against their corrupt oppressors. In the following year he wrote that independence could easily be effected if the British would support the movement. Finally, in 1804, after he had given up his command in Trinidad, Picton declared to his government that the outbreak of hostilities with Spain would furnish "a fair opportunity" to "deprive her of all her Continental Colonies." "She holds them by so precarious a Tenure and the Principles of Combustion are so thickly and widely scattered," said Picton, "that a single Spark would communicate the Explosion throughout the whole of the immense Continent." [28]

Doubtless Picton's propaganda was exerting a profound and widespread influence, but he evidently overestimated the spirit of insurgency among the Spanish colonies at this time. This is clearly shown by the unfavorable reception of the Miranda expedition against Venezuela in 1806,[29] and also by the spirited resistance to British attacks upon the viceroyalty of Rio de la Plata at about the same time.

The British expeditions against the La Plata region are important both as a revelation of British policy and as an illustration of British influence upon the early revolutionary movement in Spanish America. In the summer of 1806 Sir Home Popham, without explicit instructions, led an expedition from the Cape of Good Hope, where the English had won a recent victory, against Buenos Aires, and succeeded in capturing the city. Popham was recalled and reprimanded for having left the Cape in a defenseless state and seized Buenos Aires without instructions, but the British government nevertheless praised the subordinate officials and the army for the brilliant exploit and prepared to take advantage of the conquest. At the same time plans were made to conquer Chile. But the militia of Buenos Aires, commanded by Jacques Liniers, an able French officer commissioned by Napoleon, made a brilliant counter-attack and forced the British commander, General Beresford, who had charge of the land forces, to capitulate. British reinforcements arrived too late

[28] Robertson, *Francisco de Miranda*, pp. 313-315, 331, 342, note, 355, *passim.*
[29] See above, p. 29.

to save Beresford, but succeeded in taking Montevideo, Maldo-
nado, and Colonia Sacramento. A second assault was then made upon
Buenos Aires, but it was heroically repelled by the provincials and
the English were soon compelled to evacuate the entire region. Evidently the South Americans were not yet ready to receive the British with open arms.

These attacks nevertheless had an important bearing upon the in-
ception of the revolution in southern South America. The viceroy
had proved cravenly inefficient and had been removed by the local
leaders. The citizens of the province had learned to appreciate their
own prowess. Lastly, the British had given them a taste of the benefits of a more liberal commercial policy, for large quantities of English goods had been introduced and virtual free trade had been promised.[30]

The attitude of the British government toward these operations
in the La Plata region reveals that in 1806 and 1807 it entertained
ambitions of conquest in Spanish America. In the latter part of
1807 and during the early months of the following year, however,
emphasis shifted to the notion of revolutionizing the region. Castlereagh, who had become Secretary of War and the Colonies in March,
1807, soon drew up a memorandum in which he contended that the
British could not afford to undertake "the hopeless task of conquering this extensive country." He urged that they should not allow
themselves to appear "in any other light than as auxiliaries and pro-
tectors." "In order to prove our sincerity in this respect," continued
Castlereagh, "we should be prepared to pursue our object by a native
force, to be created under our countenance, and the particular interest which we should be understood alone to propose to ourselves
should be the depriving of our enemy of one of his chief resources,
and the opening to our manufactures the markets of that great continent." Sir Arthur Wellesley held a similar view. Were the Spanish
Americans ripe for revolt? This question should have given the British statesmen pause, but they nevertheless proceeded with extensive
preparations in the spring of 1808 and the attack would doubtless
have been made had it not been for the opportune revolt of the Spanish nation against Napoleon. When news of this event reached England it was decided to-send the troops which had been collected for
America to the Spanish peninsula.[31]

Not for this reason, however, was the revolution of Spain's colo-

[30] Robertson, *Francisco de Miranda*, pp. 392–393; Moses, *South America on
the Eve of Emancipation*, Chs. XI–XII; Watson, *Spanish and Portuguese South
America*, p. 271 ff.

[31] Robertson, *Francisco de Miranda*, p. 399 ff.

nies delayed. The task of driving the French troops across the Pyrenees was not quickly performed. Meanwhile the Corsican was laying plans for the domination of Spanish America.

"Napoleon Bonaparte, . . . to you, immortal genius, to you Spanish America owes the liberty and independence which she to-day enjoys! Your sword struck the first blow at the chain which bound the two worlds!" [32] In this fashion a Mexican writer of a century ago apostrophized the Emperor of the French. The eulogy was not entirely misplaced, but the Corsican was not engaged in chain-breaking for mere love of liberty. He coveted Spanish America along with Spain as a part of a vast projected empire to be held under his despotic sway; and it was his attempt to realize these ambitions that precipitated the Spanish-American outbreak which European statesmen had long been discussing. The appearance of Bonaparte's agents in America furnished the signal for uprisings which began by the formation of *juntas* to defend the rights of the deposed Ferdinand and ended in the movement for independence from Spain.[33]

The Revolt of Brazil

It must also be noticed that Napoleon's large schemes likewise set in motion a train of events which resulted in the independence of Brazil. When he attempted to seize Portugal and depose the Braganza dynasty, the Portuguese Prince Regent, with the royal family and the court, made a hasty departure for Brazil on board a British vessel and under cover of the English fleet. Arriving at Rio, this first of the Old World rulers to visit the New, was received with no little enthusiasm. Due largely to British influence, he threw open the ports of Brazil, removed many of the restrictions from her industries, and inaugurated several other liberal reforms. In fact, by a decree of June 16, 1815, Brazil was placed on a parity with the mother country. Soon after Waterloo, however, conditions in Portugal began urgently to demand the return of the Regent (after March, 1816, the King) of the Portuguese dominions. Departing for Lisbon in 1821, he left his son Pedro in charge of Brazil. The King's arrival at the former Portuguese capital was soon followed by an effort to reduce Brazil to its former status of a colonial dependency. This aroused profound resentment among the Brazilians, and at length,

[32] The Mexican historian Bustamente, as quoted by Robertson, "The Juntas of 1808 and the Spanish Colonies," in *The English Historical Review*, XXXI (1916), 585.

[33] Robertson, *Francisco de Miranda*, p. 429 ff.; also his *Rise of the Spanish-American Republics, passim.*

on September 7, 1822, Dom Pedro was persuaded to declare for independence.[34]

Thus the movement for independence in Hispanic America was begun under the instigation and encouragement of the European Powers. In Brazil it was of short duration and independence was achieved almost without bloodshed. In Spanish America it proved much more complicated and expensive. Would Spanish Americans receive the support of the Powers which had urged them to revolt? *This* only the exigencies of European politics could determine. The omens were far from favorable in 1809.

Treading the Wine Press Alone

There is much pathos in the vain search of the Spanish-Americans for outside assistance in their movement for liberation. The English government had long encouraged them, but for more than a decade after July, 1808, its efforts were turned "steadily toward the preservation of the integrity of the Spanish dominions in both hemispheres." At one time it even went so far as to urge Miranda to endeavor to reconcile his compatriots to Spanish rule.[35] Individual Britons joined the ranks of the insurgents in hundreds and even thousands, suffering with them tropical plague and mountain chill, and, above all, contributing their unexcelled knowledge in naval matters; but direct official aid was lacking until 1823. Britain was bound by the Spanish alliance and the conservatives were in power.

It was futile to expect assistance from the Continent. French liberalism, to which they might have looked for support, was under the smothering despotism first of Napoleon and then of the Metternich system. On one or two occasions the Spanish-American patriots solicited aid from the Corsican, but in vain.[36] Nor could any who aspired to independence under native governments expect anything from the reactionary, legitimist Neo-Holy Alliance.

The Spanish Americans turned with pathetic confidence to the United States, whose political ideas and example had inspired an enthusiastic hope, but considerations of self-interest and security prevented aid from this source. A few individuals joined the Mexican patriots or followed in the wake of the immortals who sailed with Miranda in 1806, but this was all. In 1808, while harassed by both England and France and fearing that one of these Powers might

[34] James, *Brazil*, p. 111 ff.
[35] Robertson, *Francisco de Miranda*, pp. 413, 431–432, *passim*.
[36] Robertson, "The Beginnings of Spanish-American Diplomacy," in Turner, *Essays in American History*, pp. 255, 261, 262.

establish itself in Cuba, Florida, Louisiana, or Mexico, Jefferson's cabinet had found itself "unanimously agreed in the sentiments which should be unauthoritatively expressed by our agents to influential persons in Cuba and Mexico, to wit: 'If you remain under the dominion of the kingdom and family of Spain, we are contented; but we should be extremely unwilling to see you pass under the dominion or ascendency of France or England . . . Should you choose to declare independence, we cannot now commit ourselves by saying we would make common cause with you, but must reserve ourselves to act according to the then existing circumstances; but in our proceedings we shall be influenced by friendship to you, by a firm feeling that our interests are intimately connected, and by the strongest repugnance to see you under subordination to either France or England either politically or commercially.' " [37]

Agents had accordingly been chosen in order to convey these sentiments to Cuba, to Florida, and to the Mexican frontier. To one of these intermediaries Jefferson remarked: "We consider their interests and ours as the same, and that the object of both must be to exclude all European influence from this hemisphere." He was authorized to express this sentiment to the Spanish Americans and to inform them that the American government had "nothing more at heart than their friendship." [38] In conversing with the colonials in these regions the American agents may have used even stronger language. But the proceedings of this winter of 1808–1809 mark the nearest official approach on the part of the United States to any action which might be considered as offering encouragement to revolution in the Spanish colonies. When Madison entered the White House he refused to be bound by Jefferson's policy.

Spanish-American envoys who hurried to the United States upon the outbreak of the wars of independence were unofficially listened to and occasionally supplied with funds for transportation and temporary entertainment,[39] but aside from these polite considerations, which became more and more rare after the Florida negotiations got well under way, there was little departure from the narrow path of a formal neutrality. For more than a decade after the Spanish Americans initiated their independence movement they were left to tread the wine press alone.

[37] As quoted by Henry Adams, *History of the United States*, IV, 340.
[38] Jefferson, *Writings* (Memorial ed.), XII, 186.
[39] Cox, "The Pan-American Policy of Jefferson and Wilkinson," in *Miss. Valley Hist. Rev.*, I (1904), 213; see also his "Monroe and the Early Mexican Revolutionary Agents," in A. H. A., *Ann. Rept.* (1911), I, 199 ff.

The Early Policy of Britain

In examining the policy of the Great Powers toward these wars of liberation the course of Great Britain may be taken as the central theme. One of the earliest expressions of the attitude of the English government toward the revolutionary movement in the Spanish colonies is found in the instructions of Lord Liverpool, minister for war and the colonies, to British officials in the West Indies. Here Liverpool remarked:

"The great object which His Majesty has had in view from the first moment when intelligence was received in this Country of the glorious resistance of the Spanish nation against the Tyranny and Usurpation of France, was to assist by every means in His Power this great effort of a brave, loyal, and high spirited People, and to secure if possible the Independence of the Spanish Monarchy in all Parts of the World. As long as the Spanish Nation persevere [s] in their [its] resistence to their [its] invaders, and as any reasonable Hope can be entertained of ultimate Success to their [its] Cause in Spain, His Majesty feels it to be his Duty according to every obligation of Justice and good Faith, to discourage any proceeding which may have the effect of separating the Spanish Provinces in America from the Parent State in Europe;—the Integrity of the Spanish Monarchy upon principles of Justice and true Policy, being not less the object of His Majesty than of all loyal and patriotick Spaniards." [40-41]

These instructions were penned on June 29, 1810. Accordingly, when agents of the Venezuelan insurgents arrived in England less than two weeks later and asked for a conference with Marquis Wellesley, the secretary of state for foreign affairs, it was refused on the ground that England was bound to Spain by the alliance of 1808. These agents then declared their loyalty to Ferdinand VII, whereupon audiences were granted. Wellesley urged the Venezuelans to forget their grievances, accept a reconciliation with Spain, and support the mother country in its magnificent struggle against Napoleon. He refused to accept their view that Venezuela could render Spain more efficient aid under an independent government than by a reunion with the authorities sent over by the provisional government of the peninsula, but he eventually promised to use his good offices

[40-41] As quoted by Robertson, "The Beginnings of Spanish-American Diplomacy," *loc. cit.*, p. 240.

to promote "an amicable adjustment" between the Venezuelans and the metropolis, as well as to protect them from France so long as they refrained from a break with Spain.[42]

Thus by the summer of 1810 British policy toward the revolting colonies had been clearly formulated. It can be summed up in a few words: moral opposition, a hint of mediation, and protection from France. During the next few years, however, a modification occurred. English policy moved to a position of neutrality and a willingness to mediate upon a liberal basis.

The British ministry made honest and persistent efforts to preserve neutrality. In 1814 a treaty was negotiated with Spain binding the English government to prevent its subjects from furnishing "arms, ammunition, or any other warlike article to the revolted in South America."[43] In the fall of 1817 the Prince Regent of England issued a proclamation warning his subjects not to participate in the war between Spain and her colonies and threatening all offenders with the penalties of felony prescribed by the old statutes of George II. In the summer of the following year other proclamations were issued; and in 1819 a Foreign Enlistment Act was passed making it an offense to enlist in England for foreign service or even to enter the foreign service at all. By this latter step it will be observed that the British ministry established the principle that "neutrality demands more than an observance of existing laws; it demands that adequate laws shall exist."[44]

Yet in spite of all these measures, many British subjects joined the ranks of the Spanish-American insurgents. This, however, is an indication of the weakness of the British judicial system rather than of an unneutral disposition on the part of the ministry. When a filibuster's arrest and trial is placed in the hands of his peers he always benefits by every sentiment of sympathy toward the cause he is attempting to serve.[45]

Castlereagh and the Spanish Colonies

That the British government made conscientious efforts to mediate between Spain and her revolting subjects, there is ample proof. "One of Castlereagh's first duties at the Foreign Office [1812] had been to define the British position. The Cortes had tried to win British assistance by the offer of special privileges for her commerce.

[42] Robertson, "The Beginnings of Spanish-American Diplomacy," *loc. cit.,* pp. 243–247.

[43] Paxson, *The Independence of the South American Republics,* p. 182.

[44] *Ibid.,* pp. 188–189.

[45] *Ibid.,* pp. 64, 103, 186, *passim.*

The reply had been definite. The offer of mediation had been accepted, but certain conditions had been laid down as an indispensable preliminary to negotiation. All secret advantages were rejected; the mediation was to apply to all the colonies; and (most important of all) force was not to be used." [46] Spain declined to accept mediation on these terms and England steadfastly refused to undertake it on any other.

While Madrid continued to approach the London government in the hope that it might relent, Spanish agents sought mediation elsewhere and on a basis more favorable to Spain. When in the summer of 1817 it appeared that Russia and possibly France might undertake the task, even going so far as to employ armed force, Castlereagh was considerably perturbed. Accordingly, on August 28 he made the first announcement of his policy to the European Powers. The importance of this statement warrants an extensive quotation:

"Although the Prince Regent has felt it his duty to observe a strict neutrality throughout the contest which has agitated the South American Provinces, His Royal Highness has never ceased to entertain an anxious desire that that great continent might be restored to tranquillity under the ancient sovereignties of the Crowns of Spain and Portugal. The Prince Regent has looked to this object with the more earnestness from the regret with which His Royal Highness has seen ancient authorities subverted—from the peculiar interest which He feels in whatever may concern the dignity and welfare of the illustrious families whose possessions are thereby endangered, and from a firm persuasion that the continent of South America must long remain a prey to its own internal convulsions, before it can assume any separate form of regular government capable of providing for the happiness of its own inhabitants or of adequately maintaining relations of peace and amity with other states. It is, however, the opinion of the Prince Regent that this desirable object can be obtained by a speedy settlement of all existing differences, and by the restoration of a perfect understanding between the Crowns of their Catholick and Most Faithful Majesties, and further by each determining to adopt a system of government within their respective dominions favourable to the interest and congenial to the feelings of the natives of these countries; it being obvious that whatever may have been the original of the Colonial System of either Crown, it has become in the progress of time, inapplicable to countries of such extent and population . . ."

[46] So says Webster, "Castlereagh and the Spanish Colonies," in *The Eng. Hist. Rev.*, XXVII (1912), 79, but early British policy requires further investigation.

Castlereagh then stated once more the conditions upon which mediation ought to proceed: (1) Spaniards and Spanish Americans should be placed on an equal footing before the law; (2) the colonies should be granted free trade with all nations, "Spain enjoying, as the parent state, a fair preference . . . ;" (3) Spain should offer the insurgents a general amnesty and an armistice; and (4) the Spanish government should agree to a satisfactory treaty with Great Britain on the slave trade.

In conclusion, Castlereagh put forth what amounted to a solemn warning that force was not to be used. He said: "H.R.H. cannot consent that His mediation shall under any circumstances assume an armed character . . . ; nor can H.R.H. become the guarantee [sic] of any settlements that may be effectuated, to the extent of undertaking the obligation of enforcing its [sic] observance by acts of hostility against either of the parties. His intervention must throughout be understood to be confirmed within the bounds of good offices, and the employment of that just influence which must belong to any great power when laboring only to promote the welfare of an allied sovereign and his people . . ." [47]

Thus as early as August, 1817, Great Britain in effect announced that she "would allow no European interference except on such terms as she chose to dictate." Castlereagh had dared take this bold step in part at least because he and Metternich had virtually become diplomatic allies. Russia, unwilling to oppose England under these circumstances, ceased for a time to insist upon her projects of forced mediation. Indeed, a year later, at the Congress of Aix-la-Chapelle, Castlereagh actually secured the acceptance of his basic principles regarding mediation between Spain and the colonies, and Russia went so far as to try to persuade Spain to accept them. But the Spanish government persisted in its obstinacy and nothing was accomplished. [48]

Soon afterwards the British cabinet found cause for some alarm in the intrigues of France and the attitude of the United States. First came disquieting rumors of a plot to place Bourbons under French auspices over quasi-independent kingdoms in Spanish America. Next occurred the liberal revolution in Spain, followed by the prospect of European interference with France as a possible agent. While these important events were taking place in Europe it appeared evident that the United States was moving gradually to-

---

[47] As given by Webster, *op. et loc. cit.,* pp. 86–87.

[48] *Ibid.,* XXVII, 88–89; XXX, 635–636. Russia appears never to have seriously considered the use of armed force.

ward recognition of the new states in Spanish America. The administration was being urged to take this step by liberal public opinion, by commercial interests, and by the factional opposition of Henry Clay. As early as 1810 the United States had begun to send commercial agents to the revolting colonies. Later, in 1817, preparations were begun for dispatching a committee of investigation, and the envoys of the United States in Europe were instructed to drop hints to the effect that the United States was preparing to recognize the insurgent states. At the same time Henry Clay began to deliver his Pan-American orations in Congress. The government was now held in restraint only by the Florida negotiations and uncertainty regarding the intentions of Europe. Early in 1819 it went so far as to invite an understanding with Great Britain on the question of recognition. Castlereagh's opposition to the employment of forced mediation and the rift in European diplomacy had become known at Washington. But Castlereagh refused to coöperate with the United States on recognition. Then came news that Clay had put through the House (May, 1820, and February, 1821) resolutions in favor of sending diplomatic representatives to the Spanish-American states. Then came also a copy of Monroe's message of March, 1822, announcing that this step was soon to be taken. This set the British commercial world about Castlereagh's ears. Some action must be taken, they urged, else British trade would be driven from the Spanish-American markets by the United States.

Confronted thus by the schemes of France and by the ambitious haste of the United States, what was Castlereagh to do? By the close of 1821 he apparently came to the conclusion that the difficulties between Spain and her colonies could be settled only on the basis of the latter's independence. He did not seriously object to the recognition of the independence of Spain's former colonies. What he did oppose, however, was the *recognition of republics* in the New World or the establishment there of monarchies *under the patronage of France*. He had formerly sought to hold the United States in check by the declaration that successful European mediation was imminent, and assurances that force would not be used nor United States commerce subjected to discrimination. When this device at last lost its virtue he actually turned to France with a proposal of coöperation in the establishment of New World monarchies. But France rejected the overture. Castlereagh then announced (May, 1822) his intention of modifying the English navigation laws and establishing official commercial relations with the insurgent governments. He also instructed himself, in view of the approaching Congress of Verona to which he was to be a delegate, to fight to the finish any project for combined armed intervention by the European Powers in the affairs of Spanish America. He then committed suicide and left posterity to conjecture whether, if he had attended this congress of the Powers, he would have promoted the establishment of independent monarchies in the Spanish Colonies and secured a concerted announcement of intention to recognize monarchical governments in Latin America and no other.[49]

The Policy of Canning

Castlereagh's mantle fell upon George Canning, who, though somewhat less conservative than Castlereagh, was by no means eager to change the Spanish-American policy of his predecessor. Commercial recognition had already been granted (June, 1822). Canning thought that political recognition could await further developments, and he hoped that these developments would lead to the establishment of independent monarchies in the New World, although he did not object to a few republics as counterbalances to European despotisms.

But the attitude both of the United States and of the British merchants, as well as the procedure of France, rendered delay somewhat hazardous. The British merchants were determined not to allow their trade to be diminished either by Spanish restrictions or by Yankee competition. France's resolution to suppress the liberal uprising in Spain could not be shaken by the Duke of Wellington, Canning's diplomatic agent at the congress which met at Verona late in 1822. The summer of 1823 witnessed the triumphal march of the French army across Spain. Were Frenchmen returning to the Iberian ambitions of Napoleon?

Already during the closing weeks of 1822 certain French diplomats had talked ominously of placing the French fleet at the disposition of the Spanish government for the purpose of conveying Spanish troops and a Spanish prince to America. On December 13th the *Journal des Débats* announced that French naval support had been promised for the purpose of establishing Bourbon monarchs in Mexico and Peru. During the following spring and summer discussion of the project continued, and France appeared to be considering the use of force in order to carry it out. In September, 1823, Canning apparently became convinced that France had "all along meditated a direct interference in Spanish America." [50]

[49] Webster, *op. cit.*, XXX, 637 ff.
[50] Harold Temperley, *The Foreign Policy of Canning* (1925), p. 109.

Would the resolution not to recognize the insurgent states of America until they had set up monarchies have to be abandoned? Aware of the alarm of the United States with reference to the designs of Russia and the Neo-Holy Alliance, Canning turned to Richard Rush, minister of the United States in London.

"Is not the moment come when our governments might understand each other as to the Spanish-American Colonies?" Canning inquired. "And," he continued, "if we can arrive at such an understanding, would it not be expedient for ourselves and beneficial for all the world that the principles of it be clearly settled and plainly avowed?

"For ourselves we have no disguise.

1. We conceive the recovery of the Colonies by Spain to be hopeless.

2. We conceive the question of the recognition of them as independent states to be one of time and circumstances.

3. We are, however, by no means disposed to throw any impediment in the way of an arrangement between them and the mother country by amicable negotiation.

4. We aim not at the possession of any portion of them ourselves.

5. We could not see any portion of them transferred to any other Power with indifference.

"If these opinions and feelings are, as I firmly believe them to be, common to your government with ours, why should we hesitate mutually to confide them to each other, and to declare them in the face of the world?

"If there be any European Power which cherishes other projects which look to a forcible enterprise for reducing the Colonies to subjugation on the behalf or in the name of Spain, or which meditates the acquisition of any part of them to itself by cession or by conquest, such a declaration on the part of your government and ours would be at once the most effectual and the least offensive mode of intimating our joint disapprobation of such projects. It would at the same time put an end to all the jealousies of Spain with respect to her remaining Colonies [i.e., Cuba and Porto Rico], and to the agitation which prevails in those Colonies, an agitation which it would be but humane to allay, being determined (as we are) not to profit by encouraging it . . ." [51]

While Rush sought advice from Washington, Canning sent out consuls as well as commissioners to America. He also summoned

[51] As quoted in *ibid.*, pp. 110–111.

Polignac, French ambassador in London, and demanded explanations with reference to French intentions. During interviews which occurred on October 9, 1823, Canning made three important declarations: (1) "England would recognize the Spanish Colonies if any attempt was made to restrict her existing trade with them;" (2) England would consider any foreign interference in the contest between Spain and her colonies "as a motive for recognizing" them "without delay;" (3) England, on account of her Spanish-American interests, was not inclined to enter upon a joint deliberation on "an equal footing" with the other European Powers, and would not do so unless the United States were invited to participate.[52]

The Monroe Doctrine—Its Reception and Influence

With a fairly definite idea of British attitude but without knowledge of the Polignac interview, Monroe and his cabinet proceeded to discuss and formulate the policy of the United States. The result of their deliberations was the Monroe Doctrine. It differed from Canning's proposals to Rush in several important respects: it was not a joint declaration; it contained no self-denying clause; it interdicted European colonization as well as European political interference in the Western Hemisphere; and it announced a sort of doctrine of two hemispheres. Several motives led these statesmen to prefer independent action. It was necessary to issue a warning to Russia regarding the Pacific Coast. It was feared that a joint statement might tend to make the United States, in appearance if not in reality, a mere tail to the British kite, to the great diminution of American prestige both in Europe and in America. And lastly, Adams was indisposed to bind the United States never to acquire Spanish-American territory.[53]

This independent course did not involve great risk to the United States because the Neo-Holy Alliance probably did not seriously contemplate the use of force in Spanish America, because these allies could not have agreed among themselves and with Spain as to the specific manner in which and purposes to which force would have been directed even if they had determined to use it, and because Britain would have borne the brunt of the opposition to any drastic measures which might have been undertaken. As for Russian designs

[52] Harold Temperley, *The Foreign Policy of Canning*, pp. 115-118.
[53] Adams, *Memoirs*, VI, 177; McCorkle, *The Personal Genesis of the Monroe Doctrine*, pp. 85-87; and see on the whole background of the Doctrine, Temperley, *The Foreign Policy of Canning*, p. 103 ff.

on the Pacific Coast, they seem to have been of no importance at this time. Russian territorial ambitions were directed mainly toward the Balkans. Even as early as December, 1822, the Russian government had evinced a willingness to come to terms with the United States on the Alaskan boundary issue.[54] The distinguished English specialist on Canning's foreign policy concludes that the evidence is inadequate to support the contention that the European alliance or any member of the alliance seriously considered armed intervention in Spanish America between 1818 and 1824, but he is inclined to believe they did.[55] Carlos A. Villanueva and Dexter Perkins, on the other hand, are positive that the use of force in the Spanish colonies was never seriously considered by the Neo-Holy Alliance, or by any government within it.[56]

In France—to begin with the Continental Power which had the greatest and most sustained interest in Spanish America—there had always to be reckoned with a strong sentiment among the liberal and mercantile classes in favor of recognizing the insurgent governments. The French ministry favored the solution of the Spanish colonial problem by the establishment of Bourbon monarchies in America, but a resort to compulsion was not seriously contemplated. Dexter Perkins, who has explored the European archives on this subject, says: "There seems to have been an optimistic belief that the colonies would welcome such an arrangement . . . That it might be necessary to use force . . . seems hardly to have occurred to the leaders of French policy . . . There is not a sign that any offer of material aid was ever made at Madrid."

"The project of independent Bourbon monarchies"—quoting again from Perkins—"was not considered, indeed, a project of aggression. It was a means of reconciling legitimacy with French commercial interest. It was dependent on the opening of the colonies to the trade of the world. It was, in the language of Villèle, a project 'to render more tolerable to France by the new markets open to her commerce the sacrifices which she had made and would still have to make in Spain.'" Moreover, during the Canning-Polignac interview France gave "a binding pledge against the use of force."

[54] Temperley, *The Foreign Policy of Canning*, p. 493, note 1.
[55] Temperley, "French Designs on Spanish America in 1820–5," *The English Historical Review*, XL (January, 1925), 34 ff.
[56] Perkins, "Europe, Spanish America, and the Monroe Doctrine" in *The Am. Hist. Rev.*, XXVII (1922), 207 ff.; Carlos A. Villanueva, *La Monarquia en América* (1913?)

The attitude of the other Continental Powers in the autumn of 1823 was no more aggressive. Prussia, as always, was indifferent. Austria was by no means committed to armed mediation. Metternich "had no Utopian ideas as to the reconquest of Spanish America. In July he had told Wellesley, British ambassador at Vienna, that all projects of the kind were hopeless, and that Spain would do well to confine her efforts to the preservation of Cuba. Somewhat later he declared to the Russian representative that Spain should limit her efforts to the retention of the colonies which still remained faithful and . . . compromise with those which, on terms of mutual advantage, might consent again to become subject to her. Finally, in November, he addressed to the Spanish government itself a long memorandum in which he urged such a policy upon it. Platonic counsel was Metternich's sole expedient in the premises." Moreover, the Russian government appears to have settled upon "no positive line of action." In November, 1823, Czar Alexander appeared to be in favor of delay. "Everything is confusion in America," he remarked to the French ambassador. "Let us leave this chaos for a while to reduce itself to order." The Continental Powers had determined upon only one measure when Monroe issued his message, and that was that a congress should be summoned to consider the colonial question! Moreover, Spain's attitude was intransigent throughout. Very rarely did she listen to the advice of the allies or fall in with their plans.[57]

What was the contemporary reception and influence of the Monroe manifesto in Europe? Important to note at the outset is the fact that it made the greatest impression in December and January when European diplomats and publicists believed that it had been inspired by Great Britain. It is also significant that, although there was some uncertainty as to its real intent, there was a widespread belief that the United States would use force to prevent European political interference or colonization in America. And lastly, the pronouncement aroused some apprehension regarding the possible influence of American liberalism upon the European political system itself.

The message was favorably received by the London press, which assumed that the principles set forth "would be acceptable to England." "The general interpretation was that the United States had announced that they were prepared to repel intervention by force of arms." The non-colonization clause was interpreted as applying specifically to Russia. There was only one discordant note. The *Star* (December 27) interpreted the message as meaning that the United States was resolved even to prevent Spain from reconquering her

---

[57] Perkins, *op. et loc. cit.*

colonies. It also attacked the protest against European colonization, declaring that it expressed a wish on the part of the United States to monopolize the colonization of the Pacific Northwest and "every other part of the American continent in a similar condition."

Perhaps this journal expressed the view of Canning [58] and of certain other members of the cabinet. Every important English statesman outside of the cabinet, however, appeared to agree with the general sentiment of the press. In Parliament Brougham declared that the message of Monroe should bring great joy, exultation, and gratitude to "all the freemen of Europe"; that its influence was "decisive on the subject"; and that he hoped British ministers would follow "so noble and illustrious an example."

"The reports of Monroe's message and of its reception in England created a stir in the newspapers of Paris." Press opinion was divided; the conservative and administration journals were hostile, while the more liberal papers assumed a friendly attitude. The administration journal *L'Etoile,* for instance, objected to the substitution of the *de facto* principle for that of legitimacy, rebuked the upstart Monroe for his impudence toward European potentates, and inquired what title the temporary president of an insignificant nation had to justify the claim of "immediate control" over the "Two Americas from Hudson's Bay to Cape Horn." It contended that the manifesto signified that the United States would oppose Spain's efforts to reconquer her colonies, Portugal's exercise of sovereignty over the empire of Brazil, and England's planting of new settlements in Canada or Nova Scotia. It also called attention to certain phrases in the message which were hostile to the "politics" of the Great Powers. *Le Constitutionnel,* on the other hand, saw in the message a magnificent expression of liberalism: "There one reads all that we ceaselessly repeat; there one sees put into practice all the principles which we proclaim." The United States was not going to stand by while the European alliance or even Spain herself attempted to reconquer the Spanish colonies.

The French Foreign Secretary, Chateaubriand, was at first inclined to believe that Monroe's message had been inspired by Canning. He subsequently changed his view, but as late as February 17, 1824, he was of the opinion that the Canning and Monroe declarations signified their intention of opposing by force of arms the intervention of the Continental Powers in Spanish America. Yet, on January 1, Chateaubriand had suggested to the British ambassador at Paris that the message of Monroe justified a joint representation of

[58] See *post,* pp. 56, 68.

the Powers "against the prohibition of future colonization on the Continent of America"; and, somewhat later, he had remarked to Polignac: "Mr. Canning can have no more desire than I to favor military insurrections, the sovereignty of the people, and all the beautiful things which Mr. Monroe tells us about *de facto* government." Perhaps Chateaubriand's views regarding the doctrine did not differ widely from those of other members of the French Government.

Neither Russia nor Austria permitted any freedom of the press at this time. Their views must be obtained from the correspondence and memoirs of their statesmen. All that can be said in regard to Russia is that the "speech of Mr. Monroe . . . excited" a "sensation." During the early months of 1824 the Czar and certain of his counselors and diplomats urged intervention in the Spanish colonies.

Information regarding the reception of the message by the Austrian government is much more adequate. We have the comments of the Austrian consul-general in New York, of Metternich's able ambassador at St. Petersburg, of Friederich von Gentz, and of Metternich himself. The consul-general was uncertain as to whether the message constituted a threat. The ambassador saw in the pronouncement a means of alarming Britain by representing that it was but the expression of a design on the part of the United States "to place herself at the head of a confederation which would embrace the whole hemisphere." Gentz and Metternich commented at greater length.

Gentz declared (January 13, 1824) that reconquest was now hopeless, if indeed it "had not already become impossible." He hoped that "great statesmen" would "consider carefully and profoundly what must be done with that new transatlantic colossus which was formed from such dangerous, hostile elements, not so much because of the material safety of Europe (for this cannot be menaced from that quarter for the next fifty or one hundred years) as for the moral and political preservation of the Old World upon its present basis . . ." Gentz accordingly favored a congress for the purpose of adjusting the relations between Spain and the independent states of Spanish America. Thus the Austrian Councillor of State saw the matter in the light of his legitimist views and of his opposition to liberalism.

The same was true of Metternich, except that he was even more conservative. Monroe's "speech . . . confirmed him in an opinion he had before entertained, that great calamities would be brought upon Europe by the establishment of these vast republics in the New World . . . He did not say that the present race [generation] would witness these calamities, but it was one of the first duties of Government to direct its views to the welfare of Posterity . . ." He did not see how any of the European Powers, granted that their commercial interests were secured, could favor the independence of America, "although circumstances might compel them to acquiesce in it." He thought it "would be highly advantageous to Europe" if the monarchic principle "could be preserved by vesting in his Catholic Majesty a nominal authority over those possessions, or by constituting them independent Monarchies in the persons of Individuals of the Spanish Royal Family." "The children of Europe" must be prevented from becoming "the adults of America." [59]

Such were the comments of European statesmen and publicists. What influence did the pronouncement have upon their actions? It appears only to have confirmed the Spanish monarch in his obstinacy. To him it was decidedly not "a flaming sword at the gateway of the New World." He recalled the envoys which he had sent to pacify the insurgents and made a last desperate effort at reconquest. He also favored the calling of a congress of the Powers on the subject.

The Continental statesmen likewise clung to the idea of a congress. France and Austria attempted to use the message to persuade Great Britain to participate in such an assembly, but Canning steadfastly refused, and his refusal shattered the project of a formal gathering of the Powers. For several months subsequent to the publication of Monroe's message, however, the colonial question engaged the attention of the Continental ambassadors at Paris. In the course of numerous conferences it became clear that Russia alone favored the granting of material assistance to Spain, and even Russia had virtually given up the idea by May, 1824. On May 13 Nesselrode instructed Pozzo, Russian ambassador in France, to the effect that "though the Allies, by a strict interpretation of their doctrines, might be bound not to refuse a direct assistance in men and ships to Spain, that power will readily see that so rigid a reconstruction [sic] of their engagements will serve no useful purpose while England maintains its present attitude." The conclusion of Nesselrode is typical. All the leaders of Europe "paid more heed to London than to Washington." The Polignac memorandum was far more influential than the Monroe Doctrine.

[59] On the contemporary European reception of the Monroe Doctrine, *cf.* William Spence Robertson, "The Monroe Doctrine Abroad in 1823–24," in *The American Political Science Review*, VI (1912), 546 ff.; Harold Temperley, "Documents Illustrating the Reception and Interpretation of the Monroe Doctrine in Europe, 1823–4," in *The English Historical Review*, XXXIX (1924), 590 ff.

The use of force did not seem feasible, but the Continental Powers did not for this reason forbear to employ moral pressure. Some of the French merchants were urging recognition and the French government at one time appeared disposed to act separately and grant it, but on March 31, 1824, the Ambassadors' Conference secured from Chateaubriand the statement that "France had decided not to recognize the Spanish-American colonies." In the following August the diplomats solemnly advised Spain to put forth her best efforts to reconquer the insurgents, suggesting Mexico as the most likely object of attack. The Russian ambassador urged for the last time that Spain be actively assisted by the Continental Powers, but "Metternich wanted to do nothing, and France was afraid both of England and of the United States." In October and November the ambassadors recommended that France should not evacuate Spain—a recommendation which the French government followed and thus gave Canning one of his best arguments for recognizing the new states. The conference also prevented Prussia and the Netherlands from immediately sending consuls to Spanish America. And lastly, it advised Spain not to recognize the colonies but to seek a working agreement along commercial lines, and not to give way on the Cuban issue but to refuse to accept the guaranty proposed both by England and the United States as an inducement to recognize the Spanish colonies. In both instances these recommendations were followed. The last meeting of the ambassadors was held on August 17, 1826. The influence of the conferences had been entirely moral.[60]

Meanwhile French intrigues in Spanish America continued. Neither Canning's declarations to Polignac nor the Monroe manifesto gave them the *coup de grâce*. In January, 1824, a French naval squadron appeared off Rio de Janeiro and offered to assist Dom Pedro to put down an insurrection. In July French war vessels moved ominously about the ports of Chile and Peru. In 1824 Colombians were alarmed at French designs and as late as 1825 Frenchmen continued to discuss the project of establishing a Bourbon prince in Mexico. More important than any other were French activities in the West Indies. In June, 1824, the governor of Martinique was instructed to defend Cuba and Porto Rico against any external attack as well as to interfere to suppress any revolt against the legitimate authority. Apparently France was eager to occupy Cuba. In July, 1825, the Martinique executive not only entertained and

---

[60] On the influence of the Monroe Doctrine, consult Perkins, *op. et loc. cit.;* Harold Temperley, "Canning and the Conferences of the Four Allied Governments in Paris," in *The American Historical Review*, XXX (1924–1925), 16 ff.

rationed a Spanish force on its way to Cuba, but actually escorted it from Martinique with French ships. Shortly before a naval squadron had been sent across the Atlantic under the pretext of collecting a debt from Haiti. Both Canning and Adams were alarmed. Prompt remonstrances from England and the United States put an end to this and "all further projects." [61]

Thus it may be said that the Monroe Doctrine exerted some influence in frustrating the designs of the European Powers, and did so without involving great risk. The failure of the Powers to intervene was due largely to the obstinacy of Spain, inability to agree upon a plan, and the opposition of England. Moreover, it appears that Adams, who was mainly responsible for the doctrine, felt at the time that he was not assuming great risk. Unlike Calhoun, Monroe, Madison, and Jefferson, he did not believe that war was imminent. His manifesto as a matter of fact was aimed mainly at Russia, whose subjects appeared to be casting covetous eyes upon the Pacific Northwest and whose minister had just given him a lecture upon the sacredness of absolutist principles. Adams did not believe Russia or the alliance would fight. If they should really do so, there was the British navy; and, after all, the message of Monroe was so framed as not to commit the United States irrevocably to hostilities. He "could safely blow a blast on the republican trumpet, while sheltered behind the shield of England." [62]

[61] Temperley, "French Designs on Spanish America . . . ," *loc. cit.*
[62] *Id., The Foreign Policy of Canning,* p. 127. See also Adams's *Memoirs* (C. F. Adams, ed., 1874), VI, 185, *passim.*

CHAPTER IV

EARLY RIVALRIES OF THE UNITED STATES AND BRITAIN SOUTH OF THE RIO GRANDE (1)

For almost thirty-five years subsequent to the promulgation of the Monroe Doctrine, and particularly between 1823 and 1827, the United States and Great Britain were energetic rivals in Hispanic America. In order to defeat the projects of the Neo-Holy Alliance, Canning had invited the coöperation of the United States, but this did not mean that the two branches of the Anglo-Saxon family were in complete accord. The British foreign secretary was more provoked than pleased by the Monroe Doctrine. Its protest against the armed intervention of the Continental Powers tended to support Canning's policy, but this protest was accompanied by two other ideas which gave him no little concern. The message forbade future colonization in America by European powers, and it expressed the view that America and Europe were separate worlds. These notions were acceptable to Canning neither in their commercial nor in their political implications, and during the remainder of his life (1823–1827) he made a vigorous effort to counteract them. With this effort and the counter effort of the United States the present chapter and the one which follows are mainly concerned.

Early Evidences of British Jealousy

Hispanic America had long been considered an important potential market for British goods. Certain profound economic changes which occurred during the first two decades of the nineteenth century made it even more desirable that Englishmen should dominate this market. During the previous century British industries had undergone a marvelous development. British exports had mounted from an annual value of £1,505,285 in 1701 to £41,717,000 in 1801, and her industries had reached a very efficient stage compared with those of the rest of Europe. But while the opening decades of the nineteenth century saw no decline in efficiency, they did witness a decline in the total of British exports, for they amounted to less than

54

£37,000,000 in 1822. This had been due largely to the impoverish-
ment of Europe by the Napoleonic Wars and an increasing tendency both in Europe and in the United States to encourage home
industries by the erection of tariff walls. The effect of the tariff was
particularly evident in the sum total of British exports to the United States where the duties levied by the law of 1816 were perhaps
responsible for a decline in the importation of English goods from a
little less than 12,000,000 pounds sterling in 1815 to less than
4,000,000 in 1820. These circumstances enhanced the value of Spanish-American markets, and British trade with these countries tended
to increase rapidly, reaching a total value of a little more than
£5,500,000 in 1822 and more than £7,500,000 in 1823. The United States, with a total of Hispanic-American trade of more than
$26,500,000 in 1822 and of almost $31,000,000 in the following year,
was Britain's most formidable commercial rival.[1]

English capital was likewise interested in Hispanic America. Save
for French investors British capitalists met few competitors south
of the Rio Grande during the first half of the nineteenth century.
Most of the new governments immediately negotiated loans with
British banking houses, and English investors soon became deeply
interested in the mining industry and other enterprises of Hispanic
America. In 1836 a member of the British parliament stated that his
countrymen had investments valued at seventy million dollars in
Mexico alone.[2]

Trade and investments may be profoundly influenced by government policy and hence are closely bound up with politics. Their
interrelation in Great Britain is clearly revealed in the contemporary
discussions of the British press and of British statesmen. An examination of these will likewise show a lively apprehension of the
United States and render evident the motives underlying later British procedure in the Western Hemisphere.

The outburst of the London *Times* on the occasion of the Florida
Purchase has already been noted. When the agent of the Colombian
insurgents in Europe suggested (1823) that the Spanish-American
states might accord commercial priority to foreign states in the or-

---

[1] Lawson, *The Relation of British Policy to the Declaration of the Monroe
Doctrine* (1924), pp. 13, 78–79; Chandler, "United States Commerce with
Latin America at the Promulgation of the Monroe Doctrine," in *The Quar-
terly Journal of Economics*, XXXVIII (1924), p. 481.

[2] Barlow Hoy, in the House of Commons, August 5, 1836. Hansard's *Parliamentary Debates*, Vol. 35, p. 928. See also, Great Britian, *State Papers*, index
under the various states of Hispanic America; *Cambridge Modern History*,
X, 307.

der in which they extended recognition, the *Times* returned to the attack. It accused the United States of catching "at the promised good, by hastening her formal act of recognition." At the same time it contended that the United States would "thus . . . forestall the merchants of Great Britain in the trade with South America." Coming to the assistance of the *Times*, the *Examiner* inquired whether anything could be "more disgraceful in the British Ministers than to let the North Americans, with nothing like our motives, and some natural feeling to the contrary, get the start of us in establishing a profitable connection with the immense, fertile, and improving States of Southern America." [3]

Similar sentiments were expressed by the petitions of British merchants and by the friends of these merchants in parliament. As early as 1819 a member of the House of Commons sought to modify British policy by describing the possible action of the United States. Revealing something of jealous contempt on his own part, he said: "Although a sop has, for the present, been given to Cerberus, by the cession of the Floridas to the United States, the policy of the government [at Washington] will not long be able to restrain the wishes of the people, but be compelled to join this popular and patriotic cause; an event which will at once consummate the independence of South America." [4] In September, 1822, a memorial signed by a group of London merchants prayed for government support on the ground that American citizens threatened to drive British trade from Spanish-American markets. [5]

Still more convincing evidence of British jealousy may be found in the memorials penned by George Canning in his attempt to convince the British Ministry of the advisability of extending recognition to the revolting colonies. Here he gives as one reason for this step the large investments of English citizens in Spanish America. He then continues: "The other and perhaps still more powerful motive is my apprehension of the ambition and ascendancy of the U[nited] S[tates] of Am[erica]: It is obviously the policy of that Gov[ernmen]t to connect itself with all the powers of America in a general Transatlantic League, of which it would have the sole direction. I need only say how inconvenient such an ascendency may be in time of peace, and how formidable in case of war." [6] After he had at last

---

[3] November 30, 1823, as quoted by Lawson, *op. cit.*, p. 99.

[4] As quoted by Paxson, *The Independence of the South American Republic* (1916), p. 192.

[5] Lawson, *op. cit.*, p. 87.

[6] As quoted by Temperley, "The Later American Policy of George Canning," in *Am. Hist. Rev.*, XI (1906), 781.

forced his recognition policy through the cabinet he wrote to Granville: "The deed is done, the nail is driven. Spanish America is free; and if we do not mismanage our affairs sadly, *she is English*." [7]

Indications of Jealousy in the United States

Thus it will be observed that in England the United States was looked upon as a formidable rival from the political as well as from the commercial point of view. Although apprehension of England was not so keenly felt in the United States, there are indications of its existence. In his observations on Mexico published in 1824 Poinsett pointed out the alarming extent to which the British were taking possession of the commerce and the economic resources of the country.[8] A year later, on the eve of his departure for Mexico City where he was to serve as minister, one of his friends, doubtless adapting himself to Poinsett's mood, playfully remarked: "Make a good commercial treaty for us and take care that John Bull gets no advantage of you—if anything get the weather gauge of him . . ." [9] Henry Clay, when making a desperate bid for political advantage by advocating the recognition of the Spanish-American insurgents, taunted John Quincy Adams with his dependence upon England. "If Lord Castlereagh says we may recognize, we do; if not, we do not," [10] said Clay, and he evidently hoped to profit by the popular dislike for England. The jealousy of the mercantile interests of the United States was revealed by the following remark of the New York *Commercial Advertiser*: "A few days since we took the liberty, in a short paragraph, to call the attention of the American merchants to the vast markets about to be opened to the enterprise of the world, in the late American colonies of Spain; and we now beg leave again to direct their attention to the same subject, as we all are apprehensive notwithstanding our propinquity to them, that the vigilant and indefatigable John Bull will get the start of us." [11] The influence of suspicion of British motives in preventing Monroe's administration from accepting Canning's proposal of a joint declaration against the intervention of the Continental Powers in Spanish America has already been referred to. Adams, who felt this suspicion most keenly, remarked: "The object of Canning appears to have been to obtain

[7] Quoted in *ibid., loc. cit.*, p. 796.

[8] *Notes on Mexico* (1824), p. 69.

[9] Quoted in Manning, *Early Diplomatic Relations between the United States and Mexico* (1919), p. 48, note 28.

[10] Latané, *The Diplomatic Relations of the United States and Spanish America* (1900), p. 59.

[11] November 30, as quoted by Lawson, *op. cit.*, p. 99.

some public pledge from the government of the United States, . . . against the acquisition to the United States themselves of any part of the Spanish-American possessions." He also feared that by such a joint declaration the United States would diminish its prestige and fall too much under the influence of Great Britain.[12] These illustrations will suffice to reveal the existence of apprehension of England in the United States. Had Canning's disposition been fully known, doubtless much more uneasiness would have been displayed.

During the four years following the promulgation of the Monroe Doctrine this mutual suspicion and rivalry between the two branches of the Anglo-Saxon family revealed itself on numerous occasions. In the contest for trade and a dominant political influence in Hispanic America, Great Britain, under the leadership of George Canning, was the more aggressive rival, but the United States, once the combat had been joined, frequently managed to return blow for blow. The struggle is illustrated in the Oregon issue, in the attempts at mediation between Argentina and Brazil, in the discussions regarding the status of Cuba, in the attitude of the two governments respecting the Panama Congress, and, clearest of all, in the procedure of the agents of the rivals in Mexico.

In the contest Britain had almost every advantage: the prestige of a great and victorious nation, better trained diplomats, the good-will of Spanish Americans won by the aid of hundreds of British subjects in the Wars of Independence, her great ability to supply the markets of the New World, capital to lend the struggling new republics. The United States, on the contrary, had only the advantage of being a republic and of having granted prior recognition—and even the former constituted a disadvantage in certain regions where the leaders were strongly monarchical in sympathy. It may be doubted whether the United States was so deeply interested in Latin America as a whole as was England. Latin-American trade was important, but not vital. The expanding domestic market was capable of consuming the slowly accumulating commodities of our infant industries. The statesmen at the helm in 1823–1827 were not dominated by an ambition to become the head of an American League of Nations. Their recollection of Washington's Farewell Address and of Jefferson's advice against "entangling alliances" was too vivid. It was with great difficulty that they made up their minds to send representatives to the Panama Congress of 1826. Only in Cuba and Mexico did they have a

[12] *Cf.* his *Memoirs* (C. F. Adams ed., 1874), VI, 177 ff.; and for further evidence of this jealousy of England, see W. R. Manning, *Diplomatic Correspondence of the United States Concerning the Independence of the Latin-American Nations* (1926), index under Great Britian.

vital interest. England's presence at Panama and mediation at Rio de Janeiro and Buenos Aires was in defiance of the idea of two hemispheres, but there was a great difference between the moral interposition of England and the force or menace of the reactionary Neo-Holy Alliance. The United States was mainly interested in immediate national security. It had not precisely determined upon a republican crusade or the erection of a Chinese wall. There were no Don Quixotes in the White House or the State Department.[13]

The Wider Aspect of the Oregon Issue

In dealing with the rival claims of Britain and the United States in the Oregon country Canning was not a little concerned with the bearing of the question upon British influence and prestige in America. He did not fail to see the value of Oregon either intrinsically or in its relation to the Chinese trade, but he often referred to the matter in connection with the "ambitions and overweening views" of his rivals. Thus, while instructing the British minister in Washington (1826), Canning took occasion to remark that "the avowed pretension of the United States to put themselves at the head of the confederacy of all the Americas and to sway that confederacy against Europe (Great Britain included) is *not* a pretension identified with our interests, or one that we can countenance or tolerate." It was in fact largely for the purpose of supporting British prestige and bringing the English boundary as close as possible to that of Mexico that Canning insisted upon the forty-ninth parallel.[14] The United States was just as persistent in urging its claims, but the all-American aspect of the contest was probably not so clearly perceived by American leaders.

Rivalry in the La Plata Area

The war between Argentina and Brazil over the lower eastern bank of the Rio de la Plata—a heritage of the old Spanish-Portuguese dispute—gave Canning an opportunity to counteract the notion of non-intercourse between Europe and America. He took advantage of the occasion to teach these states to lean upon England. Both belligerents had appealed to the United States for aid under certain contingencies, but our policy of non-entanglement had led the Washington govern-

[13] Temperley, *The Foreign Policy of Canning*, pp. 162–163, holds a somewhat different view.
[14] Temperley, "The Later American Policy of Canning," *loc. cit.*, pp. 794–796.

ment to refrain from action and maintain neutrality. The efforts of the United States minister in Brazil to carry out this policy offended the Brazilian government and apparently placed the United States in a position where it could not have served as mediator had it desired to do so. Canning, on the other hand, was diligent in his attempts to mediate the dispute; and although he did not live to see it brought to a successful conclusion, his efforts laid the basis for a satisfactory settlement under British auspices in 1828.

Canning was particularly anxious regarding the outcome of the struggle because he feared that the Spanish-American states might organize a republican league and overthrow the Brazilian monarchy. In this event he believed that England would lose an important point of contact with the New World, and since Emperor Iturbide (of Mexico) had already fallen, there would be no monarchy left in America to cure the "evil of universal democracy." Almost from the beginning Canning feared that his plan of mediation was likely to be interfered with by his American rival, for he remarked that "jealousy" of Great Britain had been "openly inculcated by the publick press of the United States . . . , and no doubt secretly by their diplomatic agents." [15]

Mutual Suspicions Regarding Cuba

Canning and the American cabinet harbored mutual suspicions of each other's designs upon Cuba from the time when he took charge of the British Foreign Office until death ended his career. On October 11, 1822, Canning wrote the English ambassador at Washington of various indications that the United States desired to seize Cuba, but cautioned him against imputing such a design to the administration lest the charge suggest the very evil "which it deprecates." [16] In 1825 he suspected that the United States was searching for an excuse to occupy the island; for at this time he remarked that "The Yankees may be just the rogues that we have always hitherto taken them to be, but which I was willing to hope they might have resolved to be no longer." [17] In 1826, still uneasy with respect to the ambitions of the United States, Canning instructed the special agent of the British government to Panama to warn the Spanish-American states that a concerted attempt on their part to drive the Spaniards out of Cuba might end in the occupation of the island by their North American neighbor.[18]

[15] Temperley, "The Later American Policy of Canning," pp. 783–785; Lockey, *Pan-Americanism* (1916), pp. 250–260, 460–462.
[16] Temperley, *op. cit.*, p. 789.
[17] Manning, *op. cit.*, p. 127, quoting Canning to Liverpool, August 6, 1825.
[18] Temperley, *op. cit.*, p. 792.

There is just as convincing evidence of suspicion of the Cuban designs of Great Britain among American statesmen. In the autumn of 1822 Monroe's cabinet was alarmed at the prospect of the seizure of Cuba by England. On December 17, John Forsyth, American ambassador at Madrid, was directed to investigate the rumor that Britain was treating with Spain for the island and, in case he found it true, to declare that the United States desired Cuba to continue in Spanish hands. In June, 1823, Jefferson declared in a letter to Monroe that Cuba's "possession by England would be a calamity," and he suggested that she might be persuaded to join the United States in a guaranty of the island to Spain. With respect to Canning's proposal to Rush in August, 1823, Madison suspiciously inquired: "What is the extent of Mr. Canning's disclaimer as to 'the remaining possessions of Spain in America'? Does it exclude further views of acquiring Puerto Rico, etc., as well as Cuba?" And so the apprehension continued. Just as the great English statesman passed away the United States minister at Madrid wrote that in case of war with Spain England was planning to revolutionize Cuba and the Canary Islands in order "to establish British influence" there and "in the end, probably, to obtain territorial possession of them." If indeed such a project was entertained, it was perhaps in line with plans previously suggested by Canning, for on October 6, 1826, he had written to Liverpool: "One single word I must add in the deepest secrecy. God forbid war; but if Spain will have it, ought not we to think of the Havannah? Where else can we strike a blow? and what other blow would be so effectual? It would settle all better than half a dozen Peninsular campaigns." [19]

The anxiety of both England and North America was increased by the mysterious procedure of France in the West Indies and by the more or less open schemes of Colombia and Mexico to deliver Cuba from the Spanish yoke. Each branch of the Anglo-Saxon family sought to restrain the other by disavowing any designs upon Cuba, expressing a desire that the island should remain in the possession of the mother country, and declaring that it could not permit it to fall into the clutches of any other Power. England tried to commit the United States and France to a triple guaranty of the island to Spain; and the United States, unwilling to enter into this covenant with Britain, attempted to enlist the European Powers in a concerted endeavor to secure the recognition of the insurgent states at Madrid, and thus put an end to the plans of Mexico and Colombia and place at rest all anxieties over the fate of Cuba. In this latter project the European states manifested a real interest, but they found Spain

[19] As quoted in Manning, *op. cit.*, p. 161.

as indisposed as ever to agree to any compromise that the revolting colonies would accept. Nevertheless these very rivalries of the Powers saved Cuba to Spain, for, as the London *Courier* remarked, Cuba had during these early years become the "Turkey of trans-Atlantic politics, tottering to her fall, and kept from falling by those who contend[ed] for the right of catching her in her descent." [20] Colombia and Mexico might have precipitated a crisis by invading the pearl of the Antilles, but they were first dissuaded by England and the United States and afterwards rendered impotent by domestic discords. [21] During the diplomatic contest England scored at least one point over the United States. At the Panama Congress which assembled in June, 1826, she was able to present herself as far less meddlesome and selfish in her Cuban policy than the United States had been.

The Panama Congress

Indeed, the rivalries of the two Powers in Hispanic America never appeared more clearly than in connection with this congress. Edward J. Dawkins, whom the British government in response to the invitation of Colombia sent as representative to Panama, was instructed, among other things, to urge the new states to adopt British principles of maritime law, and to do so with vigor. "You will take care to have it duly understood," said Canning, "that our determination to act upon these principles . . . will not be altered by any resolution or combination of States of the New World" any more than it "has been shaken by European confederacies." Canning then remarked that England would not object to the perfection of a Spanish-American alliance, but that "any project for putting the U. S. of North America at the head of an American Confederacy would be highly displeasing" to her. "It would be felt as an ill return for the service which has been rendered to those States, and the dangers which have been averted from them, by the countenance and friendship, and publick declarations of Great Britain; and it would too probably at no very distant period endanger the peace both of America and of Europe." [22] Thus it was to be Dawkins's duty to advance Britain's maritime interests, to detach the United States from a position of leadership, and to teach these young states to lean upon the experienced arm of Britain.

In one respect, it must be repeated, Canning misinterpreted American psychology and overestimated the ambitions of the United

[20] As quoted in Callahan, *Cuba and International Relations* (1898), p. 140.
[21] Manning, *op. et loc. cit.*
[22] See excerpts from these instructions in Temperley, *op. cit.*, p. 787.

States in the Western Hemisphere. The majority of Americans were too completely converted to the notion of no entangling alliances to accept even the dignified position of head of a Pan-American league, nor were they desirous of discriminating against the European Powers in the markets of Hispanic America. But the interests of mother and daughter nevertheless conflicted at numerous points, as will clearly appear from an examination of the instructions of the delegates of the United States to the Panama Congress. They were directed, for instance, to insist upon the most-favored-nation principle, a broad definition of the rights of neutrals in time of war, and a restriction of the power of blockade. They were also instructed to urge that "whatever may be imported from any foreign country into any one American nation or exported from it in its own vessels may, in like manner, be imported into or exported from the same nation" in vessels of other nations. Lastly, they were directed to encourage these new nations to resist European interference or encroachments and to strengthen their faith in republican institutions.

That the commercial phase of these instructions was aimed at Great Britain, there is no doubt. This fact is supported by the numerous references to the experience of the United States during the recent war (1812). It appears just as clearly in the following comments taken from the body of these instructions:

"At all times there has existed more inequality in the distribution among nations of maritime than of territorial power. In almost every age, some one has had the complete mastery on the ocean, and this superiority has been occasionally so great as to more than counterbalance the combined maritime force of all other nations, if such a combination were practicable. But when a single nation finds itself possessed of a power anywhere which no one, nor all other nations, can successfully check or countervail, the consequences are too sadly unfolded in the pages of history. Such a nation grows presumptuous, impatient of contradiction or opposition, and finds the solution of national problems easier, and more grateful to its pride, by the word than by the slow and less brilliant process of patient investigation. If the superiority be on the ocean, the excesses in the abuses of that power become intolerable . . ." [23]

Nor did the British fail to grasp the significance of these instructions. After they had been made public, in 1829, the London *Times*

[23] For the entire instructions, see *International American Conference*, IV, 13 ff.

remarked: "There is an obvious anxiety throughout these long documents to assume . . . that all 'American' states are to constitute a system and a community of their own, recognizing interests and establishing maxims for their common regulation as affects each other, and for their separate, exclusive, nay, repulsive use, as regards the other nations of the world. The first obvious consequence of such a scheme, if adopted by Mexico and the states of South America, would be to place the United States at the *head* of the new federation, in virtue of superior strength, maturity, safety, commercial and political resources." [24]

A pamphlet published in England at about the same time presented a similar view. Its author declared that the United States had urged "infant states without maritime force, without the possibility of becoming maritime states for many generations, if at all," to adopt in their relations with Europe the "highest pretensions, which, in the maturity of her naval strength, the United States herself ever ventured to urge—and even then without the remotest hope of success." Instead of advising these budding nations to cultivate the most friendly intercourse with Europe and to avoid meddling where their interests were not concerned, the United States had said: "Take the highest ground in your negotiations with Europe, that an old-established, powerful state would propose. Insist that free ships shall make free goods. Demand also a definition of blockade." Nor was this all "Having recommended to the new states that they should call upon us, to renounce in their favor, a belligerent right which we have never yet conceded to any other power, the elder branch of the American family further suggests to them the experiment of prevailing upon us to make a slight inroad into our navigation act. One of the principles of this code is, that we admit from other nations their own produce in their own shipping, or in our own; but in no other, unless such produce be again exported from this country. Thus, a ship of the United States brings us cotton or tobacco from New York; but she cannot do so from Colombia; it must come from the latter country either in a Colombian or a British ship. Now, the government of the United States says to these young republics, 'America is one continent—insist in your treaties with Europe that it is one nation—and that it shall be so considered for all commercial purposes—that we, your elder brethren, may come to your ports, and be the carriers of your produce.' " [25]

[24] Issue of May 18, 1829, as quoted by Lockey, *op. cit.*, p. 420.
[25] As quoted by Lockey, *op. cit.*, pp. 420–421.

Again the Briton exaggerated the pretensions of his American kinsman, but it must be admitted that there was a real conflict of policies and that if the United States had lined the young American Powers up with her in these important matters of maritime policy she would have struck a telling blow at British naval ambitions. These comments of the British press but marked the persistence of the apprehensions of Canning.

What did the two rivals achieve at Panama? So far as the United States was concerned it may be summed up in a word: nothing. The delegates appointed by the Washington government never put in their appearance at Panama. One died on the way; the other had not set out before news came of the adjournment of the congress to meet at Tacubaya. In view of the conflicting ideas and interests of the United States and the young Spanish-American nations, it was perhaps well that these representatives did not arrive. The British agent was present at Panama from beginning to end. Although he did not attend the deliberations of the congress, he appears to have held frequent informal conferences with the delegates. What he did may be ascertained from his own accounts and from the correspondence of the other delegates.

Dawkins reported that on June 26, 1826, he found the Colombian representative, Pedro Gual, somewhat cold and skeptical regarding the good wishes of England toward the Spanish-American states. This mood was quite in contrast with the attitude of Gual on numerous previous occasions when Dawkins had made his daily visit. At length the British agent discovered the cause for the change. Gual had been reading the dispatches of Alexander Everett, United States minister at Madrid. In these Everett asserted that the British government through the British minister in Spain, a certain Mr. Lambe, had made only very feeble efforts to secure Spanish recognition for the insurgent states. Everett said, among other things, that Lambe had had in five months only one or two conversations with the Spanish government on the question of recognition. He then went on to remark: "No offer of formal mediation has been made by England since her recognition of Mexico, Colombia, and Buenos Aires. Indeed her interest as a commercial and manufacturing country, is now on the other side. The longer the war continues, the longer she enjoys monopoly of the Spanish-American market for her fabrics, and the more difficult will Spain find it to recover her natural advantages upon the return of peace. England will, therefore, probably be very easy in regard to this matter, and will leave Spain to pursue, unmolested, the course she may think expedient. I suggested this point both to Mr. Zea head of the Spanish foreign office and to the Russian minister. . . . They both admitted the justice of my remarks . . ." [26] Here was a delicate situation and Dawkins was much concerned. He set to work diligently, and soon convinced Gual that Everett was mistaken. Indeed, Dawkins reported that British ascendancy at the Congress was completely recovered. Gual soon began to speak quite freely "of the imprudence of the United States, of the errors committed by Mr. Everett, and of the mischief which may be done by the indiscreet publication of his correspondence." Indeed, the Colombian delegate even went so far as to promise to bring before the congress a project for mediation through Great Britain! Summing up the general results of his efforts, Dawkins noted that the opposition in Mexico and Peru had prevented the United States from obtaining its much desired commercial treaties. He also declared that the general influence of the United States was no longer to be "feared." "It certainly exists in Colombia," said Dawkins, "but it has been very much weakened even there by their protests against an attack upon Cuba, and by the indiscretions they have committed at Madrid." [27]

Thus Dawkins's despatches show that he was very busy in his attempts to counteract the influence of the United States. Reports of his work by delegates of the Spanish-American states do not differ materially from those of the British agent himself. Briceño Méndez, of Colombia, characterized the conduct of the British agent as "noble, frank, and loyal." "We have had no cause for complaint against Mr. Dawkins," said Méndez, "and no reason to distrust him; on the contrary all the delegations manifested toward him very flattering remarks of respect and consideration. We Colombians, particularly, were the object of his special attentions and I am not ashamed to confess that my famous friend and colleague, Señor Gual, received greater consideration than any of the rest . . . He [Dawkins] limited himself to counseling that we show respect for the institutions of other countries, whatever they might be; that we not only avoid everything that might serve to increase the fears and misgivings which Europe already had relative to revolutionary principles, but that we make an effort to demonstrate that republicanism in America is not what France professed under a republican régime; that we do not confirm the suspicion that we are aiming to form a separate political system in opposition to Europe, but that we confine ourselves to looking after our own interests and to providing for our

[26] Everett to Clay, Oct. 20, 1825, *Sen. Doc.* No. 68, 19 Cong., 1 Sess (Ser. 127), p. 84.

[27] Temperley, *op. cit.*, pp. 788–789, 793.

national security; that above all it was important that we give proof of a love of peace and of a disposition to embrace it, even though it were at the cost of some pecuniary sacrifice . . ." [28] Manuel Vidaurre, one of the Peruvian delegates, says that Dawkins urged the Spanish Americans to "proceed in such a way as to avoid coming into conflict with the system of Europe, as well as to avoid arousing the prejudices of America," presumably designating by the term "America," the United States, but this hardly appears to accord with British attitude at the time.[29]

[28] As quoted by Lockey, *op. cit.*, p. 375. Elsewhere Méndez says that Dawkins suggested that the Spanish-American states ought to consider paying Spain from "sixty to eighty millions" as the price of recognition. (*Ibid.*, pp. 373–374.)

[29] *Ibid.*, p. 372.

CHAPTER V

EARLY RIVALRIES OF THE UNITED STATES AND BRITAIN SOUTH OF THE RIO GRANDE (II) (CONCLUDED)

Mexico the Buffer

THAT Canning considered cordial and intimate relations with Mexico the key to his "later American policy," Harold Temperley has clearly shown. In one of his memoranda urging British recognition of the Spanish-American states Canning said: "I believe we now have the opportunity (but it may not last long) of opposing a powerful barrier to the influence of the U[nited] S[tates] by an amicable connection with Mexico, which from its position must be either subservient to or jealous of the U[nited] S[tates]. In point of population and resources it is at least equal to all the rest of the Spanish colonies; and may naturally expect to take the lead in its connections with the powers of Europe . . ." After he had converted the British cabinet to his viewpoint he wrote his friend John Hookham Frere: "The thing is done . . . The Yankees will shout in triumph; but it is they who lose most by our decision. The great danger of the time—a danger which the policy of the European System would have fostered, was a division of the World into European and American, Republican and Monarchical; a league of worn-out Govts., on the one hand, and of youthful and stirring Nations, with the United States at their head, on the other. *We* slip in between; and plant ourselves in Mexico. The United States have gotten the start of us in vain; and we link once more America to Europe. Six months more—and the mischief would have been done."[1]

These statements had been made late in 1824 and in January, 1825. In December, 1822, two years before the British cabinet came to the recognition decision, Canning had accepted the offer of Patrick Mackie to go to Mexico at his own expense on an informal mission. In July and August, 1823, Guadalupe Victoria, as agent of the

---

[1] Temperley, "The Later American Policy of George Canning," *loc. cit.,* pp. 781–782.

provisional government which had followed the overthrow of Iturbide, held four informal conferences with Mackie. Nothing of great importance was accomplished or could be accomplished, considering the nature of Mackie's mission; but the Mexicans were pleased with British attentions and considered this event the beginning of diplomatic relations between the two countries.

Just before the end of the year (1823) other British agents arrived in Mexico. They were Hervey, O'Gorman, and Ward, who had been sent out by Canning (1) to report on the advisability of recognition, (2) to assure the Mexican government that Great Britain did not desire dominion over any portion of Spain's former colonies in America and would not allow them to fall "under the dominion of any other power," and (3) tactfully to encourage the establishment of a monarchy in case they found Mexican leaders favorably disposed. This commission was so blinded by enthusiasm for Mexico's cause that it reported a stable government after only three weeks' observation and in spite of the fact that an important revolution was then in progress. A few days later Hervey actually guaranteed a loan to support the government in the crisis. For this act he was recalled and Morier was sent out in his place.

Finally, on January 3, 1825, Canning announced his intention of recognizing the new states of Spanish America. On the same day he prepared instructions to guide his Mexican commission in the negotiation of a commercial treaty. By April 6 these agents had negotiated an agreement which aroused great enthusiasm among the Mexican leaders. Indeed, it was so favorable to Mexico and so at variance with British policy that Canning refused to accept it.

But the fact that these British agents had, in their friendly fervor for Mexico, allowed themselves to exceed their instructions did not immediately become known in Mexico City. Throughout the year 1824 and a good portion of the year 1825 the Mexican leaders repeatedly revealed sentiments of gratitude and cordiality toward England. In April, 1824, a public celebration of the birthday of the King of England was seriously considered. Early in the following January Lucas Alamán, Mexican minister of foreign relations, evinced in his report to congress great partiality for Great Britain, giving her the chief credit for checking the designs of Continental Europe and mentioning the United States only incidentally. On the last day of May, Henry George Ward, a member of the British commission, was granted an enthusiastic reception as *chargé d'affaires* of the English government in Mexico. In a brief speech which President Victoria made on this occasion he expressed profound gratitude for the services of Britain, referring to her as the great nation which was accustomed to sustain the liberties of the world. British popularity in Mexico was rising to a flood.

On the other hand, the influence of the United States was on the wane. The struggle for independence in Mexico, as in the remainder of Spanish America, had awakened interest and sympathy among the people of the United States. Some had offered their money, others their swords, in the contest. The government itself adopted a neutral policy, but soon announced the determination to extend recognition and oppose European designs of reconquest. Iturbide, head of the first independent government in Mexico, had expressed admiration for Clay and gratitude for his services in Mexico's behalf in the United States Congress. He had likewise predicted intimate relations between the United States and Mexico for the future. The provisional government which followed Iturbide's brief reign had evinced an equally friendly attitude, and Mexico's first republican constitution had been closely modeled after that of the United States. But these early promises of cordiality were not entirely fulfilled, for the Mexican leaders soon found grounds to suspect the aggressiveness of the United States. Don Luís de Onis, agent of the Spanish government in the United States since 1809, had filled the Mexican archives with alarming accounts of the purposes and ambitions of the Americans of the North and had even published in 1820 a memorial representing both the government and citizens of the United States as entertaining the desire to expand southward immediately to Panama and ultimately to all the regions of the New World. These reports must have been sufficient to arouse distrust among the Mexican leaders. The menacing attitude of North American frontiersmen and utterances of dissatisfaction with the Louisiana boundary which came from the press and platform of the United States deepened this distrust into anxiety; and before the first minister of the United States arrived in Mexico the Mexican envoy at Washington had been directed to ascertain the attitude of the Adams administration respecting the question of limits between the two countries.[2]

Joel R. Poinsett, who reached Mexico early in May, 1825, in the capacity of envoy extraordinary and minister plenipotentiary of the United States, was not slow to grasp the situation. From Vera Cruz, on May 5, he wrote: "The British government has anticipated us . . . Their treaty is made, and . . . has been ratified by the lower house . . . It is now before the Senate . . . no doubt appears

[2] For the preceding paragraphs, Manning's *Early Diplomatic Relations Between the United States and Mexico* (pp. 1–88) has been the main reliance; but see also *La Diplomacia Mexicana. Pequeña Revista Historica* (1925), pp. 9–12.

to be entertained of the result." [3] As soon as he reached Mexico City he managed to obtain a copy of the British treaty.[4] President Victoria's response to Ward's presentation speech filled Poinsett with envious apprehension. It convinced the American envoy that the time had come to place the attitude of the United States toward Spanish America "in its true light." Accordingly, he took advantage of his public reception, which took place on June 1, to congratulate the Mexican leaders upon the adoption of a republican form of government, to remind the audience of the sympathetic interest with which the people of the United States had viewed the struggle of their neighbors for independence, and to point out that England, in her official procedure toward Mexico, had only followed the example set by the United States. Three days later he remarked in a letter to Clay that the British had evidently "made good use of their time and opportunities." He then went on to explain that the Mexican president and three members of his cabinet were pro-British, but he also noted, hopefully, that "we have a respectable party in both houses of Congress" and that a "vast majority of the people" were friendly toward the United States and suspicious of Great Britain.[5] Longer residence in Mexico merely served to deepen these convictions. "I am made sensible every day," said Poinsett on August 5, 1825, "of this disposition to court the favor of Great Britain by taking as little notice of the United States as possible." [6]

That the American envoy's summary of the situation was essentially correct is borne out by the testimony of the British *chargé* himself. Ward wrote to Canning, on September 30, as follows: "Mr. Pointsett [sic], upon his arrival here, found His Majesty's Government in possession of that influence to which it has so just a claim. He found the President and Ministers, satisfied with the conduct of England, and her character standing high with the generality of the people . . . Although the idea of an intimate union between the former colonies of Spain had long been entertained, nothing was further from the wishes of the Mexicans than to see the United States included in this fraternal bond." [7] In brief, the two agents agreed respecting the sentiments of the executive and his cabinet and disagreed only with reference to the uncertain attitude of the people.

---

[3] Poinsett to Clay, No. 1, Mex. Desp., Vol 1 (State Dept., Bureau of Indexes and Archives).

[4] *Ibid.* to *ibid.,* No. 2, May 28, 1825, *ibid.*

[5] *Loc. cit.*

[6] *Loc. cit.*

[7] Public Record Office, London, Foreign Office, 50, Mexico, Vol. 14. Hereafter cited as F. O. 50 (14), Mexico, etc.

Poinsett's instructions had directed him, among other things, to negotiate treaties of commerce and limits, respectively, and to encourage republicanism in Mexico. He soon concluded that he could not accomplish any of these things until a transformation had been effected in the Mexican cabinet. He therefore appears to have associated himself with the opposition with a view to influencing both the Mexican executive and the Mexican congress. He encouraged the formation of lodges of York Rite Masons which were soon made to constitute the chief political machinery of the opposition party. By the latter part of September, 1825, a cabinet change somewhat favorable to the interests and ideals of the United States had been accomplished. Soon afterwards Canning returned the British-Mexican treaty of April 6, 1825, unratified. It was now Ward's turn to become alarmed.[8]

The British *chargé* immediately began to send to his chief accounts of American designs and ambitions which corresponded exactly with the apprehensions which Canning had expressed at the time he was pressing his recognition policy through the British cabinet. "It is the great object of the United States," Ward had written a few days before the Mexican cabinet reorganization took place, "to convince the natives of Spanish America, that there exists between them and their brethren of the North, a community of interests, in which no European power can share." "I think it highly probable," he added, "that they will take the earliest possible opportunity, of cultivating any disposition . . . which might be turned to account, in event of a rupture, at any future period, with Great Britain."[9] After Ward had obtained a more complete revelation of Poinsett's view and influence, he reported: "The formation of a general American federation, from which all European Powers, but more particularly Great Britain, shall be excluded, is the great object of Mr. Poinsett's exertions." And he admitted that "many members of both chambers" had been induced to favor the project and were desirous of sanctioning it by a treaty.[10] Ward viewed with no little anxiety the plans for the proposed Panama Congress, for he looked upon this gathering as the possible occasion for perfecting these Pan-American ambitions. He was particularly alarmed at the prospect that Poinsett would use his influence to secure as one of the Mexican delegates to Panama, or possibly as head of the Mexican Foreign Office itself,

---

[8] The most authentic account of Poinsett's operations in Mexico will be found in Manning, *op. cit.*, p. 190, *passim*. The present writer has also had access to the sources cited by Manning.

[9] Ward to Canning, No. 32, September 6–22, 1825, F. O. 50 (14), Mexico.

[10] Despatch of September 30, 1825 (most private and confidential), *loc. cit.*,

Señor Michelena, who had been recalled from London at Canning's suggestion and was therefore decidedly anti-British.[11]

Contests of Ward and Poinsett

Under any circumstances it would have been Ward's duty to counteract the influence of the United States in Mexico. With reference to Mexico and indeed to all Spanish America, as has already been noted, the interests and ambitions of the two branches of the Anglo-Saxon family appeared to be widely divergent. Now that Ward perceived the purposes and the power of Poinsett he was spurred to even greater exertions. Convinced that the United States had three objects in view—namely, to stultify European projects and influence in America, to secure Mexican territory, and to negotiate a commercial treaty which would embody the maritime principles of the United States and grant important privileges to its merchants— and that all of them were opposed to British interests, the British *chargé* set himself all the more firmly to checkmate every move of the American envoy.

The next two years, accordingly, witnessed a continuation of the spirited contest between Ward and Poinsett. Neither employed methods entirely above reproach and both professed an unwillingness to enter the fray, but Ward appears to have been more aggressive and uncompromising. "I cannot but regret that the Agent of the British government should imagine that whatever influence I may acquire here must of necessity be averse to the interests of the nation he represents." [12] "I never have and never will oppose the establishment of friendly relations between the new American States and Great Britain on such principles as are not hostile to the United States." [13] This was the spirit of Poinsett. At the same time Ward declared: "Nothing could have been further from my wishes, on Mr. Poinsett's first arrival, than to enter into any contest of this description." [14] But once the diplomatic struggle had begun, the British agent pursued his supposed foe relentlessly. If Poinsett sought to put through his negotiations by a sort of alliance with the *Yorkinos*, it appears that the British *chargé*, with more caution and greater finesse, associated himself with the opposing party. Ward charged that Poinsett resorted to intrigue and slander in order to

---

[11] Ward to Canning, No. 51, Oct. 31, 1825, F. O. 50 (15), Mexico.
[12] Poinsett to Rufus King, Oct. 14, 1825, Mex. Desp., Vol. 1.
[13] *Id.* to Clay, July 12, 1826, *loc. cit.*
[14] Ward to Canning, *Most private and confidential*, Sept. 30, 1825, F. O. 50 (14), Mexico.

mar the domestic felicity and destroy the influence of a fair favorite of President Victoria, but he admitted that he had made use of this favorite in order to carry out his purposes with the Mexican government. He accused the American envoy of encouraging the publication of propaganda calculated to foment suspicion against Great Britain and advance the commercial and political ideals of the United States, but Poinsett alleged that Ward had published literature designed to prevent the negotiation of a satisfactory commercial treaty and Ward's own correspondence shows that he expended funds in preparing a map of Texas and in reprinting the abusive Onis memorial,—and this solely with the view of adding fuel to the flame of Mexican suspicion toward the United States. Each diplomat gave banquets and omitted to invite his rival in order that the occasion might be used to disparage and destroy the influence of the nation whose minister was conspicuous for his absence. Ward eagerly seized upon every opportunity to discredit Poinsett, carrying to the Mexican president numerous reports of the American envoy's utterances and making frequent appeals to the personal prejudices of this chief executive. Recalled early in 1827 at his own request, the British *chargé* reported with evident exultation that Poinsett had not been invited to the farewell reception given in his honor.[15]

The Commercial Treaty

It was with reference to a commercial treaty and a boundary agreement that Ward raised his uncompromising hand most effectively against the United States. Shortly after his arrival in Mexico Poinsett approached the Mexican government in regard to the main objects of his mission. Separation of the boundary issue and the commercial pact was soon agreed upon. Poinsett then pressed the latter question in the hope of a speedy settlement. He first sought perfect reciprocity, but he met with firm opposition on this point and eventually surrendered it. The part played by Ward in this first disagreement, his own letter reveals: "From M. Esteva, I learnt, at an early period of the negotiations, that perfect reciprocity was at first insisted upon . . . Against this, I of course told him that I should protest, as Mexico had refused to assent to it in the treaty with Great Britain, and assigned the non-existence of this reciprocity as a plea for her refusal. It certainly did not exist in a greater degree between Mexico and the United States, and consequently the principles, which had

[15] These generalizations are based upon the letters of Ward and Poinsett, too numerous to cite in detail, extending from September, 1825, to the close of 1826.

been applied to us, must be applied to them. To this M. Esteva gave his full assent . . ." [16]

Having put aside for a time the question of reciprocity, Poinsett then insisted upon the most-favored-nation clause. The Mexican government was not opposed to this policy in general, but it desired to make an exception in favor of the Spanish-American states. President Victoria was ambitious to play a leading rôle among these states and he believed that Mexico's prestige would be advanced by granting this preference to them. Moreover, this exception had been admitted in the British treaty of April 6, 1825. Accordingly, the Mexican negotiators once more took a firm stand. Poinsett called upon Ward in the hope of securing coöperation. He knew that the British *chargé* had formerly protested against this exception but had received no response to his note. He now urged him to demand an immediate reply, but the astute and suspicious Ward declined to grant the favor. He had learned from Poinsett's conversation that this discrimination in the interest of the Spanish-American states displeased the American envoy so much that he would never consent to negotiate a treaty which embraced it. He had also received from the interview the impression that Poinsett felt that the concession would tend to impede the Pan-American schemes of the United States.[17] Accordingly, Ward not only developed a sudden unwillingness to insist upon a removal of this exception in favor of the Spanish Americans, but he even began to regret that he had ever made a protest at all. An impediment which tended to delay the negotiation of a Mexican-American treaty, and at the same time was looked upon by Poinsett as interfering with his project of unity among the states of the Western Hemisphere, ought not to be removed by the hand of a Briton!

A conversation which Ward had with Señor Esteva, who had taken some part in the negotiation of the treaty in question, further confirmed the British diplomat in his view. Esteva reported that he and Poinsett had had a violent discussion regarding the extension of this special privilege to the former colonies of Spain, Esteva urging the British treaty as a precedent and Poinsett contending that the United States and England should be on an entirely different footing. Esteva reported also that Poinsett, losing his temper, denounced the "accursed policy" of Great Britain, which he declared to be based upon the maxim of "Divide ut imperes," upon the desire to stifle the "American feeling in America" at its birth; and then terminated

[16] Ward to Canning, No. 32, Sept. 6, 1825, F. O. 50 (14), Mexico.
[17] *Ibid.* to *ibid.*, No. 42, Sept. 27–28, 1825, *loc. cit.*

negotiations until he could receive further instructions.[18] Ward's further conduct in the matter may best be described in his own language: "I had protested against the clause in question; and reserved to His Majesty's Government the right of taking, with regard to it, such measures as might be deemed expedient:—Circumstances occurred afterwards, connected with Mr. Poinsett's views here, which induced me to withdraw this note, in order to prevent the conclusion of a treaty between Mexico and the United States, on terms which I could not but regard as detrimental to the interests of great Britain; and I have even gone so far, on more than one occasion, as to express to General Victoria my opinion, that His Majesty's Government would admit of the exception in favor of the former Spanish colonies, provided the United States were obliged to submit to it likewise:—My object in taking this step has, indeed, been attained, and the treaty with the United States is still pending in consequence of it. . . ."[19]

Poinsett really did terminate negotiations on September 28, 1825, until he could receive further instructions from Washington. When these came they merely upheld his view regarding the clause granting special favors to the other American states of Spanish origin. Believing that a show of haste would be impolitic, Poinsett did not approach the Mexican government on the commercial question until May, 1826. Soon afterwards the Mexicans accepted the most-favored-nation clause without modification. Evidently the government was now more favorable to Poinsett, who, encouraged by this fact, determined to press a point which would tend to operate against Great Britain. He attempted to exclude from the advantages of the principle, "free ships make free goods," the vessels of all nations which refused to accept this principle. This would have been a double blow at British maritime pretensions. Poinsett found, however, that the Mexicans feared to admit this exception while their treaty with Great Britain was still in process of negotiation and ratification. Unwilling to make the provision a *sine qua non,* he finally consented to accept the treaty without it. The pact was finally completed on July 10, 1826, almost a year after the negotiations had begun.[20] That Ward had been largely responsible for the delay is fairly certain.

It is one thing to consent to negotiate a treaty; it is quite a different thing to ratify it. This part of the procedure was put off until long after Poinsett ceased to be United States minister in Mexico. The delay was due largely to indisposition on the part of Mexican

18 Ward to Canning, No. 42, Sept. 27–28, 1825, *loc. cit.*
19 Ward to Canning, No. 68, Dec. 15, 1825, *loc. cit.*
20 Manning, *op. cit.,* p. 220 ff.

leaders to consent to a commercial treaty before a boundary agreement had been accepted by the United States. They insisted upon the synchronous ratification of the two treaties because they feared the territorial designs of the United States.[21] This raises the question as to whether the British *chargé* had anything to do with the fomentation of this apprehension. To this point attention must now be turned.

Texas and the Boundary Issue

As early as September 6, 1825, Ward reported to Canning that he had "more than once alluded" to the migration of "American backwoodsmen" to Texas in "conversations with M. Alaman and Esteva," and had urged upon them the importance of putting a stop to the evil "at the very commencement." [22] On November 7, following, he went over the whole affair with President Victoria, laying before him a map which showed all of the American settlements and a detailed report on Texas, charging that Poinsett was endeavoring to influence the Mexican congress to take the whole matter out of the executive's hands by relinquishing control over the public lands to the several states, and suggesting that the subject ought to be given immediate attention. At the end of a long interview the Mexican president came to the conclusion that a commission should be sent to Texas at once in order to report upon the situation. Soon afterwards Ward heard that General Mier y Terán had been offered the headship of this commission.[23] Aware that Terán was strongly anti-American and fearing that he might decline the offer on account of pique over his failure to obtain appointment as minister to England, Ward hurried to the General and persuaded him to accept the position. "I have little doubt that the affair will now be very speedily arranged," exulted the British *chargé*. "The President has given General Terán the manuscript map of Texas which I left with him. . . . If General Terán goes to the frontier, there will be no occasion for any further interference on our part, as he will, I know, send in a report which will open the eyes of the congress, and make them fully aware of the danger with which they are threatened." [24]

[21] Manning, *op. et loc. cit.*

[22] *Loc. cit.*

[23] In fact Ward appears to have been instrumental in persuading the Mexican chief executive to appoint Terán. "It was partly at my instigation that the Countess [Regla] interfered in favor of General Terán, and it was principally owing to her exertions that General Victoria['s] dislike to him was overcome" (Ward to Canning, *Separate and Private*, March 25, 1826, F. O. 50 (20), Mexico.)

[24] Ward to Canning, No. 54, November 15, 1825, F. O. 50 (15), Mexico.

But time was to reveal that Ward was far too jubilant. Terán's appointment was indeed soon accepted by the Mexican chambers, but there was much delay in fixing his salary and general allowance and still further delay in completing the equipment of the commission. It was not until November 10, 1827, that he left the city of Mexico and it was March 1, 1828, when he arrived at San Antonio de Bexar. Meanwhile the British *chargé* suffered great anxiety respecting the fate of Texas.

Early in December, 1825, Ward was deeply aroused by a rumor that Poinsett was negotiating for a vast tract of land which would "give the Americans complete possession of the Gulph of Mexico, from the Floridas, to within a little distance of Sota la Marina, and Tampico." "I have . . . seen both the President and Mr. Esteva upon the subject, and done my utmost to make them sensible of the imminence of the danger with which they are threatened," said Ward. At the same time he complained of the difficulty of making Victoria "or any Mexican sensible, either of the value of Time, or of the necessity of applying an immediate remedy to an evil of so rapid a growth." That Ward's interest was not confined to the welfare of Mexico is evident from his contention that "His Majesty's Government can never see with indifference the whole Northern coast of the Gulph of Mexico, and the best ports which this country possesses on the Atlantic side, . . . fall into the hands of the Americans, who would thus acquire the means, in the event of a rupture with England, of destroying our whole trade with the Gulph." [25]

Nor did the British *chargé* confine his efforts to goading the Mexican government to action. Early in 1826 he lent his aid to two projects designed to counteract the influence of the American settlers along the northern frontier of Mexico. Due largely to Ward's efforts General Wavell, an English subject, obtained a large grant south of the Red River and east of the Sabine, with the express purpose of colonizing it with Europeans and cutting the American line of communications. At about the same time Ward composed a petition for an Englishman by the name of J. D. Hunter who sought permission to settle upon the international frontier some thirty thousand Indians. Speaking of the latter scheme, the British envoy remarked: "Hunter having assured me that they are well able to comply with their engagements, and determined to resist all encroachments on the part of the Americans, . . . I thought that a better opportu-

---

[25] Ward to Canning, No. 64, December 10, 1825, *loc. cit.*

nity would not easily be found of opposing a formidable obstacle to the designs of the United States upon Texas . . ." [26]

When Ward perused a copy of the commercial treaty between Mexico and the United States which a Mexican friend placed in his hands on the day following its signature, he ceased to be alarmed with regard to the purely commercial phase of the contest. In this respect he considered the pact virtually harmless. He was worried, however, by the fact that it contained no article specifically defining the boundary. In fact, he intimated that he would have interfered if he had not been misinformed about the matter. Now that the treaty had been signed, however, he declared that he would not oppose its ratification. Indeed, there was now no need of opposition. He had already, as he himself said, "done everything in" his "power" to bring to the Mexican government a realization of the danger of losing Texas. Once thoroughly aroused, apprehension with respect to this region was all that was required, as the sequel proved, to defeat the treaty. For two reasons, both of them connected with the Texas issue, the Mexican congress refused to ratify the agreement. Ward must share a portion of the responsibility for its defeat.[27]

The Texas question itself seems not to have caused Ward any more anxiety until the early days of February, 1827, when he received news of the Fredonian Revolt. He predicted that the declaration of independence which, according to reports, the Fredonians had made was but the first act in a drama which would end in the incorporation of the region between the Sabine and the Rio Grande into the American Union. He declared that this had been the "great object" of Poinsett's mission. "As to the probability of the Territory in question being ultimately thrown into the hands of the United States, by the step now taken by its Inhabitants,—there can be little or no doubt," said the British envoy. He also reported with evident satisfaction the determination of the Mexican government to send an army into Texas and suppress the insurgents. "It is possible," remarked Ward hopefully, "that this display of vigor in the first instance may terminate the affair at once; and with a view to this I urged the President strongly not to underestimate the importance of the contest, nor to imagine that in these adventurers,—because they were adventurers, he would find a contemptible enemy:—I told him that they were Men reckless of danger,—excellent Marksmen, and so perfectly acquainted with the Country, that they would be able to meet upon their own ground, more than double their number of Regular Troops;—In short, that too much caution could not be displayed, until a Force was assembled, sufficient to bear down all opposition." [28]

In the course of the interview between Ward and the Mexican chief executive, the latter let it be understood that he intended, through the Mexican minister in London, to make "some communication" to the British government regarding the designs of the United States upon Texas. Ward appeared to be anxious to forestall such application unless it should prove absolutely necessary. He accordingly returned to England, whither he had been recalled on account of financial extravagance, by way of New York, where he consulted with Charles R. Vaughan, British minister to the United States. He found Vaughan thoroughly convinced that the United States had not "connived at the conduct of the New Settlers" in Texas [29] and "decidedly of the opinion" that both the American Executive and the American Congress accepted the boundary "as fixed by the Treaty of Onis." This latter fact he communicated to President Victoria. At the same time he wrote Canning that "unless it should be Your [his] Pleasure to renew the Subject, You will [he would] have no further Trouble, at present, respecting a Question which I [Ward had] brought before You [him], perhaps prematurely, from a fear lest the Interests of Gt. Britain should be ultimately affected by it. While it remains [remained] in its present State, the Measures lately taken by the Mexican Govt leave [left] no Ground for Apprehension as to the Result." [30]

The Aftermath

Thus ended Ward's Mexican mission, but not the currents which he set in motion during his residence. These were to have far-reaching results. He had spared no effort in stimulating Mexican apprehensions with respect to the ambitions of the United States and the menace of the American "backwoodsmen" in Texas. He had expressed his conviction "both publicly and privately, that the Great End of Mr. Poinsett's Mission" was to "embroil Mexico in a Civil War, and to facilitate, by doing so, the Acquisition of the Provinces

[28] Ward to Canning, No. 34, *Confidential*, February 21, 1827, F. O. 50 (31*), Mexico.

[29] Vaughan to Canning, No. 7, February 25, 1827, F. O. 5 (233), America.

[30] Ward to *ibid.*, Separate and Private, June 20, 1827, F. O. 50 (32), Mexico.

to the North of the Rio Bravo, by the United States." [31] Such suspicions, once implanted in the Mexican mind, could not be rooted out by any private letters to the Mexican chief executive. He had been instrumental in causing the Victoria administration to send to Texas a commission headed by Terán, of whose unfriendly attitude toward the American settlers he was well aware. He had spread propaganda tending to convince the Mexican reading public of the greed and perfidy of their neighbor. The effect of these acts was irrevocable.

The sequel of Ward's machinations may in some sense be observed in the Mexican attacks upon Poinsett. They certainly may be read in the reports of Terán and in the Mexican regulations based upon them. Soon after arriving in Texas this commissioner began to compose alarming accounts of conditions in the province. In a private letter to President Victoria, written from Nacogdoches on June 30, 1828, he remarked: "The whole population here is a mixture of strange and incoherent parts without parallel in our federation: numerous tribes of Indians, now at peace, but armed and at any moment ready for war . . . ; colonists of another people, more progressive and better informed than the Mexican inhabitants, but also more shrewd and unruly; among these foreigners are fugitives from justice, honest laborers, vagabonds and criminals, but honorable and dishonorable alike travel with their political constitutions in their pockets, demanding the privileges, authority and offices which such a constitution guarantees. The most of them have slaves, and these slaves are beginning to learn the favorable intent of the Mexican law toward their unfortunate condition and are becoming restless under their yoke, and the masters, in the effort to retain them, are making that yoke even heavier; they extract their teeth, set on the dogs to tear them in pieces, the most lenient being he who but flogs his slaves until they are flayed . . ."

Terán then went on to give the following warning with reference to the attitude of the American settlers toward Mexico and the Mexicans: "It would cause you the same chagrin that it has caused me to see the opinion that is held of our nation by these foreign colonists, since, with the exception of some few who have journeyed to our capital, they know no other Mexicans than the inhabitants about here, and excepting the authorities necessary to any form of society, the said inhabitants are the most ignorant of negroes and Indians, among whom I pass for a man of culture. Thus, I tell myself that it could not be otherwise than that from such a state of affairs should arise an antagonism between the Mexicans and foreigners,

[31] Ward to Canning, Private, March 31, 1827. F. O. 50 (31*), Mexico.

which is not the least of the smoldering fires . . . I have discovered. Therefore, I am warning you to take timely measures. Texas could throw the whole nation into revolution." [32]

A despatch to the Mexican minister of war on November 14, 1829, contained a vehement philippic against American politicians and frontiersmen. "They begin," said Terán, "by assuming rights, as in Texas, which it is impossible to sustain in a serious discussion, making ridiculous pretensions based on historical incidents which no one admits—such as the voyage of La Salle, which was an absurd fiasco, but serves as a basis of their claim to Texas. Such extravagant claims as these are now being presented for the first time to the public by dissembling writers; the efforts that others make to submit proofs and reasons are by these men employed in reiterations . . . in order to attract the attention of their fellow-countrymen, not to the justice of the claim, but to the profit to be gained from admitting it. At this stage, it is alleged that there is a national demand for the step which the government meditates. In the meantime, the territory against which these machinations are directed, and which has usually remained unsettled, begins to be visited by adventurers and *empresarios;* some of these take up their residence in the country, pretending that their location has no bearing upon their government's claim or the boundary disputes; shortly, some of these forerunners develop an interest which complicates the political administration of the coveted territory; complaints, even threats, begin to be heard, working on the loyalty of the legitimate settlers, discrediting the efficiency of the existing authority . . . ; and the matter having arrived at this stage—which is precisely that of Texas at this moment—diplomatic manœuvres begin . . . He who consents to or does not oppose the loss of Texas is an execrable traitor who ought to be punished with death . . ." [33]

A subsequent letter written under Terán's direction to the Mexican Minister of War early in January, 1830, reveals an even more decided distrust of the United States and of the loyalty of the American colonists in Texas. In fact, he went so far as to charge the United States government of collusion in the Fredonian Revolt of 1826–1827. "General Terán does not doubt," says the despatch, "that the United States will carry out its project of possessing Texas at the first opportunity, which to them will be as soon as they think we are

[32] As quoted by Alleine Howren, "Causes and Origin of the Decree of April 6, 1830," in *The Southwestern Historical Quarterly,* XVI (1913), 395–398.

[33] *Ibid.,* p. 400 ff.

torn by civil strife . . . ; either they would incite the American population of Texas to revolt, as they tried to do in 1826 at Nacogdoches, or else force would be used to support these pretended claims . . ."

The writer then proceeds to outline a plan for checkmating the influence of American settlers in Texas and binding the region more closely to the central government. The encouragement of European and Mexican settlers and the increase of the army were the most important recommendations. He then concluded: "General Terán thinks it not impossible that the government of the United States of the North, on perceiving a firm determination on our part to hold our own and to support and improve Texas, will begin to carry on its work openly; therefore it may be expedient to act quickly and place ourselves on the defensive as soon as possible. The ratification of the treaty concluded in Mexico, and designating the boundary between the two nations, should afford the time required for the adoption of the above measures . . ." [34]

The man under whose eager scrutiny these reports ultimately fell was none other than Lucas Alamán, of whose pro-British sentiments Poinsett had often complained. Several upheavals in Mexico politics had brought him for the third time to the headship of the Foreign Office. On January 14, 1830, he sent to the chief executive a preliminary statement based upon the document last analyzed. He had nothing new to offer save a suggestion that Great Britain be invited to make a declaration against any design of the United States upon Texas. On February 8 he transmitted his famous report to Congress. Except for three recommendations Alamán simply reiterated the charges and suggestions of Terán. On April 6 Congress accepted his report virtually as presented. [35] At last the Texans were to be taken in hand, and this at the very time when their seven-year tariff exemption had expired and when colonists for the most part with a free-trade philosophy were beginning to feel the weight of a revenue system compared with which the "abominable" duties of the United States act of 1828 were mild indeed. And the official who was desig-

---

[34] As quoted by Alleine Howren, "Causes and Origin of the Decree of April 6, 1830," in *The Southwestern Historical Quarterly*, XVI (1913), pp. 407–408, 412.

[35] For a careful discussion of the origin of this law, see Howren, *op. et loc. cit.* An English translation of Alamán's report will be found in *House Ex. Doc.* No. 351, 25 Cong., 2 Sess., p. 312 ff.

The influence of the British may be seen even in this report. Alamán remarks: "Some of them [the Americans] have said that Providence had marked out Rio Bravo as the natural boundary of those States, which has induced an English writer to reproach them with an attempt to make Providence the author of their usurpations. . . ."

nated to enforce and carry out all these measures was the same Mier y Terán who owed his connection with Texas affairs to Henry George Ward! Events now moved with all the inexorableness of fate toward the Texas revolution. For precipitating this event it is fair to assume that the British *chargé* was partially responsible.

Britain's Official Responsibility

Were Ward's activities in Mexico duly authorized by the British government? The evidence is somewhat indefinite, but conclusive. Canning's American policy, which had as its keynote, the checkmating of the influence of the United States by the establishment of British predominance in Mexico, surely must have been known to Ward. This fact being granted, Canning probably thought detailed instructions not only unnecessary but even, under certain possible conditions, inconvenient. Certainly it would be safer to allow Ward, with his general knowledge of the views of his chief, to rely upon his own discretion. If the *chargé* got his chief into trouble the *chargé* could be disowned; if he carried out measures which without undue risk would advance the interests of Great Britain these might be turned to advantage.

The correspondence now available indicates that this was Canning's general attitude. He revealed considerable indisposition to respond to Ward's urgent importunities for detailed directions. On December 9, 1825, Canning wrote: "As the sailing of the packet of this month is fixed for tomorrow, after having been once put off, I am loath to detain it again . . . I will write you by the next packet, or sooner, by a ship of War.

"In the mean time, I have only generally to express my approbation of your zeal, in H. My's service, of the judgment with which you have regulated your conduct, and language, under circumstances of great difficulty and delicacy, and of the ability with which your Despatches are drawn." [36]

Again, early in January, 1826, Canning found himself indisposed to detain the Mexican mail! "I will not, however, omit the opportunity," he said, "of assuring you generally that your conduct, in the very difficult and trying circumstances, which you have had to encounter, has been such as H. Mys. Govt. for the most part approve; and that even where, under pressure of an urgent necessity to decide in very doubtful cases, you may have decided otherwise than either the event or subsequent reflection may have justified, you may rely

[36] F. O. 50 (9), Mexico.

upon it that there is no disposition to judge you otherwise than with indulgence . . .

"I must also add specifically that in all that relates to the watching and counteracting of the Intrigues of the American Minister Mr. Poinsett, you appear to have exercised a judgment as sound, as your zeal has been meritorious." [37]

Lastly, there is no indication that Canning ever reprimanded Ward for publishing and circulating a map of Texas and the De Onis memorial with a view to arousing suspicion regarding the designs of the United States and its citizens; [38] and a few years after the death of the great English statesman one of his devoted followers who had special knowledge of his American policy said in the House of Commons: "If the United States have declared that they cannot allow the island of Cuba to belong to any maritime power in Europe, Spain excepted, neither can England, as the first of those maritime powers—I say it fearlessly, because I feel it strongly—suffer the United States to bring under their dominion a greater portion of the shores of the Gulf of Mexico than that which they now possess." [39]

Further evidence appears to be unnecessary. There is little room to doubt that Great Britain fully approved Ward's procedure. During this early period, at least, she was strongly resolved to defeat the American ambitions of the United States, whether territorial, commercial, or political.

Great Britain's Early Victory

So in the years immediately following Monroe's trumpet blast the two Anglo-Saxon nations engaged in spirited rivalry at various points in the New World. In general it must be admitted that Great Britain was the victor both politically and commercially. Her success in Mexico, the La Plata region, and Panama has already been pointed out, and her superior political position finds further illustration in the contemporary journals and state papers of Hispanic America. When publicists and statesmen expressed gratitude for services in the past or hopes for support in the future, England usually came in for first mention. England probably held first place in their esteem in 1827. As early as July, 1824, Canning was styled "even in the [Chilean] Senate, by all the Officers of State, 'The

[37] Instructions of Jan. 6, 1826, F. O. 50 (19), Mexico.
[38] Planta to Ward, June 20, 1826, *loc. cit.*
[39] William Huskisson, *Speeches* (ed. 1831), pp. 579–580. Speech of May 20, 1830.

Redeemer of Chile.' " When the Mexican minister of foreign affairs talked of Canning's illness in August, 1827, he could not refrain from shedding tears. After 1824 Bolívar dreamed of a Spanish-American federation under the patronage of Britain. The Polignac Memorandum of Canning was valued more than the Doctrine of Monroe and the navy of England more than the shield of the United States.

In fact, the interpretation which the United States placed upon the Monroe Doctrine during the first months after its promulgation was in some sense a disappointment to the people of Hispanic America. The statesmen south of the Rio Grande naturally revealed some curiosity as to the exact meaning of the pronouncement, as well as an eagerness to give it an application favorable to their interests. The Colombian government, having been alarmed by French activities, called for assistance in July, 1824. Secretary of State Adams replied that the President did not believe that an intervention of the European Powers now threatened. Whenever he decided that such danger was imminent he would lay the matter before Congress. In any event, the United States "could not undertake resistance to them by force of Arms, without a previous understanding with those European Powers, whose Interests and whose principles would secure from them an active and efficient coöperation in the cause. . . ." "The employment of a Spanish force in America, while Spain is occupied by a French army and . . . under the influence of France and her allies, does not constitute a case upon which the United States would feel themselves justified in departing from . . . neutrality. . . ." Somewhat later the Brazilian government, no doubt encouraged by Monroe's message, appealed to President Adams. It asked him to sign a convention to preserve the Brazilian nation against any attempt at reconquest by Portugal or any other European Power. It also suggested that the United States and the states of Spanish America unite in a league of defense against the Neo-Holy Alliance. Secretary Clay replied that the Monroe Doctrine would not be involved in the attempt of a mother country to reconquer her colony and ignored the reference to other European Powers. A short time previously, Poinsett had explained to Mexico that the Monroe Doctrine was merely a pledge binding on the Chief Executive, but not on the nation unless sanctioned by Congress. The President of Mexico understood this to mean that "the Memorable promise of President Monroe" was "disclaimed." "We have no longer any sort of Guarantee or Promise, on the part of that Government, to take part in the Contest, if a Third Power should become an Auxiliary of Spain," remarked the Mexican Executive. Lastly, in response to a plea for assistance in possible contingencies, Henry Clay informed the government of the United Provinces of La Plata that the Congress of the United States alone could decide whether the Monroe Doctrine would be enforced, and that the doctrine did not constitute a pledge which foreign nations might call upon the United States to fulfil.[40]

Such were the early interpretations of Monroe's manifesto. In them is found little of the purple glow of republican enthusiasm. They certainly could not have added to the prestige of the United States in Latin America. It is no reflection upon the intelligence of statesmen south of the United States that they looked upon England as a better friend and champion.

Canning likewise obtained a degree of commercial hegemony. Before his death he had negotiated satisfactory commercial treaties with Buenos Aires, Colombia, Mexico, and Brazil. As late as 1829 the United States had secured only three—i. e., agreements with Brazil, Colombia, and Central America. British trade with Latin America was nearly three times that of the United States in 1827.

Britain's early opposition to the commercial expansion and the political influence of the United States in Latin America had been in no small degree a success.[41] Never again, however, could that term be applied without qualification to the attempts of British statesmen to oppose the policy of the United States in this region.

[40] Temperley, *The Foreign Policy of Canning,* p. 162 ff.; Lockey, *Pan-Americanism,* p. 223 ff.; W. S. Robertson, "South America and the Monroe Doctrine," in *The Political Science Quarterly,* XXX (1915), 82 ff.

[41] Temperley, *op. cit.,* pp. 156–162.

CHAPTER VI

BRITAIN AND THE SOUTHWARD EXPANSION OF THE UNITED STATES (1830–1856)

As in the previous period, the European Powers most deeply concerned in the southward extension of the United States between 1830 and 1856 were Great Britain, France, and Spain. None of these had greatly modified its former attitude toward the westward and southward sweep of the United States. The vast territorial acquisitions of the young republic since its independence had served rather to increase their apprehensions. Great Britain continued to play the leading rôle and Mexico continued to be the scene of rivalry, but Central America became more important and occasionally there was a shift to Cuba, Santo Domingo, and even some of the South American states.[1]

The continuance of Canning's devoted followers in English politics kept his Mexican policy before the public. On May 20, 1830, William Huskisson told the House of Commons, as has already been noted in another connection, that England could never "suffer the United States to bring under their dominion a greater portion of the shores of the Gulf of Mexico than that which they now possess." He was greatly alarmed at the ambitions of the United States and regarding the security of the balance of power and British maritime supremacy in America. He remarked that the Americans had their eyes not only upon Texas but upon the eastern coast of Mexico also. He urged the government to renewed effort in behalf of Spanish recognition of Mexico. "Let Mexico be at ease in respect to attacks from Spain," he said, "and she will soon become a valuable ally of this country [Great Britain], with all her interests bound up and identified with the best interests of Great Britain in the New World. On the other hand, let her remain much longer in her present harassed and exhausting condition, and the poverty of her treasury,—the necessity of making head against those attacks, may throw her into

---

[1] Rivalries in Santo Domingo and South America were of minor importance. For the attitude of Spain and a fuller discussion of the rôle of France, see *post.* Chs. VIII, XII.

the arms of the United States, and force her to sacrifices which would inevitably bring on a maritime war, unless this country be prepared to abandon her colonial empire, her commercial pretensions, and, with them, her maritime ascendency in the New World." [2]

Britain and the Texas Issue

When news of the Texas revolution reached England the supporters of the Canning tradition immediately brought up the matter in the House of Commons. On August 5, 1836, Barlow Hoy moved "that an humble Address be presented to his Majesty, praying him to direct, that such measures may be taken as may seem proper to secure the fulfilment of the existing treaty between this country and Mexico; and to prevent the establishment of slavery and traffic in slaves in the province of Texas, in the Mexican territory." Hoy's speech in defense of his motion constituted an appeal to merchants, capitalists, and humanitarians. British merchants had "embarked 70,000,000 dollars in the Mexican dominions. . . . Neither ought the importance of the possession of the mining districts by America be lost sight of by this country. The mines of Texas were of immense value. . . . Unless Mexico was assisted, as she ought to be by this country, she would be so weakened as soon to become an easy victim to the ambition of the United States. . . ." Again, "There could be no doubt, that if Texas were added to the [American] Union, the basis of the connexion would be to establish slavery, and the slave-trade, permanently, in that province." Would Great Britain, which was now spending more than a million pounds sterling per annum in suppressing and abolishing slavery, render that whole expenditure useless by a refusal to interfere in Texas? Moreover, if the United States should acquire this fertile region it would thereby be "brought within six weeks sail of China"; and, besides, "would not Cuba and the other Spanish possessions in the Gulf of Mexico then soon fall a prey to the United States?" He therefore contended that England "ought to afford every species of assistance to Mexico, not only by remonstrating in an amicable manner with the United States, but by sending out a naval force to assist Mexico against Texas, and to prevent aggression by the United States."

Hoy's motion was seconded by none other than Henry George Ward, now the representative for St. Albans in the House of Commons! Ten years had not dimmed his memory regarding his Mexican experiences, nor had the assurances given by Vaughan in 1827 modified his views respecting the purposes and methods of the United

[2] Huskisson, *Speeches* (1831), III, 585-586.

States. He was sure that American political leaders were operating in collusion with American frontiersmen to deprive Mexico of the fertile lands of Texas. "There were two considerations which ought to weigh with" British statesmen in regard to the Texas issue. "The first was the question of general policy—whether it were advisable to allow the United States to pursue a system of aggrandisement without any endeavour on our part to check them, and to allow the extension of their territory to the Rio Bravo . . . in such manner as to obtain for them the absolute command of the Gulf; for certainly the acquisition of Texas would give them that command, and would enable them with half a dozen privateers to shut us out entirely from our present trade with Mexico, leaving us no route whatsoever by which to maintain a commercial intercourse with that country save that leading around Cape Horn to its western coast. . . ." The other consideration was that of "moral feeling which must influence every Gentleman acquainted with the condition of Society in the Western States of the Union, and every Gentleman aware of the incalculable misery which the system of slavery, there prevailing, inflicted upon so many millions of human beings. The question to be decided under this view of the subject was whether, for the purpose of maintaining that demoralizing system, they would allow the annexation of . . . Texas to the United States. . . . The result of the annexation of the province . . . would be the creation of nine additional slaveholding States, with eighteen" Senators representing them "at Washington; and that circumstance would put an end to all hopes of doing away with a system which formed the most degrading feature in the whole frame of the United States. He thought the subject was one which deserved the most serious consideration . . . and on that account he earnestly supported the motion."

The reply of Viscount Palmerston, head of the British Foreign Office, indicated that he refused to take the danger seriously. He declared that an address to the Crown at that time would be "in some respects unnecessary, and in other respects premature." "With regard to the political branch of the subject, undoubtedly the probability of the province of Texas being added to the United States . . . would be a subject which ought seriously to engage the attention of the House and of the British public. But with regard to that question he did not think that the events which had so far occurred, afforded any ground to think that there was at present any such probability" as to call for the motion under consideration. "He had too high an opinion of the honour and good faith of the government of the United States not to believe that it would act up to the declarations it had made upon the subject." He ignored the matter of slavery in Texas and expressed doubt as to the existence of any important slave-trade with the province. Nor did he answer the inquiry which Hoy had made with reference to the question whether Mexico had sought the good offices of England in order to prevent the acquisition of Texas by the United States.[3]

Thus it will be seen that in 1836 the devoted followers of Canning, and even Palmerston himself, looked with disfavor upon the southward expansion of the United States. They disagreed only with respect to the immediate probability of such expansion. It will likewise be observed that British support of the Mexican government had become almost traditional in the Foreign Office. During the next decade, however, Texas gradually took the place of Mexico in the American policy of Great Britain.

There were many good reasons for English interest in this new state. It might in the future serve both as a barrier between the United States and Spanish America and as a producer of raw cotton which would relieve British manufacturers from their embarrassing dependence upon the southern states of the American Union; and, if it could be induced to adopt free labor and free trade, it might be a means at one and the same time of advancing British commerce, legitimate and illegitimate,[4] and of striking a blow at the slavery interests of the United States.

Thus, although at first the government of Great Britain appeared to be desirous of seeing Mexico reconquer Texas, by the close of 1838 it decided that reconquest would be extremely difficult, if not impossible. Thereafter it was held that further continuation of hostilities between Texas and Mexico would result in injury to British interests which had now come to be important in both countries. Accordingly, the Foreign Office undertook to mediate between the combatants and to persuade Mexico to recognize her revolting province, although England herself delayed recognition until 1842 in the vain hope that the abolition of slavery in Texas might be exacted as a price for this favor. Meanwhile the United States and France had extended recognition, but Mexico had remained obdurate and was still brandishing threats and wasting money on the Texas question. In all this there was cause for regret and irritation to Great Britain, but the ministry, lulled into a sense of security by the refusal of the United States to annex Texas in 1837 and by what it supposed was a growing sentiment among the Texans them-

[3] Hansard, *Parliamentary Debates,* 3d Series, XXXV, 928–942.
[4] It was felt that Texas might be made the base for extensive smuggling into the United States.

selves against incorporation into the American Union, felt that there was no real cause for alarm. Toward the close of 1843 they were rudely shaken from this false assumption of security.

The shock was occasioned by reports from British diplomatic agents in the United States and Texas that the government at Washington had informally but earnestly suggested union to the struggling young republic, and that President Tyler's annual message hinted at annexation. London immediately sounded out Paris and an agreement for a joint protest was reached. Early in May, 1844, the British government was further perturbed by the notice that the United States and Texas had signed an annexation treaty. Just before the close of the month the British secretary of state for foreign affairs had a very earnest interview with Patrick Murphy, the Mexican representative at London. The report of this interview, drawn up by Murphy and corrected by the head of the British Foreign Office runs as follows:

"Lord Aberdeen [the British Foreign Secretary] expressed a wish to see Mexico acknowledge the independence of Texas. 'If Mexico,' he said, 'will concede this point, England (and I have reason to believe that France will join her in this determination) will oppose the annexation of Texas and moreover *he would endeavor that* France and England will unite in guaranteeing not only the independence of Texas, but also the boundary of Mexico. On the other hand should Mexico persist in declining to recognize Texas, the intentions of England to prevent the annexation of that country might not be put into execution.' Upon my remarking that it was not at all probable [that] the American Government would be willing to drop the annexation affair, even should the American Senate reject the Treaty for the present, Lord Aberdeen replied that *provided that England and France were perfectly agreed,* 'it would matter little to England whether the American Government should be willing to drop this question or not, and that, should it be necessary, she would go to the last extremity in support of her opposition to annexation; but that for this purpose it was essential that Mexico be disposed to acknowledge the independence of Texas.' " [5]

A few weeks later Aberdeen announced to the Texas diplomatic agent in London that England and France would be willing to unite with Texas, the United States, and Mexico in a diplomatic act designed to secure Texas independence, prevent annexation, and

[5] As quoted in Smith, *The Annexation of Texas* (1919), pp. 389-390.

guarantee the Texas-Mexican boundary. Smith, the Texas agent, inferred from the interview that England and France were prepared to use force to compel Mexican acquiescence, and that the United States was not expected to come into the plan.

Was England really willing also to undertake a war with the United States in order to preserve the independence of Texas? The memorandum quoted above suggests that she was, in case France could be committed favorably. A letter from Aberdeen to Bankhead, written on the last day of the year 1844, further indicates that such was England's resolution. Bankhead was instructed to warn Santa Anna's cabinet that its proposed invasion of Texas would "paralyze the exertions by which Great Britain and France were prepared to uphold the Independence of Texas against the encroachments of the United States, even at the risk of a collision with that power." [6]

But England's scheme depended upon the attitude of France, Mexico, and Texas. In the summer of 1844 Texas and France appeared to be willing to coöperate, but Mexico refused to comply with the demands made upon her. Soon afterwards Britain decided to await the result of the elections of November, 1844, in the United States. By the time when news of the election of Polk on an expansion platform reached Europe, the French government had been forced by popular clamor to decline to support England in further opposition to the United States. Aberdeen then definitely stated to Murphy what had been implied in his position all along; namely, that England alone would not engage in a war with the United States over the Texas issue. Soon afterwards news that the annexation resolutions had passed the United States Congress reached London. Aberdeen thereupon decided to make one more effort to prevail upon Mexico to acknowledge Texas and to persuade Texas to give a pledge not to enter the American Union. This decision was followed by eleventh-hour attempts of British diplomats in Texas and Mexico to accomplish these ends, with results which are well known. All of Aberdeen's instruments had failed him: France had refused to lend aid to the extent of the employment of armed force; Mexico had procrastinated in the matter of recognition; and Texas had at last voted to accept the very destiny which Great Britian had been so eager that this republic should escape.

The Mexican War

Nevertheless Mexico had not yet perceived the futility of expecting European aid in her difficulties with the United States. On July 30,

---

[6] As quoted in Smith, *The Annexation of Texas*, p. 394.

1845, after the annexation of Texas had been consummated, the Mexican government sent identical despatches to its ministers in Paris and in London. They were instructed to say that Mexico had no recourse left but war with the United States; that she felt she would be unworthy of a place among civilized nations if she failed to prosecute hostilities with vigor; that fourteen thousand troops were now on their march to the frontier and six thousand more were shortly to follow them; and that Mexico had been led by their former interest in Texas to hope that the governments of France and England would lend the cause of the Mexican nation their sympathy and moral support. To Murphy in London was sent another "most secret" instruction stating that the Americans had officially announced a determination to seize the Californias and directing this agent to request Britain's "co-operation to prevent the loss of that important part of her territory." [7]

Aberdeen and Sir Robert Peel evinced profound interest in preventing California from falling into the hands of the United States. The former consented to sound France once more on the matter of guaranteeing Mexican territorial integrity, and held out a somewhat indefinite promise of alliance with Mexico. On February 1, 1846, Murphy summed up the situation as it appeared to him: "Our position under present circumstances appears to me to be as follows: England will do nothing, either directly or indirectly, to forestall the usurpation of California so long as the Oregon question remains unsettled. If war breaks out, all difficulty on the part of this Cabinet will have ceased, and there is no doubt that one of their first objects will be, in that event, to prevent that usurpation. If on the contrary the dispute over Oregon is amicably settled, England will find herself more free to act in respect to California,—openly and directly in case France continues in the line of policy she has just adopted and lends her aid,—or indirectly by means of some plan of colonization in California." [8]

The reports of the British agents in Europe and the comments of the British and French press appear to have led the Mexican government to anticipate European aid. From what they could learn of the Oregon issue, Mexican statesmen were fully confident that it would end in a trial of arms between the United States and England. Accordingly, when news of the clash with the troops of Taylor in the Rio Grande-Nueces region reached Mexico City it found the Mexicans all the more eager for the combat. They argued somewhat as follows:

[7] Rives, "Mexican Diplomacy on the Eve of the War With the United States," *The Am. Hist. Rev.*, XVIII (Jan. 1913), p. 287.

[8] *Ibid.*, pp. 294–295.

"Our honor will be vindicated by a brilliant stroke beyond the Rio Grande; European intervention will then occur; the United States will have to pay a round sum for Texas; and we shall obtain a fixed boundary, guaranteed by the leading powers of Europe, that will serve as an everlasting dyke against American aggression." [9]

Time of course soon revealed that Mexico had sadly miscalculated. A few days after the outbreak of the war the Oregon dispute was pacifically adjusted, and Great Britain—whether restrained by indisposition to engage in hostilities with the United States or by inability to commit France, it is not now possible to say—flatly refused to lend aid.

On June 1, 1846, Aberdeen directed Bankhead to inform the Mexican government that Great Britain could not depart from the policy of non-interference. ". . . The annexation of Texas to the United States, which had long been foreseen and pointed out to the Govt. of Mexico by Her Majesty's Govt. and which the timely recognition of Texas by Mexico, so often insisted on by Great Britain, could alone have prevented, has been consummated; and the further encroachment of the United States on the Mexican territory, which was equally foretold by Her Majesty's Govt., has been realized. Meantime Mexico, although menaced, and now indeed, as we learn, actually engaged in hostilities, on her Texan Frontier, has been precluded by her internal dissentions and the penury of her finances from effectually providing against the emergency in which She is involved. . . .

"Were Great Britain to interfere in that quarrel, She would involve herself in a war with the United States; and not only that, but She must necessarily play the part, not merely of an auxiliary, but of a principal, in such war; that is, She would find herself engaged in a war with a Nation with which She would have no personal cause of quarrel, in behalf of a Nation and Govt. which She has repeatedly warned in the most friendly and urgent manner of their danger, and which, solely in consequence of their wilful contempt of that warning, have at last plunged headlong down the precipice from which the British Govt. spared no efforts to save them. . . .

". . . Her Majesty's Govt. will always be found perfectly willing and desirous to give Mexico every proof in their power of their

---

[9] Smith, *The War with Mexico* (1919), I, 112–116.

It should also be remembered that even before the clash took place between American and Mexican troops south of the Nueces, the executive government of the United States had resolved upon war. The motives—alleged and real—were a desire for territory and the settlement of claims.

earnest wish to save her, as far as it may yet be possible, by friendly interposition, from the fatal consequences of the policy which her successive Govts. have for many years past been so unfortunately induced to pursue towards Texas and the United States." [10]

Britain was mainly concerned, after the war had once begun, in a speedy return to peace. During the early months of the struggle she made two vain overtures looking toward mediation, and, later, when Nicholas P. Trist, the American peace commissioner, arrived in Mexico he found British diplomatic agents ready to coöperate with him in securing the acceptance of the olive branch by the unsteady Mexican government. These agents were not authorized, however, to go so far as to guarantee the integrity of the Mexican territory remaining after American demands had been met. Moreover, this proposal of British guaranty was energetically rejected by Trist. Thus Mexico was left to defend her new boundary without any pledge of assistance from abroad.[11]

Britain and the Mexican Policy of the United States (1848–1856).

Britain's pledge of 1825, that she would not permit the seizure of Spanish-American territory, had been tried and found wanting. England, when the test came, was unwilling to assume the responsibility of a war with the United States in order to save Mexico. This did not mean, however, that all support of the country against the United States was to be withdrawn. The Foreign Office was still resolved to employ all the resources of diplomacy to prevent the domination or absorption of Mexico by its neighbor on the north. The years immediately subsequent to 1848 were to offer ample illustration of this resolution.

The British government was still deeply interested in Mexican commerce and in the investments of its citizens in Mexico. These would be gravely injured, it was thought, if the United States should acquire the mines of northern Mexico, exclusive transit and colonizing privileges on the Isthmus of Tehuantepec, or additional Mexican territory bordering on the Gulf of Mexico. Accordingly, the Foreign Office gave its attention first and foremost to defeating real or apprehended designs of the Yankees in these regions.

With reference to the Isthmus of Tehuantepec, British diplomacy brought pressure to bear upon Mexico in order to prevent too liberal concessions being made to the United States and to persuade the

10 Rives, *The United States and Mexico* (1913), I, 162–163.
11 Smith, *The War with Mexico*, II, 238, 301–304; Rives, *The United States and Mexico*, II, 601 ff.

Mexican government to place the region under a joint guaranty of America and Britain. Overtures looking toward the latter arrangement were also made to the United States, but with little success. The Clayton-Bulwer Treaty was considered by Washington as sufficient impediment to the perfection of interoceanic communications. Indeed, Britain once urged that Article VIII of that agreement applied to Tehuantepec. Fortunately for the harmony of the two branches of the Anglo-Saxon family, the persistent improbability that the canal could be completed rendered the contentions over the affair largely theoretical.[12]

In regard to territorial matters, England could only discourage Mexico from projected sales and urge a pacific policy toward the United States in order that the catastrophe of 1848 should not be repeated. These steps were taken time and again between 1848 and 1856, the British agents showing their concern by keeping the closest possible watch over all Mexican-United States negotiations regarding territory. On one occasion, indeed, the British and French ministers in Washington, in obedience to instructions, sounded Secretary of State Marcy on certain plans of purchase supposed to be under way. Diplomatic interposition, however, unless supplemented by financial support or material aid in some other form, could be of little service. More than once Mexico sought in vain for British, and indeed French and Spanish backing, but the Foreign Office constantly refused to grant it. In fact, Great Britain was not even willing to authorize a suspension of the payments on the Mexican bonded debt in order to prevent Santa Anna from selling what has become known as the "Gadsden Purchase." Hence British efforts to prevent the alienation of Mexican territory to the United States were confined to uttering forebodings and arousing suspicions.[13] Such efforts in reality had very little weight. The United States failed to acquire Mexican domain after 1854, not so much because Mexico's political leaders had set their minds firmly against selling it, as because American political leaders could not agree upon the terms of purchase or indeed upon the desirability of purchasing territory at all.

[12] Foreign Office to Doyle, No. 20, June 25, 1852, F. O. 50 (250), Mexico; *ibid.* to *ibid.*, No. 3, January 14, 1853, F. O. 50 (257), Mexico; *ibid.* to *ibid.*, No. 17, April 27, 1853, *loc. cit.; ibid.* to *ibid.*, No. 99, Oct. 31, 1854, F. O. 50 (265), Mexico; *ibid.* to *ibid.*, No. 13, March 1, 1855, F. O. 50 (275), Mexico.

[13] *Cf.* Doyle to Clarendon, No. 69, June 2, 1854, F. O. 50 (267), Mexico; *ibid.* to *ibid.*, No. 71, July 3, 1854, F. O. 50 (268), Mexico; *ibid.* to *ibid.*, No. 44, May 3, 1855, F. O. 50 (227), Mexico; Lettsom to Clarendon, No. 33, July 3, 1855, F. O. 50 (279), Mexico; Foreign Office to Doyle, No. 21, Feb. 13, No. 71, July 1, 1854, F. O. 50 (265), Mexico; *ibid.* to *ibid.*, No. 9, February 22, 1855, F. O. 50 (275), Mexico.

The Cuban Issue

The foregoing discussion of the rivalries of the Powers in Mexico renders any extensive treatment of the contest elsewhere in America unnecessary. Indeed the motives and policies were essentially the same whether they refer to Mexico, Cuba, Santo Domingo, Central America, or other areas.

British interest in Cuba centered mainly around questions of commerce, investments, strategy, and slavery. If Cuba were prosperous, the revenues of the island might enable Spain to meet her obligations under the heavy British loans outstanding. If the island should persist in a state of constant insurgency and maladministration, this prospect would disappear. Similarly, disturbances in the island might lead the United States to annex it and this would have essentially the same result. Moreover, this latter step, like the acquisition of Mexican territory, would strengthen America's hold on the Gulf and bolster up the Southern slave power. For all these reasons, Britain set her face firmly against the acquisition of this key to the Gulf by the United States.

In opposing the expansion of the United States in this direction, however, the British government appears to have been unwilling to press matters to the point of an open break. It could insist upon the suppression of the slave trade with the island without running such a risk; and this it did. The British government, however, does not appear to have meddled with the status of slavery itself, although certain enthusiastic British abolitionists appear to have done so. Nor was it willing alone at this time to offer Spain what it had been unwilling in the last resort to grant Mexico—a guaranty of territorial integrity against the encroachments of the United States. It was prepared, however, to use its navy against the American filibusters who were launching expeditions against Cuba, and it also tried to persuade the United States to sign with England and France a tripartite guaranty insuring Spain perpetual dominion over the island. Moreover, British diplomats probably encouraged the Spanish government in its resolution not to sell the island, and they certainly urged Spain to adopt a moderate policy toward Mexico (1857–1858) largely because they feared that the United States would take advantage of a Hispano-Mexican war in order to seize Cuba.[14]

[14] Callahan, *Cuba and International Relations* (1899), p. 164 ff.; Latané, *Diplomatic Relations of the United States and Spanish America* (1900), p. 89 ff.; A. C. Dodge (U. S. Minister to Spain) to Cass, No. 56, July 25, 1857, Dept. of State, Bureau of Indexes and Archives, Despatches from Spain, Vol. 40; *ibid.* to *ibid.*, No. 59, August 22, 1857, *loc. cit.; ibid.* to *ibid.*, March 13, 1858,

But it must be admitted that all of these efforts were somewhat superfluous. Cuba was indeed retained by Spain during this critical period, but for this retention British diplomacy deserved little credit. Public opinion in the United States was divided on the proposed acquisition of Cuba, and Spain's resolution not to sell the island needed little tonic. In order to prevent the United States from annexing Cuba, Britain had employed every resource and device of diplomacy; a more profound knowledge of the situation might have saved her the trouble.

The Contest in Central America

The contest of the United States and Britain in Central America was even more energetic than that which took place in Mexico. Mexico's population was much larger, its territory more extensive, and its subsoil resources more valuable, but its strategic location for a nation interested in world commerce and sea power was not as favorable as that of Central America. Between 1846 and 1856, in particular, there took place upon the isthmus a spirited contest between the two branches of the Anglo-Saxon family which gradually became more critical until, near the end of the period, war actually threatened.

British interest in Central America began to develop long before the United States government came into existence. There were three centers of activity—Belize, the islands of Honduras Bay, and the Mosquito Shore—, but Britain did not possess sovereignty over any of these regions or any part of them prior to the proclamation of the Monroe Doctrine. British subjects had dwelt in Belize for the purpose of cutting logwood and collecting other natural products since 1662; they had alternately occupied and abandoned certain of the Bay Islands since 1642; they had maintained fitful settlements on the Mosquito Shore and more or less intimate relations with the natives of the region since the closing decades of the seventeenth century; but by a series of treaties extending from 1786 to 1814 the British government had acknowledged that it had no sovereign rights in these regions, nor were any such claims advanced until long after 1823.

In Central America, as elsewhere, the agents of George Canning expressed uneasiness regarding the designs of the United States, but American statesmen showed little concern regarding British pro-

No. 78, *loc. cit.,* Vol. 41; *ibid.* to *ibid.,* No. 95, November 10, 1858, *loc. cit.;* George M. Dallas (Minister to London) to Cass, No. 138, November 26, 1858, **Despatches from England.**

cedure in the area during the Canning era and even down to the
time when the acquisition of California became a certainty. Englishmen
had only to deal with the weak Central American governments,
and these they easily managed by setting state against state and
party against party in a somewhat ruthless fashion. Central Americans
appealed to Washington in vain; so far as the United States
was concerned, Great Britain might work with a free hand.

Between 1830 and 1848 British influence expanded in all three
of the regions which had long been the center of attraction in Central
America. As early as 1821, in fact, British settlers in Belize had
spread out to the south of the Sibun; and in 1838 the British government
declared that the southern boundary of this settlement was
the Sarstoon. At no time prior to 1848, however, did Britain consent
to consider Belize a British colony. In similar manner the
Mosquito king had been induced in 1841 to extend his dominion
far enough south to take in the mouths of the San Juan and the town
of that name; and when Nicaragua contested this claim, the British
government supported the native monarch by force of arms, renaming
the village Greytown. Lastly, after 1840 the British government
came to the support of its subjects which had occupied Ruatan,
the largest of the Bay Islands. Clearly it was England's intention
either to control the canal zone or to prevent the United States
from doing so.

At length (1846) American interest in the isthmus became aroused
by these and other British activities and by the prospect of Pacific
Coast possessions. While the Mexican War continued, however, the
United States government was loath to enter the lists against the
British in the Nicaragua region. It sent its agent instead to New
Granada, where a treaty relating to Panama was negotiated in 1846.
As the war came to a close preparations were made to deal with
the rival in Central America proper.

The United States assumed that it was the purpose of Great
Britain to acquire territory in Central America and either to dominate
the canal route or to obstruct the construction of the canal,
and immediately set about to defeat these plans. This end might be
accomplished by negotiations in Central America or in England, or
in both. Effort was exerted first upon the isthmus. Elijah Hise and
then E. G. Squier were sent to counteract British influence and encourage
united resistance on the part of the little Central American
states. They also sought to advance the interests of the United States
by the negotiation of canal treaties. But first the former agent
and then the latter found his exertions fully matched by the work
of Frederick Chatfield, the British consul-general. Canal treaties

were obtained, but on terms which the United States was not prepared to ratify. Meanwhile (1849), negotiations were opened in
England, and not without promise of achievement. William C. Rives,
recently appointed minister to France, stopped in London on his
way to the French court and had a frank interview with Palmerston,
British foreign secretary. In the course of the interview Palmerston
was convinced that the United States, aggressive as its recent career
had been, had not really resolved upon the exclusive control of the
canal route. At the same time Rives was given the impression that
the main concern of the British had been not so much to monopolize
the route as to prevent the United States from doing so. The way
therefore seemed clear for mutual concessions and compromises, and
negotiations were speedily begun.

They soon led to the Clayton-Bulwer Treaty, signed at Washington on April 18, 1850. The document was the result of a vigorous
diplomatic encounter and, as was soon revealed, meant one thing
to Clayton and an entirely different thing to Bulwer. Clayton's first
purpose in the encounter had been to clear the way for the construction of a canal by an American company which had already
obtained a concession from Nicaragua, but public opinion in the
United States had forced him later to undertake to obtain from
Britain an agreement to withdraw from Central America altogether.
The prime concern of Bulwer, who was less interested in the immediate construction of a canal, was to exact from the United States
a pledge not to expand into Central America and to do this without
giving a reciprocal pledge that England would immediately withdraw. Both diplomats thought, or pretended to think, that they
had accomplished their purpose, but it soon became evident that
neither had accomplished anything of great importance. The United
States government adopted the view of Clayton and demanded that
Britain clear out of Central America immediately. The English government accepted the view of Bulwer and made no move to get
out at all.[15]

In the meantime the nationals and agents of the two governments
in the contested area committed acts which increased the tension.
British settlers and naval officers at Greytown interfered with
American trade and transit, and American immigrants on their
way to California often became involved in altercations with the
British and their allies in Mosquitia. The agitation was heightened
in 1852 by Britain's seizure of the Bay Islands and their organiza-

---

[15] The treaty placed the potential canal route of the Isthmus under the joint
control of the United States and Great Britain and pledged both of these powers
not to acquire territory in the region.

tion into a colony. Matters developed from bad to worse until on July 13, 1854, the village of Greytown was bombarded by an American man-of-war and then burned to the ground. The act was plainly a defiance of the British protectorate over the Mosquito Kingdom which claimed jurisdiction in Greytown, and the London government might have resented it in a forceful manner had it not been engaged in the Crimean War. As it was, the United States defended the act of the naval officer and Britain could do nothing except remain firm in her Central American claims.

The climax came in the spring of 1856. Irritation in the United States was still further increased in the latter part of 1855 by John Crampton's violation of neutrality in soliciting recruits for the Crimean War while serving as minister in the United States. The United States demanded his recall, but the British ministry refused to take action. At the same time there came evidence of Britain's active opposition to William Walker and his filibusters who were undertaking the conquest of Central America and meeting with no little success because the United States winked at the defiance of its laws forbidding such piratical operations. The United States at once recognized the Walker government and broke off diplomatic relations with England. The politicians and the press congratulated President Pierce and a demand for war was heard in several quarters. The situation was most critical, especially since the war in the Crimea had just ended and left the British government free to act if it chose.[16]

[16] Mary W. Williams, *Anglo-American Isthmian Diplomacy* (1916), pp. 168–190; William O. Scroggs, *Filibusters and Financiers* (1916), pp. 108–170; John Bigelow, *Breaches of Anglo-American Treaties* (1917), p. 37 ff.

CHAPTER VII

TOWARD ANGLO-SAXON CORDIALITY (1857–1927)

BUT the crisis in Anglo-Saxon relations was destined to pass without hostilities. In the latter part of 1856 British opposition to the southward expansion of the United States began to relax and the task of circumscribing the Yankees was left to others. After more than thirty years of almost futile effort Britain slowly weakened, abandoning one by one many of the positions which she formerly maintained. It was perhaps this recession alone that prevented war.

Britain Begins to Recede (1856–1860)

Unmistakable indications of a change in the British attitude first appeared in June. A few excerpts will suffice to illustrate the view of the journals at that time. On June 14 the London *Economist* remarked:

"We could not hinder the ultimate absorption by the Anglo-Saxon republicans of the whole of Central America if we would; and we are by no means certain that we would if we could. . . . We can have no interest in upholding the present wretched and feeble governments of Spanish America. Our interest lies all the other way. We wish ourselves for no extension of territory on that continent. We are half inclined to regret that we hold any possession at all there south of the Union. Desiring no territory, we desire only prosperous, industrious, civilized, and wealthy customers.

". . . Central America peopled and *exploited* by Anglo-Saxons will be worth to us tenfold its present value. We have no fear that our countrymen will be excluded from the commerce of those provinces. We have no fear that our ships will be prohibited from crossing that isthmus when the two seas shall be joined by a canal." [1]

During the same month a writer in *Blackwood's Magazine* expressed similar sentiments. "Great Britain has no great interest

[1] As quoted in Littell's *Living Age,* Second Series, XIV, 312.

in Central America," the writer declared. "She cannot consent to be bullied out of her rights there," he said, "but otherwise she has not the least desire to check the progress of American influence in that region. . . . The paths of Britain and America do not cross. The Isthmus of the New World is the goal of Transatlantic ambition. . . . The Isthmus of the Old World is the cynosure of British policy. . . ." [2]

Before the close of the year the London *Times* fell in line. "In the eye and forecast of the States," said the editor of this journal, "all North America is theirs excepting only those portions already belonging to European Powers, or . . . under a recognized European protection." "For our own part," he continued, "we see no reason why we should resist the process, except where a British community is established and demands our aid, or where some real interest can be shown to be at stake. . . . It must be for our interest to see North America under strong, civilized, uniform, and prosperous government. . . . It does not become us to play the dog in the manger with our fast-growing progeny across the Atlantic. They have too many good reasons, as well as too many bad ones, against allowing us to stand in their way for the mere sake of mischief or pride. . . ."

At the same time British statesmen and diplomats began to express views of a similar nature. On June 16, 1856, Disraeli arose in the House of Commons to speak on the relations of the United States and Britain in America. He thought it would "be wise in England not to regard with the extreme jealousy with which she has hitherto looked upon it any extension of the territory of the United States beyond the bounds which were orginally fixed." It was not sound policy to continue to oppose the "so-called 'aggressive spirit' of the United States." Such opposition would not prevent Yankee expansion; but it would involve England in struggles which might prove disastrous. And besides, might not the expansion of the United States in America prove advantageous to England? He recalled that the annexation of California by the United States had been looked upon in the House of Commons as a calamity, but he now asked his colleagues whether that conquest had disturbed the "balance of power" and, indeed, whether any event since the discovery of America had "contributed more to the wealth, and through the wealth, to the power of this country, than the development of the rich resources of California by . . . the United States." Disraeli then proposed a sort of reciprocity plan whereby Britain, by recognizing the necessity for Yankee expansion

[2] LXXIX, 742.

in the New World, might persuade the United States to abandon the two spheres conception embodied in the Monroe Doctrine as obsolete in an age of steam and expanding trade.[3]

Thus economic considerations were exerting a strong influence upon British thought. The southward extension of the United States might bring order and higher standards of living, thereby enlarging the market for British goods; and, besides, a war with the United States over the issue of expansion would be attended by economic consequences which could not lightly be passed over. The total value of the trade between Britain and the United States amounted to more than fifty million pounds sterling, and Yankee privateers were dreaded. The editors did not fail to note these facts,[4] and the statesmen soon decided to alter their course.

The Foreign Office considered[5] the cotton trade of the United States of greater importance than the British stake in Mexico and Central America, and diplomats began to act accordingly. Before the close of the year attempts were made to harmonize English and American interests in Mexico. British holders of Mexican bonds began work on a scheme designed to divert into their coffers a portion of any cash which the United States might pay Mexico for territory. They strongly urged their plan both upon the Mexican government and the minister of the United States at Mexico City; and in the summer of 1856 Martínez del Rio, Mexican agent of the bondholders, visited Washington for the purpose of sounding certain senatorial leaders. Partly as a result of these machinations, perhaps, United States minister John Forsyth signed a treaty (February 10, 1857) providing for a loan of fifteen million dollars to the Mexican government, four millions of which were to be applied on the British convention debt. Forsyth's procedure was unauthorized and the loan agreement was not accepted either by President Pierce or by President Buchanan, but the idea made a deep impression on British diplomatic circles. After May 4, 1857, the English ministers in Mexico had standing instructions to the effect that the Mexican government would be expected to pay a portion of any sums received from the United States to British creditors and claimants.[6]

Moreover, W. G. Lettsom, who took charge of the British lega-

[3] Hansard, *Parliamentary Debates,* Third Series, CXLII, 1511–1512.
[4] See excerpts in *Living Age,* Second Series, XIV, 119, 244.
[5] Mary W. Williams, *Anglo-American Isthmian Diplomacy* (1916), p. 213.
[6] Lettsom to Clarendon, Nos. 37, 38, and 39, February 18, 1857, F. O. 50 (306), Mexico; Forsyth to Marcy, No. 24, February 10, 1857, and enclosures, Mex. Desp., Vol. 20; Foreign Office to Lettsom, No. 67, May 4, 1857, F. O. 50 (304), Mexico; Malmesbury to Otway, No. 1, March 31, 1858, F. O. 50 (319).

tion in the summer of 1856, held views not essentially different from those expressed by Disraeli and the British journalists. In July, 1857, he remarked: "I conceive that the absorption of *half* of the Territory of Mexico by the United States would inflict greater injury on British Interests than if the whole Territory were annexed to that Country." He then went on to explain the meaning of this statement:

"If half the territory of Mexico is so absorbed, Mexico, as before, will be burthened with all her present liabilities, while the resources remaining at her disposal to cover them will be diminished by one half, and in this case I need hardly remark that it will be useless to expect she will fulfil her engagements. The manner in which the revenue of Mexico is always frittered away prevents the development of the resources of the Country, while the tariff is constantly such that consumption is impeded as much as possible.

"Were the whole of the Territory of this Republic annexed to the United States the latter Country would have to assume the liabilities of Mexico, the position of the numerous British claimants . . . would be at once ameliorated, while with the general activity then pervading this Country, with the development of its resources, and with the increase of its population, new wants would arise, and these British commerce would be called upon mainly to provide for." [7]

W. Otway, who succeeded Lettsom early in 1858, evinced a strong inclination to return to the policy of Canning. His despatches were filled with alleged exposures of American greed and ruthlessness. Eagerness to set bounds to American expansion and influence was frequently expressed. In fact, Otway even went beyond any plans ever seriously entertained by Canning and urged Great Britain to undertake, either alone or in coöperation with France, to establish a protectorate over Mexico, presenting as inducements for this radical departure a glowing picture of Mexico's unlimited resources, a discouraging account of the incapacity of the Mexican people, and the shocking prospect that four million poor Indians would be reduced to most cruel servitude if ever the United States seized the country.[8]

But Otway reckoned without his host. In July, 1858, Lord

[7] Lettsom to Clarendon, No. 163, July 22, 1857, F. O. 50 (310), Mexico.

[8] See in particular Otway's despatches No. 68, of August 1, 1858; *Private*, of August 2; No. 176, of November 5; and Nos. 208, 210, 220, 228–230, of December 2, 20, and 30, 1858, respectively, in F. O. 59 (324–325), Mexico.

Malmesbury, British secretary of state for foreign affairs, had re-marked to George M. Dallas, minister of the United States at London, "that he [Malmesbury] was one of that class of statesmen who believed that all the southern part of North America must ultimately come under the government of the United States: that he had no objection to what seemed the inevitable course of things: that, on the contrary, he thought it would be beneficial as well to the population occupying the countries referred to as to the United States, and the rest of the world." [9] On January 7, following, in response to the sensational despatches of Otway, the Foreign Office notified its minister that Great Britain would not join France in a dual intervention in Mexico, but that she would be willing to take part in a quadruple action embracing Spain and the United States as well as England and France.[10]

For more than a year and one-half this continued to be the policy of Great Britain. When the United States broke relations with the reactionary government in Mexico City and soon after-wards proceeded to recognize the liberal organization of Benito Juárez at Vera Cruz, the minister of the reactionaries at the Court of St. James's urged Britain to protest and use her influence to per-suade the United States to withdraw its recognition, but the Brit-ish secretary of foreign affairs declined to act.[11] Finally, how-ever, on June 28, 1860, the English minister in Mexico was informed of the decision of England, France, and Spain to inter-vene in Mexican affairs. He was also notified that Great Britain would be glad if the United States would coöperate.[12] In July, fol-lowing, Lord Lyons, the minister of Great Britain at Washington, actually invited the United States to join the European Powers in addressing identical notes to the two governments of Mexico, advising them to find some method for a speedy arrangement of their difficulties. The United States replied that it was opposed to the interference of other Powers in the domestic affairs of the independent nations of the New World, and especially of Mexico, and communicated the substance of this reply to Vera Cruz.[13] Without specific directions for such action the legation of the United States in Mexico issued, in December, 1860, a sort of manifesto setting forth the attitude of Washington toward the projected intervention of the European Powers. "The government of the United States," said

---

[9] Dallas to Cass, No. 99, Mex. Desp., Vol. 71.
[10] No. 2, *Confidential*, F. O. 50 (329), Mexico.
[11] F. O. to Otway, No. 44, May 31, 1859, *loc. cit.*
[12] No. 57, F. O. 50 (342).
[13] Callahan, "Evolution of Seward's Mexican Policy," p. 14.

the manifesto, "does not deny to the European powers the right to wage honorable warfare for a sufficient cause, anywhere, or against any nation; nor does it deny their right to demand redress for injuries inflicted on their respective subjects . . . , but it does deny them the right to interfere, *directly,* or *indirectly,* with the political independence of the republic of Mexico, and it will to the extent of its power, defend the nationality and independence of said republic." [14] Commenting upon this document, George W. Mathew, British minister in Mexico, said: "If the position of the United States . . . is authorised and maintained, I cannot but view it as binding that country to assume the moral obligation toward other nations, of restoring peace and order in Mexico, and of preventing the recurrence of scenes, which disgrace humanity and neutralise . . . the international rights and natural commercial relations of civilized nations." [15]

But the United States had already reached a condition which rendered the fulfillment of this "moral obligation" impossible. Secession and the Civil War concentrated attention upon domestic affairs. The United States found itself in no position to establish a protectorate over Mexico or even to prevent European intervention. Britain's participation in the joint move against Mexico appears, however, to have been in no way influenced by the old motive of circumscribing the United States. Her purpose seems to have been confined to the redressing of injuries and the satisfaction of claims.

The same softening of British official attitude likewise became evident in Central American affairs. Lord Malmesbury's statement to Dallas in July, 1858, applied to Central America as well as to Mexico. Even before this Lord Clarendon had expressed similar views. As early as March 13 of the previous year he had written President Buchanan: ". . . Pray bear in mind that beyond the point of honor respecting the Mosquito Indians we possess no interest in Central America, & that, so far from wishing to create one, we would not accept such a 'damnosa possessio' as Central America if it could be offered to England as a gift." [16]

It was therefore largely a question of honor and, Clarendon might have added, of pride. British pride could not tolerate the idea of being "bullied out of rights" in Central America by the Yankees, and British honor could not find satisfaction in the abandonment of the

---

[14] *House Ex. Doc.* No. 100, 37 Cong., 2 Sess. (Ser. 1136), p. 18.
[15] No. 85, December 29, 1860, to Lord Russell, F. O. 50 (344), Mexico.
[16] J. B. Moore, *The Works of James Buchanan* (1910), X, 115.

Mosquitoes, who had looked upon England for centuries as their great and good friend, to the tender mercies of Honduras, Nicaragua, and the United States. But the crisis was compelling and Britain found a way out by direct negotiation with the Central American states.

On November 28, 1859, a treaty was signed with Honduras acknowledging the Bay Islands as the possession of this republic and recognizing its sovereign rights over that portion of the Mosquito territory which lay within its frontiers. Two months later negotiations with Nicaragua resulted in an agreement to recognize the sovereignty of this little state over the part of Mosquitia which lay within its boundaries. The British protectorate over the natives was to cease within three months and they were to be granted a sort of home rule until they should agree to incorporate themselves into the Nicaraguan republic. Upon ratification these treaties were forthwith transmitted to the United States, and Britain expressed the hope that they would "finally set at rest the questions respecting the interpretation of the Clayton-Bulwer Treaty which have been the subject of so much controversy between this country and the United States." [17]

It was a clever stroke, and notwithstanding the fact that England still retained Belize with boundaries extending as far south as the Sarstoon, President Buchanan expressed entire satisfaction with the settlement. In a message of December, 1860, he took occasion to remark: "The discordant constructions of the Clayton and Bulwer treaty . . . , which at different periods of the discussion bore a threatening aspect, have resulted in a final settlement entirely satisfactory to this government." This was probably the most cordial mention of Great Britain that had appeared in any presidential message up to that time.[18]

The historian should pause, however, to examine just what concessions Britain had granted and upon what assumptions they had been based. It will be noted that in reality only one concession had been made. The English government had decided no longer to oppose the southward expansion of the United States, and this decision had been reached upon the presupposition that the United States would not attempt to shut off British merchants from the growing markets of the regions annexed and in the hope, moreover, that the United States might eventually abandon the Monroe Doctrine. This doctrine had not been accepted, nor had joint control over interoceanic communication by way of the isthmus been relinquished.

[17] Williams, *op. cit.,* pp. 264–265.
[18] *Ibid.,* p. 266.

A Significant Domestic Change in England

It appeared for a time, indeed, that the outbreak of the Civil War in the United States would furnish occasion for a reversal of British policy. In 1862 the London government organized the Belize settlements into a full-fledged British colony and near the end of the same year approached the verge of interference in the struggle between North and South. The former step, though in line with British procedure in Central America for three decades prior to 1856, was nevertheless out of harmony with the self-denying pledge of Canning and the provisions of the Clayton-Bulwer Treaty, as likewise with the assurances given Buchanan in 1857 and 1858. The latter procedure would have been inspired in part by the feeling that the unity and continuing prosperity of the American nation would not serve the best interests of Britain, a complex mixture of economic and political motives, among which not the least would have been the conviction in conservative circles that the failure of American democracy would help to perpetuate the privileges of Britain's aristocracy.[19]

For reasons which need not be related here, the British government did not interfere in the Civil War. Union and Democracy triumphed, and almost at the same time the great reforms which took place in England "changed Great Britain from a government by aristocracy to one by democracy." Thereafter the clash of political views ceased to be an element of discord between the Anglo-Saxon nations. Economic rivalries might continue; Irish and other hostile elements in the United States might try to stir up trouble; boundary and fishery disputes might irritate; even saner Americans, blinded by "bitter and exaggerated memories," might fail for a time to see in the British nation a sister democracy holding out friendly hands to the United States; but the sister democracy was there with extended friendly hands, and this was bound sooner or later to make a difference. Moreover, after 1895 conditions in Europe and Asia were such as to impel Britain to seek cordial relations with her Anglo-Saxon kinsmen. England was confronted by powerful rivals and the support and coöperation of the United States were greatly needed. The two nations were destined to move toward an era of harmony.[20]

[19] E. D. Adams, *Great Britain and the American Civil War* (1926), *passim*.
[20] Adams, *op. cit.*, II, 303–305; Bertha Ann Reuter, *Anglo-American Relations during the Spanish-American War* (1924), pp. 17–60.

Centers of Friction

So far as Latin America was concerned, few causes of friction arose during the next half-century. British merchants continued to enjoy a large share of Latin-American trade and to invest large sums of money in these regions. Except in Cuba and Mexico, and to a lesser extent in Central America, Peru, and Chile, the merchants and capitalists of the two nations were not brought into sharp rivalry; and, even in these areas, no more than mild friction occurred. The governments themselves do not appear to have been seriously concerned, although James G. Blaine suffered some uneasiness in regard to Chile and Peru.[21]

Only with reference to the control of projected lines of communication between the Atlantic and the Pacific, the Pan-American movement, and the interpretation of the Monroe Doctrine did a clash between the two governments seem possible. In regard to these matters friction became sharpest between 1894 and 1901.

British Criticisms during the 'Eighties and Early 'Nineties

Beginning with the 'eighties the United States gradually moved toward the resolution to demand a canal under the ownership and control of the United States government and to capture a larger share of the trade of Latin America. At the same time certain secretaries of state evinced a zeal for arbitration and Pan-American congresses. All this appeared to constitute an evil omen for European trade and influence in the Western Hemisphere. What attitude would Great Britain assume toward this resurgence of Yankee aggressiveness?

For more than a decade after this aggressiveness began to show itself, a large section of the British press assumed a critical tone. Space will permit only one or two illustrations. For instance, a hostile journal like *The Saturday Review* began to criticise the proposed Pan-American congress as early as January, 1882. "If the Congress meets," remarked the *Review,* "the representatives of the petty States will probably be invited to pledge themselves against any diplomatic arrangements with Europe, or rather with England. . . . It is difficult to understand what advantage can be offered [by the United States]

---

[21] Blaine declared his conviction that Great Britain instigated the war between Chile and Peru (1879–1883) in the hope that Chile's conquest of the nitrate area would furnish Britain nationals in Chile an opportunity to exploit this commodity. Some of the diplomatic agents of the United States appear to have held the same view. (See William Roderick Sherman, *The Diplomatic and Commercial Relations of the United States and Chile,* pp. 131–132.)

in exchange for [the] political and commercial independence [of the Latin-American nations]." The journal then went on to emphasize the commercial motive of the United States in initiating this movement. It was probably designed "as a method of establishing commercial monopoly. If the whole Western Continent could be included in a customs union with prohibitive tariff, the arrangement would be extremely popular" in the United States. The Latin-American states were then warned that they had nothing to gain and everything to lose by accepting such a project.[22] *The Spectator,* usually not unfriendly toward the United States, was sarcastically skeptical with reference to the practical results of the congress of 1889–1890. "We feel a deep compassion for the delegates of the Pan-American Congress." Two dozen or more softened Spaniards "land in America, America by a thousand newspapers roars her welcome, and then they are clutched and sentenced to prison in hot railroad cars . . . and are whirled at about thirty miles an hour for six thousand miles." What impression will the Spanish-Americans take home from their "bewildering journey"? None save that of "fear, fear of this mighty race which multiplies so fast and stretches its territory so continuously, and masters all it acquires so easily, and digs such mines, and constructs such elevators, and uses the steam-plough over fields miles broad, and is so fearfully energetic that it considers a journey of six thousand miles by rail an entertainment." Then, speaking of the commercial aspect of the congress, *The Spectator* remarked: "They [the Latin Americans] do not particularly want anything that America has, importing no corn, desiring beef and no bacon, growing their own tobacco almost without cost, and getting more money than is good for them from Europe on terms on which no American will lend them a dollar. . . . We almost think . . that Spanish America will prefer Europe to North America as her business correspondent, and certainly if she does not, it will not be because she has been persuaded by the Pan-American delegates. Men employed as diplomats know how to put up with a great deal; but a tour of six thousand miles . . . offered as an enjoyment, with the steelworks of Pennsylvania thrown in as a delight," this was too much even for Latin-American diplomats![23]

In like manner *The Fortnightly Review* published an article (1891) which expressed resentment at the mediation attempts of the United States in Chile, and *The Pall Mall Gazette* (1894) criticised the North American attitude toward the Brazilian revolution. The writer whose article appeared in *The Fortnightly Review* urged that England and

Germany should mediate in the Chilean difficulty: "The great share which English and German capital has taken in the development of Chilean commerce and industry would seem to entitle these two nations above all others to take the lead in the matter." He then remarked caustically: "Some abortive attempts at mediation have recently been made, in which the United States Minister in Chile, Mr. Patrick Egan, is understood to have taken a prominent part. . . . There can be no doubt that the notorious ex-Treasurer of the Land League and the American political circle to which he owes his present post, bear no good will toward England, and it behooves us to be on our guard against all action from that quarter. Any arrangement brought about under such auspices would certainly turn out as injurious to British *prestige* and interests as its promoters could possibly contrive to make it." [24] *The Pall Mall Gazette* complained of Yankee bumptiousness in regard to Brazil in the following manner: "The Government at Washington has issued a paper declaring that Admiral Benham [of the United States Navy], besides protecting American commerce, ought to end monarchist machinations. This is the Monroe Doctrine, which is not yet codified within the law of nations. If Admiral Benham attacks a single Brazilian insurgent merely because he suspects he is a monarchist, he will be as much a pirate as Admiral da Gama [commander of the Brazilian insurgent fleet] would have been if he had fired on an American trading vessel. Brazil is no more under President Cleveland's suzerainty than the United States are under British suzerainty." [25]

Such were the complaints of British journalists during the early 'nineties. The illustrations could easily be multiplied. British sentiment and policy were not subjected to a real test until after 1895, however. The genuine test came with the insistence of the United States upon the arbitration of the Venezuelan boundary dispute, the Spanish-American War, the demand for the abrogation of the Clayton-Bulwer Treaty, and the Venezuelan imbroglio of 1901-1903.

Growing Opposition in the United States to the Clayton-Bulwer Treaty

The question of the abrogation of the Clayton-Bulwer Treaty, though not settled until 1901, was the first to occasion earnest diplomatic discussion. Soon after the close of the Civil War the United States began to act as if this treaty were not applicable to the Panama

---

[24] Quoted in *Literary Digest*, III (July 25, 1891), 338-339.
[25] Quoted in *ibid.*, VIII (February 8, 1894), 333. "The English press is almost unanimous in its condemnation of the inaction of the Powers."— *Ibid.*, VIII, 296.

route. Recovery from the Civil War and alarm at the prospect of the Panama Canal's being constructed by a French company headed by De Lesseps soon led, in fact, to an open demand for an American canal controlled by the United States. As early as 1881 negotiations were entered upon with Great Britain having this aim in view. The British government was asked to modify or grant the United States release from the Clayton-Bulwer pact. Britain resisted the attempt with irrefragable arguments. Soon afterwards De Lesseps's undertaking showed indications of immediate and certain failure. Interest in the United States then shifted to the Nicaragua route as the most promising one across the isthmus of Central America. Here it was found that Britain was still maintaining intimate relations with the Mosquito Indians, whose reserve was in close proximity to the interoceanic route. Systematic opposition to British policy was at once begun, and before the close of the year 1894 the incorporation of these Indians into the state of Nicaragua had been effected in a manner which appeared for the moment satisfactory both to the United States and to England.[26]

Meanwhile, utterances of the American press and debates in the Senate continued to reveal the growing sentiment of hostility toward the Clayton-Bulwer Treaty and an increasing demand for an American-built, American-controlled canal. But the policy of the British government was one of firmness tempered with moderation. When questioned about the matter in the House of Commons, Sir Edward Grey, under-secretary of state for foreign affairs, replied that there was no reason to suppose that the United States did not intend to abide by its treaty obligations. And his confidence was justified, temporarily at least, by the stand which Secretary Olney took a short time afterwards, when he condemned ingenious arguments designed to prove the treaty obsolete and declared in favor of "a direct and straightforward application to Great Britain for a reconsideration of the whole matter." [27] Before direct negotiations were begun, however, the first Venezuelan crisis arose and severely tested the friendly relations of the two governments.

The Venezuela Difficulty

The immediate occasion of the difficulty was a dispute between the governments of Venezuela and England over the boundary between British Guiana and its Spanish-American neighbor,[28] but

[26] Williams, *Anglo-American Isthmian Diplomacy,* pp. 288–299.
[27] *Ibid.,* pp. 276–288.
[28] The territory in dispute extended between the Essequibo on the east and the Amacura and the basin of the Cuyuni on the west.

the issues involved were more far-reaching and the final settlement of the affair was determined by factors much broader in scope. In the United States there were currents of sentiment which prompted flamboyant jingoism, but there were also saner emotions which demanded sober second thought. In England there was a resurgence of imperialism tempered by a feeling of kinship and a realization of the dangers confronted in Asia, Africa, and Europe. A bare outline of the events of 1894–1896 will make clear the wide ramifications of the subject.

Thomas F. Bayard, American ambassador at the Court of St. James's, urged shortly after he reached London (1893) that the time was opportune for the settlement of the dispute: "Great Britain has just now her hands very full in other quarters of the globe. The United States is the last nation on earth with whom the British people or their rulers desire to quarrel, and of this I have new proofs every day. . . . The . . . European nations are watching each other like pugilists in a ring." [29]

In 1894 Scruggs published his "British Aggressions in Venezuela; or the Monroe Doctrine on Trial," and the American public was ready for a second edition by 1895. Men celebrated the Fourth of July, 1895, by discussing such questions as the advisability of annexing Canada, Newfoundland, Cuba, and Hawaii, and "Will Uncle Sam eventually rule the American continent?" [30] They also had much to say about the enforcement of the Monroe Doctrine. Henry Cabot Lodge declared in the July number of *The North American Review* that the time for "decisive action" had come. The United States must control the Nicaragua canal and defend the Monroe manifesto. "The supremacy of the Monroe Doctrine should be established and at once—peaceably if we can, forcibly if we must." [31] Albert Shaw, editor of the *American Review of Reviews* (a journal which had been founded in order to promote Anglo-Saxon harmony), was about as aggressive as any of the rest. [32]

On July 20, 1895, Secretary of State Richard Olney sent off his now famous despatch. He declared that the Monroe Doctrine was applicable to the boundary dispute which had arisen between Venezuela and British Guiana, and made several other important statements besides. He remarked, for instance, "that distance, and 3,000 miles of intervening ocean, make [made] any permanent political union between any European and any American State unnatural and in-

[29] Robert McElroy, *Grover Cleveland* (1923), II, 178.
[30] *Contemporary Review*, LXVIII, 335 ff.; *The Nation*, LXI, 322, *passim*,
[31] CLX, 658.
[32] See XI, 10, XII, 133.

expedient." He also assumed the rôle of champion of the republican system in America and declared: "To-day the United States is practically sovereign on this continent, and its fiat is law upon the subjects to which it confines its interposition." [33]

Such language could only ruffle the disposition of the head of the British Foreign Office. Lord Salisbury took plenty of time to answer Olney's contentions. His reply was set down in two despatches dated November 26. He not only refused to arbitrate the Venezuelan boundary dispute, except in reference to certain limited phases,[34] but denied the applicability of the Monroe Doctrine to the question and pointedly refused to accept that doctrine. He also took exception to the statement referring to European possessions in the Americas, declaring that "the union between Great Britain and her territories in the Western Hemisphere is [was] both natural and expedient." [35]

After conferring at length on the matter, Cleveland and Olney decided that it was time to lay the question before Congress, and on December 17 the President sent in his message. He invoked the Monroe Doctrine, asked for a committee to investigate and report on the boundary, and declared further: "The dispute has reached such a stage as to make it now incumbent on the United States to take measures to determine . . . the true division line between the Republic of Venezuela and British Guiana. . . . When such report is made . . . it will be the duty of the United States to resist by every means in its power . . . the appropriation by Great Britain of any lands . . . which after investigation we have determined of right belong to Venezuela." [36]

The message and the diplomatic correspondence were at once handed to the press. They were greeted by a jingoist outburst of patriotism more extreme than ever. Outside of a few eastern cities, like New York and Boston, where business interests opposed Cleveland's bellicose policy, the Monroe Doctrine was glorified and the administration upheld. Even the former critics of the President now supported him, and the churches, excepting a few in the cities of the eastern seaboard, approved the American position while praying for peace and arbitration.[37]

[33] U. S. *Foreign Relations* (1895), I, 558 ff.

[34] He refused to arbitrate within a certain line, usually denominated the "modified Schomburgh line."

[35] *Ibid.*

[36] *Ibid.*, I, 542–545.

[37] New York *Tribune,* December 18–22, 1895; New York *Herald,* December 18–23; Chicago *Tribune,* December 19; the Portland *Oregonian,* December 23ff.; *Public Opinion,* December, 1895 to January, 1896.

Congress was already in a pugnacious mood before Cleveland's message was transmitted. The House of Representatives had been opened on December 3 with the prayer: "Heavenly Father, let peace reign throughout our borders. Yet may we be quick to resent anything like an insult to our nation." [38] A resolution in support of the Monroe Doctrine, introduced on the same day by Senator Lodge, furnished occasion for discussions which revealed at once hostility to British policy in America and a determination to control interoceanic communications across Central America. Before Senators had finished their speeches the Cleveland message of December 17 was read. It was received with applause amounting to a demonstration. The House of Representatives, without a dissenting voice, adopted a resolution embodying the President's suggestions. The Senate debated the measure for three days and then unanimously concurred in the action of the House.[39]

During the closing days of the year 1895 the British nation was equally firm in supporting the stand taken by Salisbury. Parliament was not in session, but the press, though it had little knowledge of the issue and its merits, considered it preposterous that an American commission should alone decide a British boundary dispute and that the President of the United States should propose to support its decision by resort to force. The newspapers of both parties expressed indignation. The London *Times* contended that the concessions which England was "imperiously summoned to make are [were] such as no self-respecting nation could submit to," and the traditionally friendly *Spectator* echoed the statement.[40] There was some disposition to treat the affair as a bit of electioneering strategy on the part of Cleveland. If, however, this should turn out not to be the case and the American Congress and people sustained the preposterous contention, then Britain must teach the United States a much needed lesson.[41] The London *Chronicle*, the great mouthpiece of the Liberals, was firm though a bit more moderate. "There is one answer to President Cleveland and America," it declared. "If an enlarged application of a neglected doctrine is to be enforced with all the might of the United States, at least let us be assured that the United States will make itself responsible for the foreign policy of all the petty, impetuous little states on the two continents.

The New York *World* was the only leading journal which made a serious effort on the side of peace.

[38] *Cong. Record,* 53 Cong., 2 Sess., Vol. XXVIII, Part I, p. 26.

[39] *Ibid.,* pp. 24, 25, 111–112, 420, 544, *passim.*

[40] London *Times,* December 18, 1895.

[41] *National Review* (Editorial), XXVI 579; Chicago *Tribune,* December 18, 1895 (London Correspondent).

There is no international right without a corresponding duty. . . . Unless the United States formally proclaims a protectorate over all of the South American Republics we are bound to protect our citizens." [42]

The *Chronicle* sent Henry Norman, of its editorial staff, to Washington for the purpose of investigating the state of feeling on the Venezuelan matter. His first reports were published on January 2. Through him came the news that the intention of Cleveland's message was amicable; that many who approved the President's policy did not understand it to mean war; that the churches were pleading for peace; but that a national sentiment had sprung up in support of the course outlined by Cleveland and Olney which it would be madness for England to disregard or underestimate. "Americans believe that their attitude of demanding arbitration is one with which civilized men must sympathize. In support of this the whole Union will speak with absolutely one voice. But at the same time there is an infinite desire to see an immediate amicable settlement. I repeat with every ounce of influence I possess that everybody here worth considering desires peace." Moreover, Norman reported the information, which he had gained from access to documents in the State Department, that Salisbury's stand was far more uncompromising and dogmatic than had been that of his predecessors in the Foreign Office. He pointed out, in fact, that Lord Granville had agreed to arbitrate the entire question which Salisbury had declared impossible of arbitration under any condition.[43]

And while Norman was giving the British public a correct view of American sentiment and Salisbury's policy, an important event occurred in another part of the world which was destined to exert no little influence on the outcome of the dispute regarding boundaries in South America. On December 29 Dr. Leander Starr Jameson led a small company of Rhodesians against the Boers in the Transvaal. The hostile expedition proved a fiasco and the invaders were captured on January 2, 1896. German animosity toward England immediately showed itself. German public opinion was greatly excited, the Foreign Office issued harsh warnings from Berlin, and on January 3 the Kaiser sent a telegram to President Paul Kruger of the Transvaal congratulating him upon the successful suppression of the

---

[42] As quoted in the New York *Tribune*, December 19, 1895, and in *Cong. Record*, 53 Cong., 2 Sess., Vol. XXVIII, Part I, p. 111. For Bayard's summary of the views of the British press, see Bayard to the President, December 18, 1895, in McElroy, *op. cit.*, II, 190–191.

[43] The Norman despatches were quoted in the New York *Times*, January 4 to 6, 1896.

raid.[44] The situation was serious. Japan's defeat of China in 1895 had already disturbed the Anglo-Russian balance in the Far East and Turkish massacres in Armenia had brought about a strained condition in the Near East. Clearly it was no time to risk a war with the United States, and British statesmen began to search for a pacific settlement.

When in the face of the crisis they forgot their wounded pride and set clear heads to work on the difficulty, they were able to see that the United States was interested in two considerations: the policy of arbitration which had only recently been consecrated by the signing of a dozen treaties among American states and the settlement of half as many boundary disputes in the Western Hemisphere,[45] and the Monroe Doctrine which was rapidly becoming an American fetish. Moreover, whatever it may have been formerly, the main interest of British statesmen now was the protection and preservation of English subjects in the disputed area. These basic facts having once been recognized, it was possible to propose a compromise.

On January 12 the Foreign Office sent Lord Playfair on a confidential mission to the residence of the American ambassador, with authority to make two important proposals: (1) That the United States should call a conference of all the European Powers which then had colonies in America—namely, Great Britain, France, Spain, and Holland—for the purpose of inducing them to proclaim their acceptance of the Monroe Doctrine. Britain would agree to accept it and presumably to persuade the other powers to do so, thus giving the doctrine the force of international law and removing all danger of the extension of European "influence in that Hemisphere." (2) That England would agree to arbitrate the entire region in dispute, provided only that areas already occupied should be adjudged to the government whose nationals were in undisputed possession. Bayard telegraphed these proposals to Washington with no little enthusiasm.[46]

In the meantime the public in both England and the United States had become much calmer. English journalists criticised Salisbury for his truculent despatches, and American newspapers sympathized with Britain in her South African and European troubles.[47]

[44] See Parker T. Moon, *Imperialism and World Politics* (1926), pp. 173–176.
[45] William R. Manning, *Arbitration Treaties Among the American Nations* (1924), p. 190 ff.; W. S. Robertson, *Hispanic-American Relations of the United States* (1923), p. 154 ff.
[46] McElroy, *op. cit.*, pp. 198–199.
[47] The New York *Times* condemned the Jameson Raid but was not in

When Parliament convened in February the Lords and Commons were likewise in a conciliatory mood. They declared that the appointment of an American commission to investigate the Venezuela-Guiana boundary was not an insult to Britain and that the Foreign Office could afford to coöperate with them in their investigations. They said that the Monroe Doctrine was not unusual or obnoxious, but merely the limited assertion of the principle that a state may intervene when its interests are menaced. "What other States claim to exercise everywhere the Monroe Doctrine has limited to the American continent." Even Lord Salisbury stated in the House of Lords that the interest of the United States in the dispute, in view of Venezuela's position in the Caribbean, was "no more unnatural . . . than that we should feel an interest in Belgium and Holland." Indeed, he felt that the intervention of the United States would turn out to be an advantage, for the simple reason that the United States would be likely to force Venezuela to abide by any peaceful settlement which might be reached.[48]

Moreover, the closing weeks of January found Congressmen and Senators in the United States in a saner mood, although a few jingoists continued their efforts to disturb the calm that was settling upon the country. The Senate favored neither a resolution opposing a direct settlement between England and Venezuela nor one proposing to congratulate the South African Republic.[49] The way was clear for a peaceful exit from the tangle, if only Cleveland and Olney would be reasonable.

These statesmen were far more conciliatory than their public utterances had indicated. Neither they nor their supporters had expected the difficulty to eventuate in war.[50] They were not in favor

"sympathy with those who rejoice in the troubles of Great Britain." The jingoist New York *Press* published a leader which declared that "an absolutist concert" against Britain would induce the United States to depart from its policy of isolation and come to the aid of their kinsmen. The London *Times* was "gratified" at this display of friendly sentiment. (See the London *Times*, January 6 to 13, for excerpts and comment.)

[48] Hansard, *Parliamentary Debates,* Fourth Series, XXXVII, 52, 84-85, *passim.*

[49] *Cong. Record,* 53 Cong., 2 Sess., Vol. XXVIII, Part I, 529, *passim,* 783, *passim.*

[50] On December 29 Cleveland wrote to Bayard, who had expressed some alarm in a recent letter to the President: "Great Britain has refused our request [to arbitrate] . . . We do not threaten nor invite war because she refuses—far from it. We do not propose to proceed to extremities, leaving open any chance that can be guarded against, of a mistake on our part as to the facts. So instead of threatening war for not arbitrating, we simply say inasmuch as Great Britain will not aid us in fixing the facts, we will not go

of a congress of European Powers to pass upon the Monroe Doctrine,[51] but they did not long oppose a settlement with Venezuela upon the basis proposed by Salisbury through Playfair on January 11. By July the crisis had entirely passed; by February, 1897, all arrangements for arbitration had been made. The entire boundary was to be submitted to an arbitral tribunal, but "adverse holding or prescription during a period of fifty years" was to constitute a good title. On October 3, 1899, the arbitrators announced their decision. On the whole it was more favorable to the claims of Great Britain than to those of Venezuela.[52]

British Attitude During the Spanish-American War

The first Venezuelan crisis had scarcely passed when the prospect of a war between the United States and Spain over Cuban difficulties began to loom in the distance. When the struggle began in April, 1898, it found the British public sympathetic toward the United States. Opposition to American extension into the Caribbean had long since been abandoned; the anti-British attitude of the Kaiser was driving England into the arms of the United States; the cooperation of the United States was needed in the Far East; and, moreover, John Hay, who became ambassador at London in 1898, was an Anglophile statesman not without great influence in the English capital.

Leaving the official attitude of England for more detailed treatment in another connection,[53] we may here note briefly the sentiment of the press. Its position in April, 1898, was summed up by *The Literary Digest* in the statement that the general tenor of the British journals was "in our favor." [54] The hostile *Saturday Review* noted this attitude and scolded its colleagues: "When we find the bulk of the English newspapers calling on us to admire . . . the United States

to war but do the best we can to discover the true state of facts for ourselves, with all the facilities at our command. When with all this, we become as certain as we can be . . . that she has seized the territory . . .—that is a different matter." *Then,* apparently, Cleveland thought the United States would have cause for war. (See McElroy, *op. cit.,* II, 193-195.)

Of the ten Senators who spoke on the Venezuelan question during the discussion of December 17-20, nine expressed a conviction that the matter would be settled peaceably, while only one feared war. (*Cong. Record,* 53 Cong., 2 Sess, Vol. XXVIII, Part I, p. 246, *passim.*)

[51] McElroy, *op. cit.,* II, 200.

[52] R. B. Mowat, *The Diplomatic Relations of Great Britain and the United States* (1925), pp. 258-272, presents an excellent survey of this whole question.

[53] See *post,* Ch. X.

[54] XVI (April 23, 1898), 502.

and to accord our moral support . . . , it is time to protest." [55]
Henry Norman, speaking of a possible European combination against
the United States, declared that Britons would "never stand idly by
and see a hundred millions of people who speak English trampled on
by people who speak Russian or French or Spanish." [56] Even the London *Times,* always scrupulous in matters of diplomatic decorum, did
not fail to let its sympathies be known.[57] And when the close of the
war left the Philippines in American hands this strengthening of the
position of the United States in the Far East was greeted with almost
unanimous approval.[58]

Another Important Concession

The way was now practically cleared for a renewal of the canal
negotiations, and the diplomats of the two nations returned to the
question without delay. The Spanish-American War was attended by
a growing aggressiveness on the part of the United States and the
spectacular thirteen-thousand-mile voyage of the *Oregon* around
South America emphasized the importance of a communication across
the isthmus. Besides, the United States now had very large Pacific
interests to guard. The British clearly realized this changed situation. *The Spectator* urged, as early as December 3, that Britain face
the facts and abrogate the treaty before the United States had time
to demand the step. A few weeks later Sir Charles Dilke expressed a
somewhat similar view in Parliament.[59] But neither *The Spectator*
nor Sir Charles was ahead of Lord Salisbury. Before the close of
December he had told Henry D. White, who had paid him a visit
at Hatfield, that he was willing to agree in principle to the American contention regarding the canal, provided the United States would
agree that there should be no discrimination in the matter of tolls
when the communication had been completed.[60] The matter might
have been settled at once had it not been complicated by the Alaskan
boundary dispute and the insistence of the United States upon the
right to police the canal and to stand as the sole guarantor of its
neutrality. As it was, the treaty was not signed until the close of the
year 1901. Britain then conceded virtually every demand of the

[55] LXXXV (April 9, 1898), 479.

[56] As quoted by *Literary Digest,* XVI (May 7, 1898), 562.

[57] Issues of April 21 and following.

[58] For convenient summaries see *Literary Digest,* XVII, 627, 670, and Bertha
Ann Reuter, *Anglo-American Relations During the Spanish-American War,* p.
168 ff.

[59] Hansard, *Parliamentary Debates,* Third Series, LXVI, 152.

[60] Mowat, *op. cit.,* p. 286.

United States,[61] and Washington was now practically dominant in the Caribbean.

It will be well to pause at this point, however, in order to note an important assumption, an assumption which amounted almost to an understanding—and in one instance, at least, was really an understanding—that underlay all the concessions which Britain had made since 1895. In the case of the Venezuela boundary dispute the editor of the London *Chronicle* had seized the idea when he remarked that Great Britain should not admit the contention of Olney and Cleveland unless the United States was willing "to make itself responsible for the foreign policy of all the petty, impetuous little states on the two continents." Lord Salisbury had the same idea in mind when he remarked that the intervention of the United States government would be an advantage if it should force Venezuela to abide by any peaceful settlement which might be reached. Britain's friendly position during the Spanish-American War had doubtless been based upon the hope that the American acquisition of Cuba, Porto Rico, and the Philippines would not result in injury to English economic interests but, on the contrary, that it would support these interests. So it was, likewise, in the case of the Hay-Pauncefote Treaty. Article III of that treaty provided that the canal should be "free and open to the vessels of commerce and of war of all nations . . . , on terms of entire equality." Britain had given way with the understanding that nothing was to be done officially to injure her trade in Hispanic America.

Of course the Monroe Doctrine had not yet formally been accepted: it had in fact been left by Cleveland and Olney "like a volcano suddenly thrust up in mid-ocean"; but the London government had shown some disposition to discuss a plan whereby it might be lifted to the realm of accepted international law. Unless the United States should attempt to give the doctrine an economic application so as to secure exclusive advantages for itself, it would not be likely to cause trouble. The British fleet was reduced in the Caribbean and joint control of the canal was given up. Britain had virtually recognized that paramount interest which the United States had asserted, but the concession was strategic and political rather than economic.

Recent Issues

During the next two decades only two issues arose to interrupt the harmony of the Anglo-Saxon nations in respect to Spanish-

---

[61] Malloy, *Treaties*, I, 782–784, gives text of the treaty.

American relations. The Venezuelan difficulty of 1901–1902 was not one of these.[62] The official conduct of England gave little offense and British diplomats were severely criticised by the British press for joining Germany in the attempt to coerce Venezuela. Moreover, it served as the occasion for further revelation of the assumption underlying British concessions to the United States and of the readiness of British statesmen to accept the Monroe Doctrine. Lord Avebury remarked that "the Monroe claim involves a certain responsibility" on the part of the United States to see that the nations of Latin America conduct themselves properly. Arthur J. Balfour, assistant foreign secretary, said: "The Monroe Doctrine has no enemies in this country that I know of. We welcome any increase of the influence of the United States of America upon the great Western Hemisphere." The Duke of Devonshire declared that Englishmen accepted "fully and unreservedly the Monroe Doctrine." The Marquess of Lansdowne said that British statesmen did not "have any desire to impugn" that doctrine. Joseph Chamberlain, "with bland indifference to the expressed opinion of his nominal chief" (Lord Salisbury), declared that England recognized the existence of the Monroe Doctrine and "never thought of impugning it." [63] In like manner, the procedure of the United States in the Panama revolt and the acquisition of the Canal Zone did not call forth severe criticism from British publicists,[64] and the government hastened to recognize the new Republic of Panama. The informal protectorate over Mosquitia was finally abandoned in 1906, and the Monroe Doctrine, as defined and delimited, was formally accepted by being incorporated into the League Covenant.[65]

The two issues which caused friction arose almost simultaneously and both of them related to economic matters. On August 24, 1912, the United States Congress authorized the President "to prescribe and from time to time change the tolls" levied upon the shipping which should pass through the Panama Canal. The act also provided that "no tolls" should be "levied upon vessels engaged in the coastwise trade of the United States." Against this exemption Great

[62] *Post*, Ch. XI.

[63] A. Álvarez, *The Monroe Doctrine* (1924), pp. 92–93.

[64] For convenient excerpts, see *Public Opinion*, Dec. 3, 1903; *Literary Digest*, Dec. 14, 1903.

[65] At a Pilgrim's Day Dinner in June, 1911, Sir Edward Grey, then British secretary of foreign affairs, virtually announced his acceptance of the doctrine. (*Literary Digest*, June 24, 1911, p. 1234.)

Of course a general formal acceptance of the Monroe manifesto would mean a definition of the doctrine and of its subsequent interpretations. To reach an agreement on this matter would probably prove almost impossible. If the United States should subscribe to a definition of the doctrine, it would thereby limit its expanding utility.

Britain protested on the ground (1) that it was contrary to the Hay-Pauncefote Treaty; (2) that it would increase the toll burden of the other ships using the canal; and (3) that foreign shippers would be tempted to evade the tolls by landing their cargoes at the nearest United States port and sending them the rest of the journey by the favored coastwise shipping. The protest was without effect upon the Taft administration, however, and was left over to Woodrow Wilson for solution. Meanwhile, another difficulty arose to prevent the frank coöperation of the two Powers. It was connected with Wilson's opposition to official economic imperialism in Latin America and his refusal to recognize the government of Victoriano Huerta in Mexico. In both instances the American President was running counter to the economic interests of British citizens, and particularly those of the great oil magnate, Lord Cowdray. After considerable parleying a settlement which represented mutual concession was reached. Wilson persuaded Congress to repeal the obnoxious tolls-exemption clause; Britain allowed him to have his way with Huerta, even going so far as to transfer the British ambassador from Mexico City at Wilson's request. Cowdray withdrew from the oil fields of Colombia and probably suffered losses in Mexico as a result of Huerta's downfall.[66] Both difficulties were settled without serious friction, but they should perhaps serve as danger signals for the future. The idea of an economic Open Door has underlain every concession which Great Britain has made to the United States in Latin America. Persistence in an opposite policy by the United States might conceivably lead to war.[67]

And in spite of the World War and its aftermath, the British nation has managed in large measure to maintain its economic position in Latin America. Its investments were 999,236,565 pounds sterling in 1913 and 1,139,659,470 in 1925. It purchased nearly 21 per cent of Latin America's exports in 1913 and about 18 per cent in 1925, while it furnished nearly 24 per cent of Latin America's imports in the former year and a little less than 18 per cent in the latter. Britain's Latin-American trade was $897,000,000 in 1924 and $933,000,000 in 1925, as compared with $1,937,000,000 and $2,110,951,000 for the United States and $409,000,000, and $440,000,000 for Germany.[68]

[66] J. Fred Rippy, *The United States and Mexico* (1926), pp. 335–336; Mowat, *op. cit.*, p. 328 ff.; Moon, *op. cit.*, pp. 442–443.
[67] This was the view of Sir Harry Johnson in 1913. (See George H. Blakeslee, *The Recent Foreign Policy of the United States* [1925], p. 182.)
[68] The Pan-American Union, *Latin-American Foreign Trade . . .* (1923, 1924, 1925); *Revista Económica,* XIV (San Salvador, 1927), 300–303.

CHAPTER VIII

FRANCE AGGRESSIVE AND CRITICAL (1857–1927)

SHORTLY before the British government decided to relax its opposition to the expanding influence of the United States in the Western Hemisphere, France began to reveal a more aggressive disposition. For some time subsequent to 1825 the energies of the French government were largely absorbed elswhere. French trade with Hispanic America gradually increased until it reached thirty million dollars in 1848, but only rarely was the attention of French officials directed to this region. True, they had bombarded Vera Cruz in 1838, intervened in Argentina during the same year, and joined England in a collective action against the River Plate republics in 1845, but the French government had refused to commit itself to England either on the Texas issue or on the question of interference in the Mexican War.

Maximilian and Mexico

The growing aggressiveness of France in the New World synchronized with the rise of Louis Napoleon to power. In 1851 the navies of France and England were instructed to prevent filibustering operations from the United States against Cuba, and in the following year the ministers of France and England in the United States proposed a tripartite pledge to preserve that island to Spain. In 1854 the British government admitted that it had entered into an agreement with France with reference to the navigation of the leading rivers of South America and the republics bordering upon them. Near the close of the same year the commercial representatives of the United States in the island of Santo Domingo reported Anglo-French interference to prevent the United States from acquiring trade or territorial concessions from the Dominican Republic. Early in 1855 reports reached Washington of similar interference in Ecuador. The French *chargé* had been particularly obtrusive and menacing. He had tried to dissuade the Ecuadar government from granting guano concessions to the United States and brandished the threat that the Emperor Napoleon would turn his attention toward the New World as soon as the Crimean War was concluded,

126

All this activity serves as a proper background for French intervention in Mexico. How long this enterprise had been under consideration before 1861 is not definitely known, but the suspicion of the United States was aroused as early as 1852, and by 1857 the French minister in Mexico was causing no end of apprehension. At this time the French and Spanish envoys discussed plans for checking the "expanding and unrestrainable people who occupy the north of the new hemisphere." Such discussions accurately revealed the true intent of the French project which began to be acted upon in 1861.[1]

It was in October, 1861, that the long apprehended European intervention took place. The reason announced by England, France, and Spain was a desire to avenge the outrages suffered by their nationals and force Mexico to live up to its financial obligations. It soon became evident, however, that France had ulterior designs. These were revealed in Louis Napoleon's now famous letter to General Forey which deserves to be quoted at some length:

"In the present state of the world's civilization," said the Emperor, "the prosperity of America is not a matter of indifference to Europe, because it nourishes our industries and stimulates our commerce. We have an interest in seeing the Republic of the United States become powerful and prosperous; but we have no interest in seeing it seize all of the Gulf of Mexico, dominate from there the Antilles and South America, and become the sole dispenser of the products of the New World. If the United States should become master of Mexico and consequently of Central America and the pass between the two oceans, there would indeed be no other power in America.

"If on the contrary Mexico shall achieve its independence and maintain the integrity of its territory; if a stable government is set up by means of French arms, we shall have opposed an impenetrable dike to the overflow of the United States; we shall have upheld the independence of our colonies and those of ungrateful Spain; we shall have established our benevolent influence in the center of America, and this influence shall radiate to the North as well as to the South, create immense markets for our commerce, and procure materials indispensable for our industry. . . .

"Thus . . . are now involved our military honor, the exigencies of our policy, the interests of our industry and our commerce; all oblige us to advance upon Mexico, resolutely place our flag there, and establish a monarchy—if it is not incompatible with the national

[1] See Rippy, *The United States and Mexico* (1926), p. 197 ff.

sentiment of the country—or at least a government which promises something of stability." [2]

Into the details of Napoleon's Mexican undertaking it is unnecessary to go. Owing to the hostility of the United States, the menacing attitude of Prussia, opposition in the French Parliament, and the dogged persistence of the soldiers fighting under the Mexican patriot Benito Juárez, the French troops were finally withdrawn in 1867, leaving the puppet Maximilian to the tragic fate which soon overtook him. Louis Napoleon thus suffered a blow to his prestige and resentment toward the United States was felt in certain circles of France.[3]

Indeed, since the close of the Maximilian period Frenchmen have been most persistent and bitter critics of our Latin-American policies. A survey of the French press since 1867 will reveal several other motives for this attitude besides the unpleasant memory of the Mexican fiasco.

Motives for French Criticism

First may be noted a melancholy envy produced by the fact that the United States was achieving success where France had failed. The Mississippi valley, the great treasure-house of the United States, once had belonged to France, and, moreover, the products of this enormously fertile region were appearing all over the world in competition with French commodities. This envy comes out clearly in an essay written by Comte d'Haussonville in 1905. As a descendant of Rochambeau, he had been the honored guest of the United States in 1881 at a festival commemorating the centenary of the surrender of Cornwallis at Yorktown. While in America he had taken a flying trip across the continent from New York to San Francisco. After the lapse of twenty-four years he still cherished fond memories of the delightful journey, but his pleasure at the time as well as in retrospect was somewhat marred by emotions which forced themselves upon him as he sped over the immense country. "I remember," said the Count, "that with the happy feelings of satisfied curiosity there was mingled a certain degree of melancholy when I read on the railway charts and heard pronounced by foreign lips names of cities and stations, great and small, which recalled their French origin: La Nouvelle Orleans, Saint Louis, Vincennes, Saint Geneviève, Versailles; for

[2] Translated from a copy of the original found in the archives of Marshal Bazaine. (See Genaro García, *Documentos Inéditos* . . . , XIV, 13–15.)

[3] See Halford L. Hoskins, "French Views of the Monroe Doctrine and the Mexican Expedition," in *The Hisp. Amer. His. Review, IV* (1921), 677 ff.

said I to myself: It is the French who baptized these places, but where is France?" "I experienced other feelings also," continued the Count. "While travelling across immense plains where the steam plow was at work . . . with a view to the approaching seed-time; . . . when crossing large rivers by which I knew wheat, cattle, and fruit were carried to the sea for export to Europe; or when I saw the glare of mighty furnaces and the accumulation at the depots of great vats of petroleum, I became conscious that a powerful rival was preparing himself to deal terrible blows to our agriculture and our industries, and that it would be necessary to defend ourselves against the invasion of his products." [4]

In the second place, there is something of the sentimental, the racial and cultural, behind this French criticism of the procedure of the United States in the Western Hemisphere. Filled with pride by the fact that they had been the intellectual and cultural leaders of the Hispanic-American peoples, the French were anxious to maintain this leadership unimpaired. And to this cultural sentiment was added a feeling of kinship based upon the Latin element common to the two peoples. As the Anglo-Saxons of the United States gradually encroached upon the Latins to the south Frenchmen were impelled by racial consciousness to protest against the threatened absorption.

This racial and cultural sentiment, this Pan-Latinism, was one of the motives which influenced Louis Napoleon to undertake his Quixotic Mexican expedition. Indeed, it is one of the most persistent factors in shaping French attitude. M. Reclus, writing in the *Revue des Deux Mondes* in 1868, urged Frenchmen to cultivate the Hispanic Americans. He sought to console Frenchmen with respect to the Napoleonic fiasco in Mexico by recalling that, "fortunately for France, the affinity of languages assures for her literary and scientific works a decisive influence among all the Hispanic Americans, and the grand memories of the Revolution will render them only too indulgent toward our contemporary history."—"They recognize with a sort of filial piety," added Reclus, "that they owe their emancipation to the ideas proclaimed by the men of '89; in spite of all our political blunders we inherit a part of the spirit of gratitude dedicated to our ancestors." [5] In similar vein another writer in the *Revue des Deux Mondes* (1893) pointed out that French political, scientific, and cultural ideas were in the ascendent in Mexico. Díaz's administrative system was modeled after that of the French, the Mexican civil code

---

[4] Barral-Montferrat, *De Monroe à Roosevelt* (1907), Introduction.
[5] Vol. LXXIV, p. 497.

was almost a literal reproduction of the Napoleonic code, and cultured Mexicans not only read more French than Spanish books, but actually sent their children to Paris to complete their education. These considerations filled the writer with pride, and he expressed the hope that Frenchmen and the French government would assist the Latin nationalities to defend themselves. At the same time he warned the inhabitants of Spanish America, and particularly the Indian element, that too close relations with the Anglo-Saxons would mean extermination.[6] Again, near the close of the year 1902, several French journals called upon Latin Europe to rescue its American kinsmen from the greedy maw of the United States. One of them remarked: "The nations of Central and South America must be ranked among the Latin people. A positive alliance with these peoples would be difficult perhaps, because it would arouse the suspicions of the United States. But at any rate a cordial understanding is needed, a growing intimacy of relations between the Latin peoples of Europe and those of America."[7] Still another French writer predicted in 1909 that his generation would live to see the greater portion of Hispanic America under the control of the United States. Then, he remarked regretfully, the inhabitants of this vast region would be taught English and sent to the United States to complete their studies; then Rome would be transferred to the New World and Paris would become "no more than another Athens which would begin to enter the melancholy shades of the past."[8] This motive comes out again, along with others, in Poincaré's preface to García Calderón's book on Latin America. Here Poincaré says: "May South America while cultivating herself . . . grow ever more and more hospitable to the literature, the arts, the commerce, and the capital of France. Thereby only can the great Latin family gain in material prosperity and moral authority." And lastly, it was expressed in 1912 in the following language: "The future of the Latin race is linked up with South America. . . . We have interests of the first order in the independence of the South American republics because . . . we exercise in those countries a veritable intellectual and moral preponderance, because we are their spiritual guide on the highway to progress. . . ."[9]

There is also an element of self-defense in the French attitude. The importance of the Latin Americans as allies or friendly neutrals in a general war is at once evident. But at this point we refer par-

[6] Barral-Montferrat, *De Monroe à Roosevelt*, vol. CXVI, 366–368.

[7] *Literary Digest*, XXV (Oct. 25, 1902), 530.

[8] Waleffe, *Les Paradis de l'Amérique centrale* (1909), pp. 303–304.

[9] Angel Marvaud, in *Revue politique et parlementaire*, LXIX, 437 ff.

ticularly to the American phase of the question. The French people have been uneasy lest the rising tide of Yankee imperialism should result in the loss of French Guiana and the French Antilles. These possessions were (and are), to be sure, of no great importance intrinsically, but they were remnants of empire which reminded Frenchmen of a more glorious past, and there was strong indisposition to lowering the French flag where it once had floated so magnificently.

A few illustrations of this point will suffice. It will be recalled that Louis Napoleon had this factor in mind. The apprehension arose again in 1890, in the discussions occasioned by Blaine's Pan-Americanism. At this time it was asserted that the United States had resolved to expel the European nations from all their American possessions.[10] The attempt of the United States to force England to arbitrate the Anglo-Venezuelan boundary dispute aroused even more apprehension. It was generally agreed among French journalists that the United States was taking but another step in its general policy of shutting Europe out of the Western Hemisphere. One writer, accepting this view of the matter, warned that the Yankees would find themselves in "conflict with all Europe" if they undertook a general application of "the pretension of Mr. Cleveland." He furthermore served notice that a concession on England's part in this instance would not obligate other European Powers or render them more disposed to submit to "such odious interference." [11] Another journalist, coming nearer the real motive of French apprehensiveness, remarked that the government of the United States would be likely to assume toward republican France in its dispute regarding the boundary between Brazil and French Guiana, the same attitude which had been taken with reference to monarchical England. He further alleged that of course the United States intended at an opportune time to seize all of Europe's colonies in America—perhaps, indeed, the nations of Europe, adopting Russia's policy, should sell them to the United States before it should be too late, but that he did not believe the Yankees were foolish enough to consider the year 1896 a fit occasion for this robbery. On the other hand, he felt quite sure that if France should be "forced to make a naval demonstration in the waters of Rio de Janeiro for the purpose of establishing" her "rights in the contested territories of French Guiana, the admiral commanding the American fleet would do us the honor of coming aboard the French admiral's vessel to dance." Surely the American officer would

[10] C. de Varigny, in *Revue des Deux Mondes*, XCVII (Jan., 1890), 433 ff.
[11] A. Merignac, in *Revue du Droit Public*, V (1896), 202 ff.

rather dance on a French man-of-war than over a volcano! It would be more cheerful and less dangerous![12] Indeed the anxiety of the French for the security of the remnant of their American colonies became so evident by 1898 that the German Emperor thought France might be persuaded to join a concerted action against the United States mainly on this basis.[13]

The expansion of the United States into the Pacific and its increasing participation in non-American affairs furnished the French a further motive for criticising the Latin-American policy of the Yankees. Frenchmen complained that the Yankees, at the very time when they were asserting most loudly their pretensions to a paramount interest which tended to render the Western Hemisphere an exclusive field for their exploitation, were aggressively demanding equal rights with other nations all around the world. They alleged that the United States, starting out with the modest slogan of "America for the Americans," had first expanded it into America for the North Americans and later (since 1898) into a maxim which meant no less than "America and the World for the Yankees."[14] They declared that the European Powers, while they were asking themselves where the Yankee choice would fall when their nation should be confronted by the dilemma of choosing between the Monroe Doctrine and world empire, were astounded to behold that the Yankees, after a brief delay, overlooked the dilemma and chose both! Old Count d'Haussonville remarked in 1905 that he had become much wiser regarding the Yankee menace than he had been in 1881. "The idea did not then cross my mind," said the Count, "that a day would come when we should have to occupy ourselves with still another invasion, that of the United States into the politics of Europe and the world."[15] And he was merely voicing a remonstrance that was generally felt in France up until the outbreak of the World War.

By far the most important motive for French attacks upon the American policy of the United States, however, was the economic motive. The desire to share the trade of Latin America has always been very persistent and very strong. It influenced the Hispanic-American policy of France as early as 1823, and it had been largely responsible for French recognition of the new states before the mother country had taken the step.[16] It furnished one of Louis

[12] Gabriel Couillault, in *Le Monde economique* (Jan., 1896), pp. 7–8.
[13] *Die Grosse Politik,* Vol. XV, pp. 3–6.
[14] Petin, *Les Etats-Unis et La Doctrine de Monroe* (1905), p. 436, *passim.*
[15] *Op. et loc. cit.*
[16] Dexter Perkins, in *The American Historical Review,* XXVII (1922), 207 ff.

Napoleon's justifications for his Mexican schemes in his famous letter to General Forey. Nor had France's desire to avail herself of Hispanic-American markets remained unrealized. Her trade with these countries had risen from less than three million dollars in 1825 to thirty million in 1848, to more than eighty million in 1855, and to more than one hundred and twenty-three in 1860. But during the Civil War the United States underwent a marvelous industrial transformation, the effects of which France was destined to feel, before many years, in the m'arkets of Hispanic America. The Hispanic-American trade of France was only a little over one hundred and forty-four million in 1896, even less than this in 1900, only one hundred and fifty-eight million in 1905, and hardly one hundred and eighty-seven million in 1909.[17] Of course the United States was not France's sole competitor in the Latin-American field (England and Germany were also very important), but Yankee shrewdness and aggressiveness were greatly feared. Their competition was always more formidable in prospect than in reality. Hence the French press was often filled with exaggerated statements of Yankee commercial designs in the New World. The Pan-American movement was decried as a Yankee scheme to erect a Chinese wall between Europe and the three Americas, and the Monroe Doctrine was generally alleged to have a decided commercial aspect.

For instance, it was said in 1890 that Blaine was preparing to prevent the economic as well as the political intercourse of Europe with America; that the Republican Party had resolved "to prohibit all importation from Europe into the New World." [18] Again, in 1893, a French writer declared that the Monroe Doctrine signified the economic hegemony of the United States in the Americas; for, said he, "in our day . . . economic interests tend always to dominate political." [19] Thereafter, this design on the part of the United States appears to have been taken for granted by French journalists.

The Policy of the French Government

Thus it will be observed that the attitude of the French press toward the American policy of the United States was generally unfriendly subsequent to 1867. But what was the official attitude of France? The documents necessary to answer this question still lie concealed in the French archives. Since the French government dur-

---

[17] Calvo, *Recueil complet des Traites* (1862), I, viii, *passim;* U. S. Dept. of Commerce, *Statistics of Foreign Trade* (1909), *passim.*
[18] *La Nouvelle Revue,* Sept. 1, 1890. Translation in *Lit. Digest,* I, 590.
[19] Claudio Janet, in *Revue des Deux Mondes,* March 15, 1893.

ing most of this period was republican in form, it is not unlikely that it was influenced by the views of the journalists. But whatever the official attitude, French procedure *a propos* the Yankee menace was necessarily influenced by the prospect of a war with the United States which an attempt to interfere in America would be likely to bring about, and still more was it affected by the international situation in Europe. The fiasco of Louis Napoleon constituted an impressive lesson in these respects. Confronted by a divided public opinion at home, by a hostile American army on the Rio Grande, and by a threatening Prussia across the Rhine, the French Emperor had been compelled to abandon his Mexican undertaking and France had to reckon with an unpleasant loss on the balance sheet of commerce and prestige. Frenchmen might well hesitate to repeat the project. And by the time the Yankees had reached the most aggressive stage of their American policy France found that England and Germany were beginning to vie with each other for the friendship of the United States, and that Russia, France's most important reliance in case of a threat from Germany or England, was indisposed to offend the leading nation in the New World.[20] In brief, due to international complications in Europe, France was in the position of a giantess with hands tied, but with tongue unloosed and wits sharpened by the very manacles which bound her hands.

All that could be done by criticism, denunciation, and propaganda, Frenchmen did; and they proved themselves the more able in these lines of effort because there was little else they could do. Pan-Americanism and the Monroe Doctrine were held up before the world in general, and before Latin America in particular, as cloaks alternately worn to cover Yankee absorption, monopoly, haughty domination, or imperialism. The Latin Americans were warned to keep up their economic connections with Europe, to cease fighting among themselves and unite, and to lend a willing ear to Pan-Hispanism and Pan-Latinism. "Washington aspires to become the capital of an enormous empire comprising, with the exception of Canada, the whole of the New World," said Waleffe.[21] The United States is destined to subject to its imperial sway all the Latin-American states which might conceivably affect the control of the Yankees over the Panama Canal, and the Big Stick and Dollar Diplomacy are its weapons, declared Angel Marvaud.[22] The United States aspires to dominate the New World from "the icy shores of the Arctic Ocean to Cape

[20] Apparently the United States experienced uneasiness in regard to French procedure in Venezuela (1881), and in Haiti (1888, 1903).

[21] *Op. cit.*, p. 3.

[22] *Revue politique et parlementaire*, LXXIX, 245 ff.

Horn," said Varigny (*supra*). "Neither Mexico, nor the states of Central America, nor those of South America, have anything to fear from the European Powers," assured Leroy-Beaulieu. "It is less certain that the government of Washington will always observe relative to the other states of America a discretion equally absolute," he added. He then urged the Hispanic-American nations not to encourage the application of the Monroe Doctrine.[23] Professor Merignhac expressed the hope that the Spanish-American states would seek the assistance of Europe against the pseudo-benevolent and self-appointed intervention of the United States.[24] The *Journal des Débats* remarked ill-humoredly that "every time a misunderstanding arises between a European power and a country in Central or South America, the United States comes to the front." "She has, however, no right to do so," continued this journal; "she is not the protectress of those republics, and would meet with more than coolness if she attempted to become so. . . ."[25] On another occasion the same publication addressed this explicit advice to the Latin Americans: "If you want *rapprochement* . . . look to your mother Spain, rather than to the great invading republic of the North."[26] And, to give only one more illustration from the period prior to the World War, the *Economiste français,* returning to the subject again and again, warned the nations of Latin America that they were in grave danger. "The simplest foresight imposes upon Latin America . . . three conditions for the maintenance of independence," declared the editor of this journal; namely, "Order and good government, peace among the various sister republics, and close economic . . . relations with Europe, from whom she has nothing to fear."[27]

Recent Comments

The World War, absorbing, as it did, all of the energies of France and demanding careful cultivation of the United States as a friendly neutral and possible ally, caused a virtual cessation of French criticism. But the change was only temporary. The tremendous struggle caused a serious decline in France's Latin-American trade,[28] to say nothing of its injurious effects upon French investments, and the United States was the main Power to benefit from French losses.

---

[23] *L'Economiste français,* Annee 23, Tom. II, 797–799.
[24] *Revue du Droit Public,* V, 202 ff.
[25] As quoted in *Lit. Digest,* XI, 415.
[26] As quoted in *ibid.,* XXIII, 51–52.
[27] As quoted in *ibid.,* XXIV (1902), 814.
[28] The relative decrease between 1913 and 1918 was more than 55%.

These facts, and the additional fact that the United States has some-times run counter to French sentiment since the close of the World War, have not placed Frenchmen in a better mood toward the policies of the White House in Latin America. Recently the French nation has returned to many of its former attitudes and methods.

Indeed, nothing which happened during the tragic days of 1914–1918 tended to decrease in any marked degree the former deep interest of France in the Latin peoples of America. Even in the dark days when resistance to the German peril demanded every ounce of French energy, Frenchmen found time to consider their relations with these peoples. In the supreme crisis the great resources and friendly disposition of Latin Americans served but to emphasize their importance to France, and French writers surveyed the commerce, investments, cultural influence, and general prestige of their nation in these lands and discussed plans for the future.[29]

The close of the World War found Frenchmen resolved to recoup their losses in Spanish America and inspired by a Pan-Latin enthusiasm ready to burst out in denunciation of the policies and activities of the United States. "One of the inevitable consequences of the European War will be a most terrible competition in the markets of Latin America. This contest will not be limited to commerce but will extend itself to all of the fields of human activities. There will be a political, financial, industrial, and intellectual contest. It is necessary to prepare for it." Thus wrote one of the journalists just as France entered the era of post-bellum reconstruction. He then went on to speak of the rival Powers, sounding the notes of Pan-Latinism and of mild resentment toward the United States:

"There are two competitors, Europe and the United States. The United States displays the Monroe Doctrine to exclude, if possible, from the southern markets European capital and production. That political doctrine includes also an economic domination. But the South prefers her liberty to a purely Geographical union. Her points of contact with North America are few; neither language nor race, nor religion, nor customs are included. She will gain little if she enters into the orbit of the United States, but on the contrary will lose much.

"The most active elements in South America today are European emigrants that have maintained close relationships with their fatherland, and the sons and descendants of emigrants who feel and call themselves 'sons of the country' but who do not wish to deny that they are Latins: latinity is not a vague and literary phrase, it is a real thing in many economic and political problems. The Latin

[29] *Cf.* G. Lafond, *L' Effort français en Amérique latine* (1917).

republics of America feel their affinity of race for the Latins of Europe. We must prepare promptly an army of young men for this new struggle, an army that does not need to be so numerous but well chosen. Only thus shall we be able to conquer the place which the Latins deserve in South America." [30]

It was not long until this resentment deepened into hostility. In 1921 *Le Correspondant* came out with an article which accused the United States of preventing Costa Rica and Nicaragua from joining the Central American Union, and two years later it printed another which maintained that the Washington government had broken up this Union with the view of dominating the little states which had tried to form it. This last article, indeed, gave a general survey of the recent imperialism of the United States and evinced a severe attitude toward our post-war procedure in Mexico and the Caribbean. [31]

By 1923 French criticism had resumed the hostile tones of 1890–1913. The centenary of the Monroe Doctrine and the Pan-American Congress of Santiago occasioned outbursts similar to those of an earlier period. Pierre Arthuys opened the discussion with a bitter article on Dollar Diplomacy. "In Latin America the United States is trying to reduce her neighbors to economic fiefs, through the agencies of trusts, financial control, loans, and political intervention," wrote Arthuys. This general thesis was then freely developed, and the discussion deserves to be quoted at length:

". . . Europe is financially pauperized and politically insolvent. Latin America cannot maintain itself and make progress without foreign aid. Its needs play directly into the hands of the Yankee graspers after power. Wall Street bankers lend money freely because it gives them the key to the door of every one of these countries. The guaranties they exact are most important and often curtail the sovereignty of the borrowing States.

"Your Yankee is a hard-headed, practical man, keenly alive to his own interests. So he insists that customs duties shall be pledged— or city revenues in case of a municipality—as security for what he lends. He likes still better to place a man of his own in charge of the custom-houses, or even of a nation's treasury. When he takes a mortgage upon the customs revenues of one of these Republics, he has his hand upon the funds that pay the salaries of presidents,

[30] *Revue Minerva,* as quoted by S. G. Inman, *Problems in Pan-Americanism,* pp. 240–241.
[31] New Series, CCXLIX (1921), 1080 ff.; CCLIV, 609 ff.

cabinets, and the civil service; for internal taxes are hardly known, and in any case difficult to collect. . . .

"Therefore it is not strange that the United States is quite ready to grant liberal financial favors to these Republics; for it places them under the Yankee's thumb. Such loans serve to balance budgets, to pay domestic and foreign creditors, and to construct public works.

"Administering the customs, standing guard over the goods that leave the country and the goods that enter it, the Americans are indeed economic masters. They can easily show favor to their own products and discriminate against those of foreign countries. Whenever they get control, they boycott our manufactures, for the United States recognizes no friends when it comes to business.

". . . All the world knows that the Governments of all the Latin-American countries except Argentina, Chile, and a part of Brazil, are unstable. The United States is not unconcerned in the revolutions which afflict them. American money has played a part in many such disturbances and has thereby created excuses for intervention and eventual subjugation. Most Mexican revolutions have been fomented by Yankee intrigues. The Republic of Panama . . . owes its existence to a revolution supported by the Americans. The civil dissentions in Nicaragua, followed by American military occupation, the seizure of Santo Domingo, the practical absorption of Haiti, the dictation to Cuba that makes it a virtual vassal of the United States, all accord with the fundamental policy of a country that represents itself in Europe as a champion of political liberty."

M. Arthuys concluded his analysis by a definition of the Monroe Doctrine and the assertion that both political parties in the United States were committed to economic imperialism. He said that the famous manifesto of the fifth President of the United States is a "hypocritical charter of North American monopoly that prevents France from exercising her own rights in America, and is but a cover for Yankee imperialism." He then paid his compliments to the parties: "It makes little difference whether Democrats or Republicans are in power in Washington. For they do not represent two parties, but two plutocracies. . . . For the American government now rests upon a monarchy of gold and an aristocracy of finance. It is the prototype of that quantitative civilization that is striving to erect a new form of feudalism in the modern world." [32]

These rather lengthy excerpts render it unnecessary to quote ex-

[32] *La Revue universelle*, January 15, 1923, as quoted by *The Living Age*, March 10, 1923, pp. 570–576.

tensively from the comments of other French journals on the centenary of the Monroe Doctrine and the rôle of the United States at the Santiago Congress. The *Temps* emphasized Latin-American mistrust of the United States, "which refuse to assume responsibility in world organizations and at the same time seek to extend their financial and political control over Mexico, Central America, and the Antilles." The United States "might prevent the conference from doing anything which goes against their imperialistic interpretation of the Monroe Doctrine, but that would draw South America closer to the League of Nations." These comments were mild compared with those of *La Liberté*, which asserted that the United States urged the plan of armament limitations with the view of rendering the domination of South America easier, spoke scornfully of loans with "Draconian guarantees" designed to promote hegemony, and declared that Pan-Americanism had got stuck on a reef. "It seems that the United States are going to confront opposition . . . when they seek to enter into a practical application of their badly camouflaged imperialism," exulted this journal. "Latin Americans have not forgotten that they are Latin. They know Latin Culture has nourished them, and that at the origin of their independent life it was the technicians and financiers of Europe who supported and aided them." [33] Only a little less severe were the comments of Louis Guilaine, who declared that the Monroe Doctrine had become an offensive policy which tended toward the complete eviction, political and economic, of Europe from the American continent and the placing of Latin America under Yankee tutelage and control. The United States was passing judgment upon the morality and the immorality of the governments of Latin America, but who was going to pass judgment upon the morality of the United States? M. Guilaine found reason to rejoice over the indications that the small nations of America were resolved to repudiàte "all imperialism and all hegemony" and find an equilibrium in American Latinism and *rapprochement* with Europe.[34]

It is needless to present further illustrations. That French criticisms have continued to the present year may be ascertained by an examination of the comments of the Paris newspapers on the recent trouble between the United States and Nicaragua. An Associated Press despatch sent out from the French capital on January 7 stated that condemnation of the United States was universal. The organs of all parties and all classes denounced American imperialism. "For

[33] As quoted by the New York *Times,* March 27, 1923.
[34] See *L'Europe nouvelle,* March 31, 1923, pp. 391-393, and June 2, 1923, pp. 688-689.

Christ and petroleum," remarked one of the newspapers in describing the motives prompting the landing of American marines. The radical *Humanité* declared that American imperialism in 1927 was becoming more dangerous than German imperialism of 1914!

An attempt to determine the amount of truth contained in these assertions—in those of the earlier as well as of the later period—cannot be made here, and in fact would be pointless so far as the main purposes of this chapter are concerned. Their bearing at this place does not depend so much upon their truth or falsity as upon their revelation of French disposition and their possible influence upon the attitude of the Latin Americans toward the United States. It can only be noted for the present that most of this French discussion of the policy of the United States in the Western Hemisphere is in the nature of propaganda and, as such, is characterized by half-truths, exaggerations, and inventions which will not stand the test of careful research. The United States has too often been made a villain in the play, and its ambitions, great as they may have been and are, have not infrequently been overstated. Frenchmen have been eager to maintain their territorial possessions unimpaired, to retain and even increase their prestige; they have felt a sort of mystical racial and cultural affinity for what they call the Latins of the New World and have been deeply concerned in their welfare; they have looked upon the United States as a possible peril to all of these interests and have therefore portrayed Yankee policies and ambitions, sometimes unconsciously but more often consciously, in rather sinister outlines.

The Influence of French Opinion in Latin America

The effectiveness of French effort would be difficult to assess in detail, but there can be little doubt that it has achieved a large measure of success. In spite of all the post-war handicaps, French trade with Latin America had about reached its pre-war proportions by 1923.[35] Nor can one doubt the influence of French writers upon the Latins of America. French books and periodicals for many years have enjoyed a wide circulation south of the Rio Grande, and most of the intellectuals have long looked to France as their guide.[36] The criticisms of the United States contained in the writings of Latin Americans are strikingly similar to those reiterated by the French and, where citations appear, French authorities are usually

[35] Robertson, *History of the Latin-American Nations* (1925), p. 573.
[36] Cf. Georges Lafond, *L'Effort français en Amérique latine* (1916) and *La France en Amérique latine* (1922).

referred to. There could be no more striking illustration of French influence than is to be found in two small books recently published. One of them was written by a Brazilian and represented an effort to counteract anti-Yankee propaganda in Hispanic America. The author occupied himself almost entirely with an analysis of the allegations of various French authors concerning American imperialism.[37] The other was the work of a Mexican and one of the most violent indictments of the Latin-American policy of the United States that has ever appeared. It was entitled *The United States versus Liberty*[38] and the majority of its citations referred the reader to French writings. The attitude of the Latin Americans toward the United States cannot be understood without taking the influence of France into account.

[37] Dunshee de Abranches, *Brazil and the Monroe Doctrine* (Rio, Imprensa Nacional, 1915).

[38] Isidro Fabela, *Los Estados Unidos contra la Libertad* (Barcelona, Talleres Gráficos "Lux," [1920]). The author had recently held a high position in the Mexican diplomatic service.

CHAPTER IX

GERMAN INTERESTS AND ACTIVITIES (1870-1927)

To arrive at the beginning of German participation in Latin-American life the historian would have to go back to the emigration movement of the early nineteenth century and even to the period of the Spanish conquest. For present purposes, however, it is hardly necessary to commence earlier than the year 1896. This date will be taken as the starting-point for the present chapter, and two important phases of the subject thus delimited—Germany's attitude during the Spanish-American War and German participation in the joint coercion of Venezuela—will be reserved for subsequent treatment.

The Basis of German Policy

Comparatively speaking, Germany did not become a factor of great importance in Latin America until near the close of the nineteenth century. Prior to that time several thousand Germans had settled mainly in Mexico, Guatemala, Venezuela, Argentina, Brazil, and Chile; several million dollars had been invested; German educators had begun to influence Chile's educational system; a few German officers were beginning to train the armies of some of the Pacific Coast states; German vessels were carrying a goodly portion of South American commerce; and the German Empire had negotiated commercial treaties with most of the nations of Latin America. It was at this latter date, moreover, that many Germans began to clamor for colonies and a navy capable of defending German interests throughout the world. By 1896 there were about 400,000 people of German descent in Latin America, while German investments in the region had reached half a billion dollars, and German trade with these countries amounted to about $146,000,000.[1]

Such was the state of German interests in Latin America at the

[1] *Cf.*, on these earlier interests and activities, Sievers, *Süd und Mittelamerica* (1914) and *Südamerica und die deutschen Interessen* (1903); Schapelle, *The German Element in Brazil;* [Austin Harrison], *The Pan-Germanic Doctrine* (1904); U. S. Dept. of Commerce and Labor, Bur. of Statistics, *Statistics of Foreign Commerce* (1909), *passim.*

close of the last century. During the next seventeen years they underwent an increase little short of marvelous. By 1913 German trade reached $470,000,000, German investments about $2,000,000,000, and German settlers about 600,000 to 700,000 souls.[2] The growth of German trade was especially noteworthy. The Latin-American commerce of no other nation grew so rapidly. The trade of the United States, Germany's closest competitor, increased 300 per cent as compared with a 325 per cent increase for Germany during the period. Moreover, the Latin-American commerce of the German nation had grown more rapidly than its total commerce, as evidenced by the fact that the latter increased only 265 per cent during the period under consideration. Add to this a large transportation business and the cultural interest which the Germans felt in the people of Latin America as in most of the other peoples of western Europe and America; note also the immense possibilities for future expansion in so undeveloped a region—and it will not be difficult to understand why Germany has frequently turned its attention to Latin-American affairs.

Latin America in the German Press

German discussions of Latin America usually assumed one or more of three forms. They pointed to the importance of protecting German investments and trade; they criticised the Latin-American policy of the United States; sometimes—and this was true in particular of the members of the Pan-German League,[3] the Navy League, the National Security League, and the German chauvinists in general—they dwelt upon ways and means of advancing German interests in such fashion as to arouse suspicion of territorial designs.

The Kaiser's now famous speech made in June, 1896, at the opening of the Kiel Canal may be interpreted as referring to Latin America, among other regions. It will be recalled that he said at this time: "The German Empire has become a world empire. Everywhere in distant quarters of the earth thousands of our countrymen are living. . . . The value of what Germany has upon the sea amounts to thousands of millions. It is your duty, gentlemen, to help

[2] On this growth see, in addition to the authorities cited in the previous note, the following; Ernst Wagemann, "Das Deutschtum in Südamerika," in *Deutsche Rundschau*, CLXII (1915), 321, CLXIII, *passim*, and "Die deutschen Kolonisten in Südamerika," in Schmoller's *Jahrbuch* (1915), I, 283 ff.; Halsey, "Investments in Latin America . . . ," U. S. Dept. of Commerce, Special Agents Series, No. 169 (1918).

[3] Mildred S. Wertheimer's, *The Pan-German League* (1924), throws a flood of light on chauvinist aspirations and policies.

bind this greater German Empire firmly to our ancestral home. . . . It is my wish that, standing in the closest union, you help me to do my duty not only to my countrymen in a narrower sense, but also to the many thousand Germans in foreign lands. This means that I may be able to protect them if I must."[4]

Of course there is no reason to assume that Wilhelm II had the slightest reference to the Anglo-Venezuelan boundary affair. It was just at this time, however, that the dispute was in its most critical stage, and it aroused in Germany as elsewhere in Europe a certain resentment toward the Monroe Doctrine. The following comment of the *Kölnische Zeitung*, indorsed by what was reputed to be the official *Norddeutsche Allgemeine Zeitung*, probably expressed the view of many Germans: "England has not come out of the affair with much honor. The bluff of the Americans was . . . a success, as it caused England to submit to the appointment of the Venezuelan commission. And now England willingly acknowledges the Monroe Doctrine. . . . We wish, however, to state right here that England stands perfectly isolated in the establishment of this precedent. Germany at least will never permit a foreign power to interfere if she finds it necessary to defend German interests in South and Central America."[5] The interference of the United States in the Anglo-Venezuelan dispute also gave Bismarck an opportunity to denounce the Monroe manifesto. "The idea which people in America have of the Monroe Doctrine is a proof of extraordinary insolence," said the disgruntled ex-Chancellor. "It is just the same as if a European state . . . were to assert that no change of frontier might take place on the European continent without its consent, or if Russia or England were to dictate in a similar manner in Asia." Such an attitude on the part of the American people represented "an overestimate of their own power and an underestimate of the strength and rights of other American as well as European nations."[6]

Two years later the Spanish-American War broke out. The German press in general was in sympathy with Spain and hostile toward the United States, but this attitude can be explained without referring it entirely to displeasure at the prospect of Yankee expansion into the Caribbean. As will appear in a subsequent chapter, official Germany, at least, was interested in the fate of the Spanish monarchy and the Philippines. Nevertheless the following expression indicates the thoughts that were revolving in certain minds. On March 5, 1898,

[4] C. F. Gauss, *The German Emperor as Shown in his Public Utterances* (New York, 1915), pp. 102–103.
[5] As quoted in *Lit. Dig.*, XIV (Dec. 5, 1896), 152.
[6] *Ibid.*, XV (Dec. 4, 1897), 952.

just on the eve of the war, Gerhart von Schulze-Gaevernitz wrote in *Die Nation:* "The more Germany is condemned to an attitude of passive resistance toward the United States, the more emphatically must she defend her interests in Central and South America. . . . Now, in matters of equity and respect for the law the Romanic peoples in America cannot be judged according to European standards; and in certain circumstances Germany will be constrained all the more to employ coercive political measures in proportion as the amount of German capital invested (in State loans, railways, plantations) in those parts increases. For this purpose we need a fleet capable not only of coping with the miserable forces of South American States, but powerful enough, if the need should arise, to cause America to think twice before making any attempt to apply the Monroe doctrine [economically?] in South America." [7] Even more aggressive was a statement which appeared in the *Hamburger Nachrichten* a few weeks later: "It is not true that the world is divided up," remarked this journal. "It never is. The whole of Central and South America is at present to be had for the right nation. German emigrants can, if they are so minded, create a German empire there. We need not directly attack any of those countries, unless they attempt to exclude the Germans. It is, however, fairly certain that they will, one after the other, cease to be independent states, simply because their people cannot manage their own affairs." [8]

The Spanish-American War appears to have stimulated German interest in Latin America. At any rate during the next few years German writers frequently discussed this region and often criticised the Latin-American policy of the United States. Professor Johannes Unold of Munich contended that the Germans were "marked by their talents and . . . achievements to be the teachers and the intellectual, economic, and political leaders" of the peoples of Spanish and Portuguese America. If Germans did not accomplish this mission, then these peoples would fall sooner or later "under the domination and exploitation of the United States." [9] One of the Berlin daily newspapers remarked that the victory so easily won over Spain had puffed up the Americans until they were beginning "earnestly to think of the political and economical annexation of South America." "This interests us," the journal went on to remark, "not only on account of our trade, but also on account of the continually growing

[7] As quoted in *The Pan-Germanic Doctrine,* p. 233. *Cf.,* also, *Conquest and Kultur,* p. 106.

[8] As quoted in *Lit. Dig.* (April 30, 1898), 534.

[9] *Das Deutschtum in Chile* (1899), p. 62 ff.

and prosperous German colonies in Brazil." [10] A German journalist, Wilhelm Wintzer, concluded a brief survey of German settlements and investments in tropical America with the following remarks: "The moral sanction of the Monroe doctrine disappeared on the day when the treaty for the annexation of the Philippines was signed. . . . Thereby America broke the tacit agreement 'Do not mix in American affairs and I will not mix in affairs outside America,' and gave us the right to set up a doctrine of Greater Germany against that of a Greater America. European interests, and with them the German, lie in America in case we have the power to support them effectively. We shall not forbear to accustom America to this point of view. . . . German emigration should not be directed to South America unless the question whether Germany means simply to obey the American order of hands off in South America is first answered in the negative." [11] In some circles, at any rate, South America was believed to be closely bound up with Germany's future, and in this connection the United States was looked upon as a sort of menace.[12]

Yet there is good evidence, on the other hand, of a growing conviction among Germans that the anti-American attitude of the German press during the Spanish-American War was an unfortunate clash of popular sentiment and national interest. For instance, von Kardorff, a member of the Empire Party, declared in the Reichstag in December, 1898, that the people of Germany should not give way to a sentimental conception which politically could not be "turned to account." "We must remind ourselves," said Kardorff, "that it is more useful to us that a great aspiring people like the Americans should win the upper hand, especially since conditions in Spain have shown themselves to be so decadent. . . . I hope that we preserve through the future the good relations with the United States which the Prussian government has maintained since the time of Frederick the Great." [13] In similar fashion—to give only one more illustration—Ernst von Halle contended in the *Preussische Jahrbücher* (January, 1902) that this unfriendly attitude toward the United States at the outbreak of the war had been "undoubtedly a political mistake," argued that Germany had far more in common

[10] *Deutsche Tages Zeitung,* as quoted in *Lit. Dig.,* XIX (Oct. 7, 1899), 441.

[11] *Die Deutschen in tropischen Amerika* (1900), p. 78 ff.

[12] *Cf. The Pan-Germanic Doctrine,* p. 229 ff. Gustav von Schmoller, *Hondels-und Machtpolitik* (1910), I, 36.

[13] As quoted by Keim, *Forty Years of German-American Political Relations* (1919), p. 234, note.

with the United States than with Spain, and urged a more circumspect policy in the future.[14]

These admonitions may have had some influence. At any rate the journalists assumed a more moderate tone during the Venezuelan imbroglio of 1901–1903.[15] Until the affair was submitted to arbitration in February, 1903, the organs of public opinion appear to have had little to say about it, merely declaring that Germany had no ulterior territorial designs. When the terms of the settlement became known, however, widespread dissatisfaction was expressed and chauvinists once more hinted of colonial ambitions in the New World.[16]

Of course the official journal of the Pan-German League, the *Alldeutsche Blätter*, might be expected to explode. In fact, even before arbitration had been agreed upon this journal had declared the Monroe Doctrine an unjustifiable "inspiration" and an "impertinence," and had denounced the Yankees in the following terms: "With a noisy cry they try to make an impression on the world and succeed, especially with the stupid. The inviolability of American soil is invoked without there being at hand the slightest means of warding off the attack of a respectable European power." [17] But the outbursts which occurred after the announcement that the claims with Venezuela had been submitted to arbitration were not confined to the Pan-Germanists. The *Neuste Nachrichten* (Berlin), for example, declared that the policy of the United States served only to encourage outrages against European nationals in Latin America and expressed strong opposition to the Monroe Doctrine.[18] Even the more moderate *Grenzboten* allowed to appear in its number for March, 1903, a long anonymous article which denounced the Monroe Doctrine and American imperialism as grave dangers to Germany's future. The writer of the article declared, among other things, that Germany could not be a passive witness to the gradual absorption of the Latin-American nations by the United States. He also pointed out that the exclusion of Germany from this vast region would mean economic and political death. "We cannot, and will not, allow ourselves to be shut out from the only portion of the globe still left to us," concluded the essay.[19]

[14] CVII, 189 ff.
[15] *Post,* Ch. XI.
[16] See *Literary Digest,* numbers for February and March, 1904.
[17] January 17, 1903.
[18] *Cf. Public Opinion,* XXXIV (February 19, 1903), 233.
[19] A good summary of this article may be found in *The Pan-Germanic Doctrine,* p. 240 ff.

But once more, as in the discussions immediately following the Spanish-American War, writers pointed out the importance of maintaining friendly relations with the United States. It was felt that England had been a "bad ally" and that the intrigue of British journalists had placed Germany in a false light before the American public.[20] The journalists of the Fatherland should not allow themselves thus to be outdone. The *Preussische Jahrbücher* for April, 1903, contained two articles dealing with the Venezuelan question. One gave an excellent survey of press reports in the United States during the episode and showed how they had been influenced by the British. Its conclusion was as follows: "All that, however, should be one more reason why Germany's public opinion and press should exercise foresight when they speak of foreign and particularly of American affairs. It does no good unnecessarily to irritate a sensitive man. And at present America is in a very irritable mood towards Germany. . . ." The other article, written by Hans Delbrück, declared that no sensible man in Germany was planning or had ever planned to establish German colonies anywhere in America or to found a kingdom as Napoleon had done in the case of the Emperor Maximilian.[21]

In general it appears that such advice as that given by the *Jahrbücher* was followed during the next decade; and yet there were some who failed to take it to heart. The Berlin *Kreutz Zeitung* continued to complain of Yankee pretensions and bluff.[22] The *Grenzboten* sometimes urged the possibility of an understanding with the United States whereby Germany might acquire colonies in the Western Hemisphere and sometimes gave utterance to denunciations of the Monroe Doctrine.[23] A famous German professor declared that the determination of the United States to keep other nations from gaining a foothold in South America "must lead to war as the only solution."[24] Klaus Wagner wrote enthusiastically of the possibility of making all South America the "habitation of German or Germanoid races."[25] Tannenberg confidently looked forward to the day when Germany should take under her "protection the republics of Argentina, Chile, Uruguay, and Paraguay," as well as the south-

[20] *Lit. Dig.*, XXV (December 27, 1902), 879–881.

[21] CXII, 120 ff., 184 ff.

[22] *Lit. Dig.*, XXVIII, 24, XXX, 250–251.

[23] See volumes for 1904, 1905, 1906, and 1912.

[24] Statement made in 1910 by Eduard Meyer. (Quoted in A. B. Hart, *The Monroe Doctrine* [1916], p. 278).

[25] *Krieg* (1906), pp. 165–166.

ern portions of Bolivia and Brazil.[26] Such statements sound menacing, but they were the exception, not the rule.

Official Attitude of Germany (1870–1914)

What of the attitude of the German government? In general it appears that at no time between 1870 and 1914 did Germany seriously consider territorial acquisitions in Latin America. Of course by no means all of the documents bearing on the subject are available to the historian. Many of them are accessible, however, and the motives shaping German policy seem to render the acquisition of American colonies without the consent of the United States well-nigh unthinkable. Important as German expansion into Latin America was, the friendship of the United States appears to have been considered even more important. This was particularly true after 1898. From that year to the outbreak of the World War conditions in Europe, Asia, and Africa were never such as would permit Germany to defy the Monroe Doctrine or to offend the United States in any way. On the other hand, the state of world politics demanded that Germany avoid driving the United States into an alliance with England and even that Germany seek such an alliance for itself. This being the case, Germany's official action in Latin America had to be confined to the promotion and protection of commerce, investments, and emigrants.

The support given by the German government to foreign enterprise and its efforts to use German emigration as a means of promoting the commerce and prestige of the empire are topics which require further investigation so far as Latin America is concerned. The negotiation of numerous commercial treaties and the rapid growth of German trade, investments, and shipping interests indicate that there was no lack of alertness. Yet in view of the energy and industry of the German people much could be left to private enterprise; and, indeed, so far as emigration is concerned it must be noted that the von der Heydt rescript forbade the departure of Prussians from 1859 to 1896.[27]

More important to the present study, and much more evident, are the various actions of the German government in defense of German nationals and their economic interests in Latin America. These defensive measures might take one or more of several forms which

---

[26] *Gross-Deutschland* (1911), p. 250 ff. Pertinent quotations from Kraus and Tannenberg are given in translation in *Conquest and Kultur,* p. 102 ff.

[27] *Mitteilungen des Deutsch-Südamerikanischen Institutes* (1915), IV, 77.

varied somewhat in severity: the blockade of ports, the bombardment of coastal towns, the seizure of custom houses, the occupation
of territory. In view of uncertainty regarding the extent of each coercive action and its possible relation to the Monroe Doctrine, the
United States was usually an interested party. Germany appears
always to have realized this factor in the situation and to have
proceeded with more or less circumspection, but rumor always played
its part and uneasiness rarely failed to evince itself in the United
States.

Two incidents, which revealed something of German policy and
attracted attention in Washington, occurred shortly after the achievement of Germany unity. In 1871 Germany planned to present to
various European Powers a proposal for joint action against
Venezuela. The satisfactory settlement of claims was the point at
issue. Before negotiations were entered upon the United States was
consulted. Secretary of State Hamilton Fish alluded to vivid recol-
lections of the Maximilian episode in Mexico and declared that the
United States, while it would not object to a collective remonstrance
against revolutionary disorders and the non-fulfilment of international obligations, would view with grave concern any attempt at
a forcible coercion of Venezuela by a combination of European nations. Such coercive action was not undertaken and the claims were
submitted to mixed commissions for settlement.[28] Three years later
the United States was disturbed by a rumor that Germany was
negotiating for one or more of the Danish West Indies. A discreet
inquiry was made and George Bancroft, American minister in Berlin, sent to his government the following emphatic statement regarding the falsity of the rumor: "As to Saint Thomas, Germany does
not want it, would not accept it as a gift; has no hankering after
that or any other West India colony; from principle avoids them;
wishes at most a coaling station in Asiatic seas, and that only in
case it can be enjoyed in security without being made a military
post. This statement I have had often from every member of the
government that could by any possibility have charge of any negotiation made for the acquisition of territory."[29] A similar denial was
made at Copenhagen.[30]

During the next two decades there appears to have been no modification of Germany's policy with respect to territorial acquisitions in

[28] Moore, *A Digest of International Law,* VI, 531; U. S. *House Rep.* No. 29,
42 Cong., 2 Sess.; Great Britain, *Accounts and Papers* (1871), LXXII (C–308),
571.

[29] *Foreign Relations* (1874), p. 439 ff.

[30] *Ibid.,* p. 368.

the Western Hemisphere. Emil Witte, German *attaché* at Washington, is responsible for the account of an incident which occurred in 1892. At that time Baron Herbert von Reuter, founder of the famous Reuter information bureau, offered the German imperial Government a 1,600,000-acre tract of land which he had just acquired from Colombia. He asked "that the German Empire should turn the tide of emigration which was flowing into the United States at least partially toward Colombia, where a new Germania across the sea would appear under the sovereignty of the old Empire." The project aroused no enthusiasm and the offer was rejected.[31] Similarly, the Kaiser revealed no inclination to acquire a stronghold in the Dominican Republic in the late summer of 1898, when the German resident agent brought the matter up. It appears that the President of this little state, filled with fear of the Americans and desirous of strengthening European interests, suggested the negotiations of a commercial treaty with Germany. In this treaty he proposed to offer the imperial Government a strip of land or an island to be used as a naval base or for other purposes. The Dominican Republic was to retain its sovereignty over the region, but it was to be placed under German management for an indefinite period. The Kaiser remarked that he would not "fall into such a trap" and expressed an unwillingness to "set himself at variance with the United States." [32]

In fact the German Government, like a large section of the German press,—and perhaps the attitude of the latter was in part determined by that of the former—decided about this time that it was good policy to cultivate American friendship. The steps taken to attain this end were numerous and most of them are well known. A direct cable was laid between Germany and the United States. Architectural and sculptural treasures were presented to Harvard by the Emperor. The Kaiser's brother was sent on a friendly visit to the United States. Americans were cordially received in Germany. Alice Roosevelt was invited to christen the Kaiser's yacht. The American squadron was very agreeably entertained at Kiel. In view of these friendly gestures and the international situation confronted by Germany, the rumors (1901) of German negotiations for the island of Margarita and harbors in Lower California [33] appear absurd. Such procedure would seem under the circumstances not only Machiavellian but foolish.

[31] *Revelations of a German Attaché* (1916), pp. 100–101.
[32] *Die Grosse Politik*, XV, 109–111. The proposal was made during the last days of August and rejected on September 3, 1898.
[33] Keim, *op. cit.*, 279.

Nevertheless these reports—joined with the common action against Venezuela to be discussed later—aroused apprehension in the United States and elsewhere in America, and Germany attempted to allay suspicions. Prince Henry was instructed not to speak of these matters on his own initiative, but in the event that American anxiety should reveal itself he was to conjure it away by calling the whole idea an absurd phantom and pointing out the many problems confronted by Germany in other parts of the world.[34] On February 28, 1903, the German ambassador in Washington emphatically assured President Roosevelt that Germany had no thought of "acquiring territory in South and Central America." [35] On March 19 von Bülow made a similar statement in the *Reichstag*.[36] Soon afterwards he set forth Germany's Latin-American policy in an interview with the agents of the press—an interview which was widely circulated in the journals across the Atlantic.[37]

On this occasion von Bülow emphatically denied that Germany officially encouraged emigration to South America or cherished the design of forming a state within a state or had any political interest in the matter whatsoever. He declared, however, that Germany desired a full share of South American trade and expressed the hope that Germans "in Brazil and elsewhere" would not "forget their mother tongue or abandon their attachment to the old country." [38]

Of course such statements have in themselves little value for the historian, but no evidence has come to light which would indicate that this was not a true expression of German interests and aspirations. Whatever Germany might have desired under a slightly different arrangement of the international chessboard, she could not under the circumstances seriously entertain any hope of immediate territorial acquisitions in the New World. Nor does any important change appear to have taken place during the subsequent decade. Germany's immediate interest in Latin America continued as formerly to be centered in the winning of trade and the protection of German nationals and investments. It is true that in the late 'nineties Germany had begun to make use of her navy to inspire respect for German rights in Latin America. Very drastic action had been taken against Haiti in 1897, the coercion of Guatemala had been discussed in 1902, and vigorous measures were again resorted to in Haiti dur-

[34] *Post*, Ch. XI, note 5.

[35] *Die Grosse Politik*, XVII, 291–292.

[36] For an English version of the statement, see Hart, *op. cit.*, p. 276.

[37] The interview was published in the *Jornal do Commercio* of Rio and the *Laplata Zeitung* of Buenos Aires.

[38] A good summary of this interview may be consulted in *The Pan-Germanic Doctrine*, p. 237.

ing the same year. This policy continued to be followed,[39] but there is no convincing evidence that it was inspired by any motive save a desire to defend Germans and their vested interests and to convince the German *Reichstag* and public of the usefulness of the fleet.

The Latin-American Policy of Germany since the Outbreak of the World War

The outbreak of the World War brought about no immediate change in the attitude of official Germany. On the contrary, it served to emphasize the importance of American friendship. Propaganda in favor of the German cause was at once begun. A special effort was made to cultivate the United States. When German newspapers severely criticised Wilson's Mexican policy, officials of the government counseled moderation, and in September, 1914, the German ambassador in Washington emphatically denied rumors that Germany intended, in the event of victory, "to seek expansion in South America." Bernhard Dernburg, presumably a representative of the Kaiser, publicly stated that if the United States desired assurances on this matter, such assurances would be forthcoming at once. "We have already laid before the Government of the United States an official note stating that Germany would not seek expansion in South America," said Dernburg.[40]

After it became virtually certain that the United States would enter the war on the side of the enemies of the Central Powers and endeavor to bring the Latin-American states into the struggle, the policy of Germany naturally veered from its former course. Thereafter its main purpose was to prevent the Latin-American states from joining the Allies and to divert the energies of the United States by causing trouble in the Western Hemisphere. And the position and influence of Germany for the first time became fairly obvious. The German nation was seen not to be without friends in any part of Latin America. The influence of that procession of military instructors, scientists, bankers, merchants, and professors who had been coming over for years was revealed. Notwithstanding the fact that the combined influence of France, England, Italy, and the United States was pitted against the Teutons, Brazil was the only important Latin-American nation which entered the lists opposed to Germany, and decidedly pro-German predilections were revealed in several states. Of course this was not a clear test, because other motives entered into the decision; but it did indicate that the Ger-

---

[39] *Lit. Dig.*, XXVIII (January 2, 1904), 24.
[40] Hart, *op. cit.*, p. 280.

mans were a power to be reckoned with in the lands south of the United States. Sympathy for Germany was probably strongest in Venezuela, Colombia, and Mexico, but it probably had more menacing possibilities in Cuba, Haiti, Brazil, and Mexico. German designs are said to have had something to do with the armed intervention of the United States in Haiti in 1916, and it was alleged, but never publicly demonstrated, that Germans instigated a revolt in Cuba in February, 1917. Fear was expressed that emissaries of the Kaiser might endanger the peace and security of Brazil and Uruguay by organizing the German element in southern Brazil, but these Germans proved either too loyal to their adopted country or too indifferent to the fate of the Fatherland.[41]

It was in Mexico that German activities created most excitement. On January 16, 1917, Herr Alfred Zimmermann, German minister of foreign affairs, instructed von Eckhardt, the representative of the Imperial Government in Mexico, as follows:

". . . We intend to begin on the first of February unrestricted submarine warfare. We shall endeavour in spite of this to keep the United States of America neutral. In the event of this not succeeding, we make Mexico a proposal of alliance on the following basis: Make war together, make peace together, generous financial support and an understanding on our part that Mexico is to reconquer the lost territory in Texas, New Mexico, and Arizona. The settlement in detail is left to you. You will inform the President of the above most secretly as soon as the outbreak of the war with the United States of America is certain and add the suggestion that he should, on his own initiative, invite Japan to immediate adherence and at the same time mediate between Japan and ourselves. Please call the President's attention to the fact that the ruthless employment of our submarines now offers the prospect of compelling England in a few months to make peace. . . ."[42]

On February 8 Eckhardt was directed immediately to broach the question of alliance to President Carranza and to suggest that he (Carranza) sound Japan. "If the President declines from fear of subsequent revenge," said Zimmermann, "you are empowered to offer him a definitive alliance after conclusion of peace, provided Mexico succeeds in drawing Japan into the Alliance." On February 20 Eck-

[41] P. A. Martin, *Latin America and the War* (1925). (See index under Germany.)

[42] As quoted in Burton J. Hendrick, *The Life and Letters of Walter Hines Page*, III (1925), 333.

hardt had an interview with the Mexican minister of foreign affairs, who "willingly took the matter into consideration, and thereupon had a conversation, which lasted an hour and a half, with [the] Japanese Minister." A fews days later the German envoy appears to have begun negotiations with Carranza. The most urgent need of the Mexican President was munitions and arms, and Germany considered plans for partially supplying this need, but suggested that it would be wise for Mexico to look to Japan and South America for these essentials. Evidently progress was being made. On March 1, however, Germany's Mexican project became public information in the United States and a little more than a month later the United States Congress declared the existence of a state of war with Germany. Shortly afterwards Carranza informed the German minister that he intended to remain neutral. "The alliance . . . had been stultified by its 'premature publication' but would become necessary at a later period." German agents then apparently turned to Francisco Villa to devise plans for setting fire to the Tampico oil wells.[43] Once more, however, their schemes met with failure. With the defeat of Germany all danger passed.

The war and its aftermath inflicted great injury upon German interests in Latin America. For three years German trade was completely wiped out, but it is now slowly recovering. In 1920 Germany shared a little more than 5 per cent of Latin America's commerce. In 1921 her portion had passed 11 per cent, and in 1922 it had reached 15 per cent, or half its total for 1913.[44] The effect of the war and reconstruction upon Teutonic vested interests and moral influence would be difficult to ascertain.

[43] For this entire correspondence, see Burton J. Hendrick, *op. cit.*, III, Ch. xii.
[44] William Spence Robertson, *History of the Latin-American Nations* (1925), p. 573.

CHAPTER X

THE EUROPEAN POWERS AND THE SPANISH-AMERICAN WAR

ANY discussion of the attitude of the European nations during the war between the United States and Spain must center mainly around the procedure of Germany. It was generally believed at the time— and the view still persists—that the German government was unfriendly toward the United States, and German diplomats were in fact prominent in the discussions which related to the war and its effects upon World Power. Contemporary newspapers of England and the United States conveyed the impression that Germany disapproved of American expansion; that the commander of the German squadron in Manila Bay conducted himself in an offensive manner; that Germany was eager to seize the Philippines; and that the Kaiser even tried to persuade the European Powers to interfere in Spain's behalf. Moreover, these journals alleged that Germany and the nations of continental Europe were held in restraint solely by the pro-American attitude of Great Britain.[1] The persistence of this view in the United States finds illustration in a recent book published by Dr. Bertha Ann Reuter. With reference to Germany's attitude she says: "Germany was very much concerned over America's intentions both in Cuba and in the East. She was in no way pleased to see the United States acquire territory in either sphere." [2]

Documents recently published by the German government[3] afford an opportunity to test these beliefs. Although the final account cannot be written until the archives of the other European nations have been searched, the main outlines of the story now appear clear. The subject quite naturally falls into two divisions: the question of European arbitration and intervention in the Cuban difficulty, and

---

[1] Cf. files of *Literary Digest*, April to December, 1898, and of the New York *Times* for the same period. For a later dispute regarding the matter, see *Literary Digest*, XXIV (February 22, 1902), 263.

[2] *Anglo-American Relations During the Spanish-American War* (1924), p. 127, *passim*.

[3] *Die Grosse Politik der Europäischen Kabinette, 1870–1914*. Most of the documents bearing upon the matter are found in Vol. XV.

the problem of the disposition of the Philippine and the Caroline Islands.

Proposed Mediation of the Cuban Difficulty

Emperor William II, upon learning that General Woodford, American ambassador in Madrid, had been instructed to protest against Spanish procedure in Cuba and urge Spain to make peace, suggested to the Foreign Office (September 28, 1897) that intervention by the European states in favor of Spain, whose monarchical system would be endangered if she should lose Cuba, might be advisable.[4] The German under-secretary of foreign affairs recommended great caution. He feared that France and England might use Germany's support of Spain in order to estrange Germany with the United States and secure commercial advantages at Germany's expense. He considered the coöperation of Russia and France an absolute prerequisite. Eulenburg, counselor on the Imperial Staff, thought that Austria, as the most natural advocate of Spain, should be induced to take the lead.[5] The Emperor agreed to this plan, remarking that the most expedient method would have to be found; that the end itself, not the means of attaining it, was the important matter. Regarding Eulenburg's apprehensions that the French Republic would not be willing to serve dynastic purposes, the Kaiser remarked that the protection of the colonial possessions of the European Powers against transatlantic ambitions might be made the basis of agreement. In like manner he approved of Bernard von Bülow's recommendation (September 30) that Austria should be urged to take the initiative, with the understanding that England and France should coöperate in the step under consideration.[6]

Accordingly, on October 7, 1897, Bülow authorized Lichnowsky, German *chargé* in Vienna, to approach Austria. Lichnowsky was instructed to inform the Austrian government—in case the matter of European intervention in the Cuban affair should be brought up again—that while Germany could not take a definite stand in advance of the other European Powers, she would be disposed seriously to consider any proposals received from Paris or London—perhaps upon Austria's suggestion.[7]

After the middle of October the whole affair entered the quiescent stage, only to become more critical than ever in the following Feb-

[4] *Die Grosse Politik der Europäischen Kabinette,* 1870–1914. XV, 3, editorial note.
[5] The Queen of Spain was an Austrian Archduchess.
[6] *Ibid.,* XV, 3–6. Bülow was Acting Secretary of Foreign Affairs.
[7] *Ibid.,* XV, 6–7.

ruary. As the real crisis between Spain and the United States approached, European diplomatic circles buzzed. The Spanish government inquired whether Germany, in order to protect the principle of monarchy, would be inclined to head a European demonstration. Bülow replied that Germany was eager to safeguard that principle, but that France must be persuaded to take the lead in intervention before Germany would be willing to support the move.[8] In like manner it soon became evident that neither Austria nor France was willing to take the first step. The Austrian Foreign Secretary thought that something should be done, but declared that the Austrian government was not strong enough to undertake the initiative. The French ambassador at Vienna revealed anxiety in regard to French colonial possessions in America and admitted that a united European demonstration was necessary. He felt, however, that Russia could not be counted upon and "showed an unusual degree of aversion to the Island Kingdom which placed obstacles in the way of necessary French colonial expansion in every quarter of the globe." [9]

Thus matters stood in February. On March 14 the ambassador of Austria-Hungary in Berlin suggested once more that Germany should take the lead against the United States. Again Bülow declined and instructed the German ambassadors in Vienna and Madrid to express His Majesty's regret that he found himself unable to lend any assistance so long as Russia and France failed to give binding promises of active support.[10] In his letter to the German ambassador in Vienna, however, Bülow made the important statement that the Emperor, convinced that a separate action of the Triple Alliance was quite out of the question in view of the stand taken by England, France, and Russia, now considered papal arbitration the only means left to save Spain.

It was, in fact, at the instigation of William II that the Pope instructed his Nuncio in Madrid to ascertain whether mediation by the Papal See would be agreeable to Spain. Having saved the Spanish monarch from taking the initiative in asking the Pope for mediation —a step which the Spanish people might have interpreted as a symptom of royal weakness—the German Emperor appears to have considered his mission finished. Thereafter he apparently preferred to leave the matter to the parties concerned.[11] After he

---

[8] Bülow to Radowitz, February 15, 1898, *ibid.*, XV, 7–8.

[9] Eulenburg to Hohenlohe, February 23, 1898, *ibid.*, XV, 8–9.

[10] Bülow to Eulenburg, March 15, 1898, *ibid.*, XV, 10–12; to Radowitz, March 17, 1898, XV, 12–14.

[11] *Ibid.*, XV, 14, 18.

learned (April 1) that the Spanish government, contrary to expectations based upon Radowitz's [12] report from Madrid (March 22, 1898), had told the Nuncio that Spain could not consider arbitration on the basis of surrendering Cuba, the Emperor wrote at the foot of the telegram: "Then there is no help for her! She will lose it anyhow!" [13]

In the meantime the Madrid representatives of Germany, Austria, France, Russia, Italy, and England were asked (March 26) by the Spanish minister of state to submit the following confidential request to the consideration of their respective governments: "The Powers should advise both Spain and the United States to settle the difficulties to which the questions embodied in Mr. Woodford's note of March 23 might give rise by accepting an arbiter, in such way that peace should not be disturbed." Bülow instructed Radowitz that the Emperor still felt that Germany should not act before France and Russia had committed themselves. He therefore asked Radowitz to report on the replies given by the other Powers.[14]

Soon afterwards (April 4, 1898) Bülow authorized Holleben, German ambassador at Washington, to participate in the diplomatic action suggested by Spain, provided all five of the ministers of the Great Powers should agree to act together. But this concession appears to have been made mainly to oblige Austria. "Since the Vienna Cabinet wishes it," was the remark of Bülow.[15] Germany must not give offense either to the Powers or to the United States, he cautioned Holleben on April 7.[16] On this latter date the representatives of the Great Powers handed President McKinley a joint note, dated April 6, urging that peace be preserved.

Thus the German government had participated in this collective action with considerable caution; and, it should be added, without expecting any satisfactory results. On April 5, Bülow had remarked to the Spanish ambassador in Berlin that the Powers were too occupied in the Far East to permit of effective measures in Spain's behalf. He personally believed that it would be better for Spain to give the Pope "carte blanche" to prevent war.[17]

The sequel showed, of course, that Bülow's misgivings regarding

---

[12] German Ambassador at Madrid.

[13] *Ibid.*, XV, 19.

[14] Telegram of March 28, *ibid.*, XV, 16–17. Woodford's note contained the threat that unless a satisfactory settlement regarding both the *Maine* and the whole Cuban affair could be reached in a few days, the President would lay the matter before Congress.

[15] *Ibid.*, XV, 19–20.

[16] *Ibid.*, XV, 20–21.

[17] *Ibid.*, XV, 20.

the influence of the Powers were well founded. Spain was eager for peace and actually directed a suspension of hostilities in Cuba, but on April 11 McKinley sent his message to Congress without any mention of this concession. A few days later the legislative branch of the government authorized McKinley to use force in Cuba. War now appeared almost inevitable.

On April 14 Sir Julian Pauncefote, British ambassador in Washington, surprised Holleben by proposing that the diplomatic representatives of the Great Powers hand the United States another collective note. Pauncefote called the diplomats together and they decided that this note should express the view that the intervention of the United States in Cuba would not be justifiable under the circumstances. In telegraphing this proposal to the Kaiser, Bülow remarked: "I personally regard such a demonstration somewhat coldly, though I, too, think it desirable that this frivolous attack be branded before the world. A step undertaken here would only decrease the prestige of the Powers, if their representatives have nothing at their command properly to repel an unfriendly answer." At this time—or later, as has been alleged [18]—the Emperor commented on Bülow's reaction as follows: "I think it [the demonstration suggested] entirely impracticable, useless and therefore prejudicial! We make ourselves as ridiculous in the eyes of the Americans as we did in those of the Greeks and the Turks, who did not care a straw about our collective notes. . . . I am against this step!" [19]

Nevertheless, Bülow immediately sounded out Russia on the proposed move. The Russian minister of foreign affairs suspected that England had suggested the plan merely to bring discord between monarchical Europe and the United States and expressed the view that non-intervention would be the best policy.[20] Thereupon Bülow instructed the German ambassador at St. Petersburg to inform the Russian government that His German Majesty was also of the opinion that "platonic steps with lame protests" would be

---

[18] The proposal of April 14 became a matter of controversy in 1902 on the occasion of Prince Henry's visit to the United States. The editors of *Die Grosse Politik* (XV, 24 note) assert that the Kaiser's marginal notes were made known to the German ambassadors in London and Petersburg on the very day that the telegram was received, but unfortunately they do not publish the documents which are alleged to prove this. On the question of responsibility for initiating the second move for intervention, see *Die Grosse Politik*, XV, 24 note, 29–30; *Revue des Deux Mondes*, CLXX, 476–478; *Journal de St. Petersbourg*, Feb. 23, 1902; G. W. Smalley, *Anglo-American Memoires* (1912), II, 178 ff.

[19] April 15, 1898, *Die Grosse Politik*, XV, 22–24.

[20] See Bülow to William II, April 16, 1898, *ibid.*, XV, 25–27.

of no advantage to Spain and serve only to impair the prestige of the Powers.[21] Soon afterwards the matter was dropped.

The negative attitude of Germany and Russia appears to have been decisive, although the position of England may have had considerable weight.[22] On April 16 Bülow remarked in a telegram to the Emperor: "This collective action had been suggested by England, which made a Russian rejection appear probable from the beginning. I thought, therefore, that it would be in accordance with your Majesty's highest intentions if I investigated only in Petersburg regarding the reception of the English proposal, so as to avoid taking a rejection exclusively on our own shoulders. The answer of Count Muraviev [Russian minister of foreign affairs] turned out as had been foreseen by Your Majesty." [23] Yet Holleben, in a letter to Prince Hohenlohe, imperial chancelor, appears to have agreed with his French colleague when the latter remarked that Pauncefote's plan was not carried out because of the "lukewarm attitude" of England.[24]

At any rate England's position must have been puzzling to some of the other Powers. Holleben wrote the German Foreign Office that the hesitation of the British government appeared "quite like a riddle," and the Kaiser commented with an "uns auch!" Hollenben's comments on this phase of the affair deserve to be quoted at some length. In the letter of April 22, to which reference has already been made, he said: "In the beginning of the Cuban conflict England showed toward the United States, probably with special regard to the Far East, a disposition to oblige, which, it is true, was platonic —at least I still think so—, but then she joined the collective action of the Powers on the seventh instant without difficulty. Soon after that Sir Julian Pauncefote was even the originator of the further steps which were planned here toward a coöperation of the Powers. . . . But nothing further has come of it, as my French colleague tells me, because of England's lukewarm attitude, which, by the way, I do not regret very much, as Your Majesty knows. Now more recently come the fraternal articles of the two presses, especially of the one here, and the banquet speeches of the American ambassador in London; also there appears here, it is believed on a secret mission,

[21] Bülow to Radolin, April 16, 1898, *ibid.*, XV, 27.

[22] The French government was also hesitant, but its attitude was thought to depend largely on the position of Russia. (See Bülow to Radowitz, March 17 and 31, *Die Grosse Politik*, XV, 12–14, 18–19.)

[23] *Loc. cit.*

[24] April 22, 1898, *ibid.*, XV, 28.

the secretary of the American embassy in London, White; but all this is ridiculed by Sir Julian Pauncefote and as far as manifestations of friendship on the part of America are concerned, he flatly declares them to be hypocritical. From the mouth of Sir Julian that is a good deal regarding America."

This description of Britain's procedure aroused the Kaiser's ire. He suggested that Pauncefote was possibly lying. He then commented on his island rival: "England wants to play the very same game that she played years ago when she admittedly provoked the Graeco-Turkish War. She stirs all the Powers to action, pretends to participate until the Powers have compromised themselves with the belligerents; then she draws back, pharisaically beats her breast, secretly joins one of the combatants—of course always the stronger —and incites it against the Continental Powers. Meanwhile, at their expense, she solicits from it commercial advantages for herself. England positively does not wish to belong to Europe, it won't throw in its lot with the Continental Powers [this clause in English], but desires to constitute an independent entity between this Continent and America or Asia." [25]

The truth regarding England's position seems to be that Pauncefote either exceeded his instructions in convening the diplomats and planning further joint action, or that the English government underwent a change in sentiment about the time that war broke out between Spain and the United States. The facts in the case cannot be determined until England and France throw open their archives.

The documents published by Germany appear, however, to make clear the attitude of that government. The Kaiser, though he was the originator of the thought of intervention, can hardly be said to have pursued an aggressive policy with reference to the matter. The German government urged mediation upon the European Powers and the Pope, but the German Foreign Office pointed out from the beginning that Germany would not lead the movement for intervention. The German government even felt that Spain should give up Cuba in order to avoid war. Throughout the whole affair the Kaiser was primarily interested in the preservation of the "monarchical principle." Possibly he would have joined the Powers in the employment of more forceful means to prevent an outbreak of war and the defeat of Spain, but to assert that he undoubtedly would have done so is to draw an inference that is not supported by the documents. [26]

[25] *Die Grosse Politik*, XV, 28–29.
[26] See Lester Burrell Shippee, "Germany and the Spanish-American War," in *The Amer. Hist. Rev.*, XXX (1925), 763.

The Question of the Disposal of the Philippines

As already intimated, the suspicion that the German government was attempting to oppose the interests of the United States deepened during the months of uncertainty when the solution of the Philippine problem was pending. At one time it was reported that Germany contemplated lending assistance to Spain; at another she was said to be preparing to support the natives; and more than once she was suspected of seeking an opportunity to take over the Philippines and the Sulu archipelago.[27]

These apprehensions were nourished both by accident and by design. The mere appearance of a German admiral before Manila with larger naval forces than had been present in former times of unrest led some of the natives to assume that this official had come to aid the Spaniards. This opinion was so generally held that simple men in such a remote place as Mariveles, for instance, even asked the German officers when they were going to proceed against the Yankees. The apparently erroneous report of an unmusical Spanish sailor that a German man-of-war, while passing an American vessel, had played the Spanish national anthem—it had probably been the American national hymn—provided further foundation for the rumor that Germany was favoring Spain; and the Spaniards, catching in their emergency at every straw, seem to have given credence to the report.[28]

It does not seem strange, in view of the current rumors and tense emotions of war-time, that Commodore Dewey should have observed German naval proceedings with considerable suspicion—especially when so many sinister reports were brought to Dewey, for the most part, it would seem, from English sources, and when tactless and hostile utterances from German newspapers and alarming reports of the British journals kept poisoning the atmosphere.[29] Yet, it should be

[27] See New York *Times,* July 13 ff.; New York *World,* July 14 ff.; *Literary Digest,* XVII (July 16 and 23), 86, 91, *passim.*

[28] Diederichs, "Darstellung der Vorgänge vor Manila von Mai bis August, 1898," in *Marine Rundschau,* I (1914), 253 ff. An English translation was published in the Royal United Service Institution, *Journal,* LIX (1914), 421–446. Diederichs's "Statement" was intended as an answer to Dewey's *Autobiography* (New York, Scribner's, 1913), pp. 252–267.

[29] Both Secretary of State Day and Andrew D. White attempted to counteract these rumors. (See Washington *Evening Star,* June 15, and New York *Staatszeitung,* June 16, 1898; also White, *Autobiography* (1907), II, 157 ff., and *Die Grosse Politik,* XV, 54 note.)

noted that, even so, the press exaggerated the friction of these two officials, for Dewey appears to have written to Diederichs on April 16, 1899, as follows: "I rejoice that our differences have been of newspaper manufacture." [30]

The documents published in *Die Grosse Politik* throw significant light on the attitude not only of Germany but of France and Russia as well. From them it is possible to trace the main outlines of the diplomacy of this second phase of the Spanish-American conflict.

Attention was drawn to the Far East by Dewey's victory over the Spanish squadron in Manila Bay. On May 11 Prince Henry of Prussia, then in command of the Asiatic squadron, cabled from Hong-Kong that the natives of the Philippine Islands had decided upon a rebellion, which would probably achieve success, and that they "would gladly place themselves under the protection of a European power, especially Germany." This the Prince had from a reliable German merchant from Manila. Three days later a cable corroborating this view was sent by the German consul at Manila. He said that Spain's sovereignty over the islands was about to collapse and that the natives, unwilling to exchange the old master merely for another in the form of the United States, were planning to strike out for independence. He pointed out, also, that they showed a predilection for Germany and might offer their throne to a German prince. He then inquired whether this sentiment should be discouraged or allowed to develop freely.[31]

Bülow immediately communicated with the Kaiser, discussing the Philippine question in all of its bearings. It was a matter of great importance, in which Russia and France as well as the United States and England would be interested, for "the control of the sea in the end may rest on the question of who rules the Philippines, directly or indirectly." Even if the Filipinos gave evidence that they were not trying merely to play off one Power against another and unanimously took up arms in favor of Germany, this would be of

---

[30] Diederichs, *op. cit.* (Eng. trans.), pp. 445–446. Jeannette Keim (*Forty Years of German-American Political Relations* [1919], p. 224, note) correctly remarks that the controversy was "of short duration" and "would have excited little comment in the United States had it not been interpreted by the American press and public to be indicative not only of anti-American sympathies on the part of Germany but also of that country's intention to annex the Philippines."

The British Admiral appears not to have considered the disagreement a matter of great importance. (See *British Documents* [ed. Gooch and Temperley, 1927], I, 105).

[31] *Die Grosse Politik*, XV, 33–34, notes.

little avail, because the permanent possession of the Philippines would depend upon sea power. Moreover, encouragement of revolution in the islands would be contrary to the "principle of legitimacy" which formed the basis of German relations with Russia and Austria-Hungary. Indeed, the establishment of a German protectorate would be likely not only to involve Germany in difficulties with the United States but also to provoke a coalition of European Powers against her. The idea of a protectorate should therefore be discarded. Division of the islands among the Naval Powers would be better, and it might meet their approval in spite of press notices which indicated that the United States was going to claim all of the Philippines and that England would not permit European interference. More acceptable to Bülow, however, would be the neutralization of the archipelago by agreement of the naval powers. He believed that this would make possible a future settlement more favorable to Germany and, for the present, leave to each party the silent hope that some day an opportunity to seize the entire group might offer itself. At any rate he felt that this proposal might be the most harmless means of securing information upon the aspirations of the nations interested. He was convinced that a successful move of any sort in the Philippines would depend upon an understanding with the United States and England—especially England, for should Britain and the United States reach an agreement regarding the islands the issue would be settled. He accordingly advised (1) that an attempt be made to ascertain whether Great Britain was eager to obtain her share of the Spanish spoils at once or would be satisfied if nobody got anything, and (2) that Admiral Diederichs be sent to Manila Bay to observe and report developments.[32]

The Emperor's comments written upon the margin of Bülow's letter show that he was in agreement with his secretary. Accordingly, Diederichs was soon dispatched to the Philippines and Hatzfeldt, German ambassador in London, was directed to sound the British government. In instructing Hatzfeldt, Bülow emphasized the fact that the Kaiser was opposed to the establishment of a protectorate, but was determined to demand an adequate compensation in case the islands should fall wholly or partially into the hands of another Power. If such compensation could not be realized at once, German diplomacy would have to direct its efforts toward the neutralization of the islands.[33]

Hatzfeldt did not act immediately upon his instructions. He had already conferred with Lord Salisbury, British foreign secretary,

[32] Bülow to Kaiser Wilhelm II, May 14, 1898, *ibid.,* XV, 33–38.
[33] *Ibid.* to Hatzfeldt, May 18, *ibid.,* XV, 39.

and had not found him inclined to discuss the Philippine question.[34] The matter was therefore dropped for a few weeks.

Diederichs with a detachment of the Germany navy reached Manila Bay on June 12. His arrival aroused excitement in the United States and was even viewed as somewhat tactless by some of the European journals.[35] But it did not cause great uneasiness in official circles at Washington. The American ambassador in Berlin was directed not to give assurances as to the Philippines and cautioned not to permit the fate of these islands to be involved with that of Samoa. A little later he was asked whether he thought it was likely that the large German force at Manila would be withdrawn or reduced, but there was not sufficient concern to follow the matter up.[36]

As already intimated, however, relations between Diederichs and Dewey soon became somewhat strained. Friction was occasioned by the failure of Diederichs to conform to the rules of neutrality as Dewey interpreted them. Near the middle of July matters reached a critical stage. Dewey became convinced that the German man-of-war "Irene" had interfered to prevent the Filipino chief, Aguinaldo, from taking Isla Grande in Subig Bay. One of Dewey's officers had also been forced to fire across the bow of the "Cormorant" in order to compel it to stop for communications. On July 10 Diederich's flag-officer came to Dewey with a list of grievances and an explosion occurred. In a fit of anger Dewey said: "Why, I shall stop each vessel whatever may be her colors. And if she does not stop I shall fire at her!" The flag-officer inquired of the irate commander whether he knew that such procedure would mean war, whereupon Dewey retorted: "And I tell you, if Germany wants war, all right; we are ready. With the English I have not the slightest difficulty; they always communicate with me."

When Diederichs reported the affair four days later he said that he attributed little importance to it, but he nevertheless remarked: ". . . I do not conceal from myself that in the future the relations between the American squadron and ours will be somewhat strained and the greatest care must be taken to avoid incidents. The Americans refuse to trust our loyalty, especially since my arrival at Manila, and their suspicion is being strengthened by the circulation of rumors to the effect that Manila is being supplied with provisions by His Majesty's ships and that there will be more energetic meddling in the war on our part in the near future." On August 2, after fuller reflection, he wrote: "I must admit that so far as I am able to

[34] *Die Grosse Politik,* XV, 39, note.

[35] Holleben to Bülow June 13 and 17, *ibid.,* XV, 41–42.

[36] Instructions of June 13, 18, and 22, MSS., Department of State, Despatches, Germany.

judge my coming here has not been favorable to the German cause. No one fails to let us know that he has seen through our alleged scheme. The Englishman was egging on in the background and so the Yankee was seized with an irritability which deprived him of calm reflection and made every movement of German ships appear suspicious. On both sides there was indignation because of the interruption of their former quiet life at Manila; perhaps also they were a little disturbed lest the partiality for Americans manifested by the English ships might be too closely observed. . . . I fear that we shall not be spared the open suspicion of having come here bent upon larger plans and of having been forced to retreat because the watchfulness of our opponents rendered the execution of our plans too difficult." [37]

Meanwhile, Germany returned for a brief interval to the plan of neutralizing the Philippines. Spain had suggested to Germany, France, and Russia that the Powers assume control over Manila, and the Spanish governor-general had gone so far as to urge Diederichs to receive the city *in depositu*. The admiral refused to act without instructions. Bülow sounded out Paris and St. Petersburg and found that the proposal was not warmly received.[38] Germany then decided to urge a division of the spoils.

By this time, however, German diplomats had become convinced that their aspirations must be realized, if at all, through an understanding with the United States and on the basis of "live and let live." On July 1 a telegram was sent to Holleben, informing him of the Emperor's purpose "to leave unused no opportunity which may [might] arise from the Spanish-American War to obtain naval stations in East Asia." The ambassador was instructed to observe closely the drift of public opinion, to ascertain the strength of annexationist sentiment, and find out what price Britain was expected to ask for her support of the United States in the Pacific. He was further directed to broach the idea of a *rapprochement* between Berlin and Washington, pointing out that Germany and perhaps Germany alone would be willing to back the territorial demands of the United States in the Far East. According to accounts in their respective newspapers, both France and Russia were opposed to the establishment of another Great Power in that region, and England was not accustomed to allow herself to get into trouble for the sake of a friend.[39]

[37] *Die Grosse Politik,* XV, 62, note.
[38] Bülow to Wilhelm II, June 21, and Consul Rieloff (Hong-Kong) to the Foreign Secretary, June 23, 1898, *ibid.,* XV, 42-44.
[39] *Ibid.,* XV, 44-45.

A few days later Berlin evinced even greater anxiety for an understanding with the United States. News got out that England was negotiating for some of the colonial possessions of Portugal; and, moreover, the English press appeared to be trying to frighten the United States into an alliance with Great Britain, using Germany as the bugbear.[40] Quite naturally Germany was alarmed, but believing that an Anglo-American alliance—perhaps supplemented by one with Japan—would be ideal for England, Richthofen, German acting secretary of foreign affairs, felt that it would be futile to try to entice Britain from this course. He held, therefore, that all efforts to prevent such an alliance should be directed toward the United States. Accordingly, he suggested that Hatzfeldt might find it convenient to confer with the American embassy in London on the common interests of their countries. He also went on to point out that an understanding with Germany would be worth more to the United States than an Anglo-American alliance. Emphasizing the fact that Germany's territorial demands would always be more modest than those of Britain, Richthofen declared that, in view of Germany's position in Europe and her limited financial resources, acquisitions on a large scale, as for instance the taking over of the Philippine group, would be quite out of the question. All that Germany wanted was naval and coaling stations in the Far East, such as were indispensable to any maritime Power.[41]

Hatzfeldt replied that the American representative in London was openly sympathetic with England and very taciturn. He feared that nothing would be gained from an interview with him, but that, on the contrary, the American ambassador would immediately communicate any German proposals to the British government. He accordingly suggested that negotiations for a German-American understanding be opened with the ambassador of the United States at Berlin.[42]

The suggestion was immediately followed. On July 9 Richthofen had a long interview with Andrew D. White, then American ambassador to Germany. Referring to a recent address of White's in which he had remarked that the attitude of Germany in the Spanish-American War had been entirely correct and neutral, he expressed

[40] *Die Grosse Politik*, XIV, Part I, Ch. 92.
[41] Instructions of July 6, *ibid.*, XV, 47–52.
[42] Despatch of July 8, 1898, *ibid.*, XV, 52–53. Hatzfeldt's conviction of Hay's British leanings was perhaps well-founded. Hay's attitude toward Germany may be observed in a letter he wrote White regarding the Anglo-German agreement respecting China, in which he said: "At least we are spared the infamy of an alliance with Germany. I would rather, I think, be the dupe of China, than the chum of the Kaiser." (Letter of November 21, 1900, quoted by Keim, *op. cit.*, p. 239, note 43.)

a desire to make the American diplomat an intermediary for an exchange of views with Washington on a possible agreement between the two countries regarding colonial issues. White expressed himself as willing to do everything he could to advance friendly relations, but he said that he was uninstructed as to the plans of his government. He frankly admitted, indeed, that he believed it had no plans. Thereupon, Richthofen, somewhat embarrassed, made in substance the following statement, which he desired White to consider as unofficial but as coming from one in close personal touch with the Kaiser:

If Germany, along with the other nations, had observed a strictly correct attitude toward the belligerents in the war then being waged, she could justly lay claim to distinction in that she had been the only power which had actually been tempted to take an opposite course. It had been to the German admiral alone that the Spanish governor-general had offered Manila *in depositu.* This official, in conformity with instructions from his superiors, had rejected the offer, but Mr. White must recognize that the maintenance of neutrality had involved particular difficulties. In the first place, responsibility for the decision with reference to European intervention in the war had been thrust upon the German Emperor. The Powers which might have been inclined to intervene had all awaited a signal from Berlin, and Spain had looked in the same direction for aid. If Germany had found ground for interference, Austria and France would have fallen in line immediately and Russia would have followed the lead of France, while Italy would have followed that of Germany.[43] Thus all the Continental Powers might have decided upon intervention. But His Majesty had seen fit to maintain a negative attitude toward every suggestion of this nature. In the second place, the sentiment of the German people might have prompted the Kaiser to take an unneutral course. While their attitude could not be described as Hispanophile, it must be admitted that it was not friendly toward America. This lack of friendliness could not be explained entirely by monarchist sympathy for the Queen Regent, on the one hand, and the feeling that the declaration of war had not been entirely justified, on the other; it had already existed to a certain extent even before the beginning of the war, and it had been caused

[43] In his secret letter to the Kaiser of May 14, Bülow had spoken of discussions in the press of Russia and France relative to possible combinations to prevent the United States from acquiring the Philippines permanently or in order to transfer them to England. Yet the reader will note that it was the German government which originally proposed mediation. Richthofen is therefore somewhat misrepresenting Germany's attitude.

less by commercial rivalry than by grievances in the colonial sphere. While the negotiation of the treaty providing for the annexation of the Hawaiian Islands was in itself not a source of discontent to the German people, they were undeniably disappointed that the United States did not thereupon cede her claims on Samoa to Germany. The latter was far from grudging America the fruits of her victory in the present war or her position in the world. On the contrary, Germany was willing to support her in the peace negotiations, provided the United States would not oppose Germany's modest aspirations. Richthofen then declared his conviction that the history of the world during the next century would in large measure be determined by a proper understanding between the United States and Germany at the close of the Spanish-American War. If the United States should take a hostile stand toward Germany and form an alliance with Britain, this would lead to a coalition of France, Russia, and Germany and a feverish enlargement of fleets. Thus the United States would be forced to maintain its armaments after the close of the war. On the other hand, a German-American agreement would be more likely to promote peace and disarmament, for there would be little danger of a war so long as Germany could find it possible through a friendly understanding with the United States to avoid joining Britain, on the one side, or Russia and France, on the other. Only by a *rapprochement* with Germany could the United States, without expenditures for preparedness and without bringing its own peculiar institutions into jeopardy, fully and completely realize its colonial aspirations.

In compliance with a request of White, Richthofen named the places which he "personally imagined" that Germany would like to obtain; namely, full possession of the Samoan and Caroline Islands—chiefly from considerations of national sensitiveness—and maritime fulcra in the Philippines and perhaps in the Sulus.

The entire interview was reported to have been very cordial, White having agreed with Richthofen in every respect. White declared that he believed the German aspirations to be legitimate and perceived in German territorial expansion a means of bringing the blessings of civilization to mankind. He recognized that the acquisition of coaling stations in the Pacific was essential to Germany, and he would support her wishes in Washington.[44]

Despatches from Holleben brought no definite information, however, for he had been unable to ascertain the colonial aims of the

[44] *Die Grosse Politik*, XV, 53–58. For Samoan negotiations, see *ibid.*, XIV, Ch. 96. White was not an imperialist, but he desired the acquisition of Hawaii and a few coaling stations in the Pacific.

United States. He reported that the parties had no fixed program, but that the administration was more disposed than the politicians to comply with German desires. He thought that the seizure of any Spanish possession by Germany would, at the moment he was writing, be considered an unfriendly act. He recommended that negotiations relating to commercial differences should be taken up at once in a spirit of cordiality, in order that all grounds for hostility might be removed.[45]

At length, on July 13, Hatzfeldt decided to discuss the colonial issue and future relations between the United States and Germany with John Hay. He found Hay's attitude far less satisfactory than had been that of White. Differing from the latter, Hay maintained that the United States had great interests in Samoa and ought not to give them up. He also hinted that, contrary to former intentions, his government might see fit to retain the Philippines. Hatzfeldt was even doubtful whether Hay would recommend to Washington a careful consideration of German interests in the Pacific.[46]

About July 25 White, apparently moved by the tone of American press items, informed Richthofen in a personal conference that his government entertained friendly feelings toward Germany, but owing to the fact that the United States held nothing in its hands as yet, a discussion of the colonial question appeared premature. As a personal suggestion White added that the situation might be improved if the German vessels in Manila Bay would move back and forth in the neighborhood instead of remaining stationary. Richthofen merely replied that these vessels had been sent solely to protect German subjects and commercial interests and that the German admiral at Manila ought to know how many vessels he needed. As a proof of Diederichs's reasonable disposition Richthofen mentioned the recent dismissal of the "Irene" from service in the Philippines.[47]

When White and Richthofen met again, the latter, with Bülow's approval, expressed regret that the American ambassador had made the remark about the German vessels at Manila. He said that if it should become known it would offend the German people, especially since the Kaiser was just as little disposed as the United States to suffer encroachments upon his rights. White begged Richthofen not to report this purely personal remark to the Emperor, but to consider it as unspoken. He declared that his only purpose had been to deprive those who had been carrying on propaganda against

[45] *Die Grosse Politik*, XV, pp. 59–60, 65–66. Despatches undated but arriving in Berlin on July 13 and 28, 1898.

[46] *Ibid.*, XV, 60–61.

[47] *Ibid.*, XV, 62–64.

Germany, particularly Russia and England, of their chief argument. For the same reason he had dictated a denial of some of their insinuations to the correspondent of the New York *Staatszeitung*. White also promised to suggest to Washington an exchange of views on the territorial question, but further negotiations between the two countries seem not to have taken place until after the opening of the Paris Peace Conference (October, 1898).[48]

Meanwhile German diplomacy busied itself in London and Madrid. The opening days of August found Hatzfeldt still of the opinion that the United States did not desire to retain any portion of the Philippines save Manila, which it desired for a coaling station. He queried whether Spain might not be induced likewise to yield such a station to Germany. He felt that the consent of England and of the United States to this might not be unattainable and expressed a willingness to approach Lord Salisbury very cautiously on the matter.[49]

But Richthofen held a different view regarding American ambitions. By August 5 he had become thoroughly aware of the waxing strength of the annexationist party in the United States. He thought, however, that England would be threatened more than Germany by the expansion of the United States into the Pacific, and that Japan might not be kindly disposed toward American intrusion. He therefore suggested to Hatzfeldt that the neutralization project should be revived. This would necessitate a coaling station for each of the protecting Powers, and it might also be the means of saving the natives from the bloody revenge which the Spaniards would exact in case the United States perchance decided to withdraw.[50]

The sequel showed that Richthofen had correctly interpreted the growing ambition of the United States, but that he had not penetrated the mind of British statesmen. Toward the last of July Salisbury had given Hay to understand that England preferred to have the United States retain the Philippines. When the German ambassador approached Salisbury, on August 9, he therefore found the Foreign Secretary's attitude so negative with reference to the neutralization scheme that he deemed it unwise to reveal that he was acting under the express authority of Berlin.[51]

But new prospects for Germany were opened up through Radowitz's report from Madrid (August 8) that Spain had about decided

[48] *Die Grosse Politik,* XV, 66–68.
[49] Despatch of August 3, *ibid.,* XV, 68–69.
[50] *Ibid.,* XV, 69–71.
[51] Hay to the Department of State, July 28, 1898, MS. Department of State, Despatches, Germany; *Die Grosse Politik,* XV, 71–72.

THE PACIFIC REALM AND AUSTRALIA ~ 1927

to dispose of all her distant colonies. Richthofen instructed him forthwith to make inquiries regarding the Philippines, the Sulus, the Carolines, and other South Sea Islands, as well as with respect to Fernando Po and the Canaries.[52] When Richthofen learned soon afterwards, however, that the Spanish-American Peace Protocol (August 12) had placed the fate of the Philippine group in the hands of the peace commission, his interest in these islands appears to have diminished. The naval detachment in Manila Bay was soon reduced and Diederichs himself was ordered to Batavia to represent Germany at the coronation of the Queen of the Netherlands. Germany still entertained some hope that the United States would not oppose her acquisition of a coaling station or two somewhere in the archipelago, but thenceforth German diplomatic activity was directed principally toward the Ladrones and the Carolines.[53]

The Ladrone and Caroline Questions

On August 13, 1898, Radowitz was instructed to make inquiries looking toward the purchase of Kusaie, Ponape, and Yap. The Spanish government deemed it unwise to make a definite disposition of these possessions while peace negotiations were in progress.[54] Nevertheless, persistent negotiations on the part of Germany led to the following provisional agreement on September 10, 1898:

"The governments of Germany and Spain have agreed that the islands of Kusaie, Ponape, and Yap, of the Caroline archipelago, shall be ceded to Germany for an indemnity the amount of which shall be fixed later. However, for the final treaty concerning the cession of said islands it will be necessary to await the decision of the conference of Paris regarding the sovereignty of Spain over the Philippine archipelago.

"Until this arrangement can be submitted to the constitutional sanction prescribed by the laws of the two countries the governments concerned pledge themselves to maintain the strictest secrecy."

The conclusion of the treaty was postponed in order that its terms might not interfere with the negotiations of the Spanish peace delegates at Paris. The stipulation of secrecy resulted from the desire not to irritate the United States as well as from the fear that a publication of the terms of the pact might arouse the ambitions of the other Naval Powers, especially England, and thus endanger the remainder of Spain's colonies. In addition to this agreement to sell

[52] *Die Grosse Politik*, XV, 72–74.
[53] *Ibid.*, XV, 74, note.
[54] *Ibid.*, XV, 74–75.

the three Carolinas, the Spanish Minister of State expressed a willingness to grant Germany favorable consideration in any future disposal of Spanish insular possessions.[55]

During the sessions of the Spanish-American Peace Conference which sat in Paris from October 1 to December 10, the Spanish government made at least two appeals for German backing against the United States. Late in October the Spanish ambassador in Paris, León y Castillo, approached his German colleague, Count Münster, and inquired whether the Kaiser would support an intervention of the Powers in favor of Spain. Münster replied that he had no instructions regarding the matter but expressed his personal opinion that pressure could be exerted neither in Paris nor in Washington. Any such move would wound the exaggerated pride of the Yankees and hence do more harm than good. Replying to Münster's report of this interview with Castillo, Richthofen informed Münster that the Spanish ambassador in Berlin had also broached this subject and had been told that Germany could perhaps serve Spanish interests best by maintaining an attitude of reserve and avoiding all incentives for American suspicion. He directed Münster to make a similar statement to Castillo, but to do it in such a way as to lead Spain to believe that the Kaiser was greatly interested in seeing her emerge from the conference with as many colonial possessions as possible, for His Majesty was anxious that Spain should cherish a sentiment of gratitude toward Germany. Again, on November 5, Spain raised a cry of indignation because the United States demanded the Philippines and the Sulu Islands and offered in return only an indemnity of two hundred million *pesetas* or less. The Spanish Minister of State urged an intervention of the Powers under the leadership of Germany and Russia, but the German Emperor, who had remarked concerning the proposal of late October that intervention was out of the question,[56] now appeared to consider such a step more absurd than ever.[57]

By November 15 it became evident that American and German interests were likely to clash in other areas besides the Philippines. At that time Münster learned from the peace commissioners that the United States desired a cable station on the Carolinas and had therefore originally intended to demand all of those islands from Spain, but out of consideration for Germany had finally decided to demand only one of them. On receiving this news Richthofen instructed Münster to inform the American commissioners frankly

[55] *Die Grosse Politik*, XV, 75–77.
[56] "Bestimmt nicht!"
[57] "!! Das fehlte noch!" (See *ibid.*, XV, 78–81.)

that if the Carolines should cease to be Spanish Germany expected that they should be transferred to her. She felt that she was entitled to the group both on account of old claims and because of large German investments. Münster was also directed to allude to the assurance of the American ambassador at Berlin in 1885 that the United States claimed none of the Carolines and would regard the extension of her power into the islands of the Pacific as contrary to her long established policy. He was authorized to say, however, that the German government would be willing to allow the United States to establish a cable station in the Carolines in case the Mariannes should prove inappropriate.[58]

Münster at once discussed the matter with Whitelaw Reid, an influential member of the American peace delegation, who assured him that German claims to the Carolines would be respected. He said that the United States desired only one island for a cable station and meant to negotiate with Spain for the one best adapted to this purpose, probably Kusaie.[59]

The report of this interview did not allay German alarm. Kusaie was deemed by Germany to be the most important of the entire group, both because of its excellent harbors and because of its situation amidst the Carolines and the German protectorates of the Marshall Islands and New Guinea. Münster was therefore advised to point out these and other circumstances and to persuade Reid to use his influence in Washington to bring about a total renunciation of the Carolines. In return, Germany was ready to make far-reaching concessions to the Boston missionary station at Kusaie, concern for which she supposed to be the only motive for America's desire to acquire the island. Münster was also directed to suggest that Germany felt that her claims to the Sulu Islands, whose Sultan had placed himself under the protectorate of the Prussian King in 1866, should take precedence over those of every other Power save Spain. If, however, the United States would fully comply with Germany's wishes with respect to the Carolines, the German government would be equally compliant and content itself with only one of the Sulus (appropriate for a coaling station). Lastly, Münster was instructed to refer to the Anglo-German treaty of 1886 which pronounced all the islands now claimed by Germany to lie within Germany's sphere of influence.[60]

Speck von Sternburg, German *chargé* in Washington, was given

[58] Münster to the Foreign Secretary, November 16, and Richthofen to Münster, November 21, 1898, *ibid.*, XV, 81–83.
[59] See Richthofen to Bülow November 22, 1898, *ibid.*, XV, 83–85.
[60] *Loc. cit.*

similar instructions. He was also directed to emphasize the fact that public opinion in Germany would be deeply offended if the United States should take any of the Caroline Islands. This would be true above all in the case of Kusaie. For the sake of their friendship since the days of Frederick the Great and in view of their future proximity in the Pacific, the United States must be urged to abandon the project. If in addition to such abandonment the United States would grant Germany one of the Sulu Islands for a coaling station, the political relations of the two nations would then be placed upon a most intimate footing.[61]

On November 28 and 30 Sternburg had interviews with Secretary of State Hay. The last of these proved more satisfactory than the first. Hay assured the German ambassador, during the second interview, that the United States valued German friendship very highly and had no intention of running counter to her wishes. The United States could not abandon the idea of securing a cable station in the South Pacific, but she would be willing to exchánge Kusaie for another island—one of the Marshall group, for instance. The American government had never intended to take all the Caroline Islands. It might even be willing to cede one of the Sulu Islands to Germany as a favor, but not in recognition of a legal claim, for the Anglo-German agreement regarding the Sulus was not deemed binding upon the United States. If Germany had any proposals regarding the matter, Hay would be glad to consider them.[62]

Early in December negotiations with Spain concerning the South Sea Islands were resumed. The Spanish government inquired if Germany would not prefer to buy all the Carolines and then settle the matter of an American cable station with the United States. Germany refused to assume this responsibility, but expressed a desire to acquire the rest of the group, the Pelew (or Palau) Islands included. She likewise evinced a disposition to purchase the Mariannes (except Guam), Fernando Po, and one of the Canaries.[63]

For dynastic reasons the Spanish government feared to dispose of the Spanish islands adjacent to the African coast when it was just losing the Philippines. It also feared that such a step would arouse English ambitions. It did, however, sign a secret provisional treaty, on December 21, which considerably enlarged the cessions provided in the secret agreement of September 10. By this December pact Spain agreed to sell to Germany, for a sum to be fixed in the future, not only all of the Carolines, but also the Pelews and the

[61] Instructions of November 26, 1898, *ibid.*, XV, 85–86.
[62] Sternburg to the Foreign Secretary, November 30, *ibid.*, XV, 86–87.
[63] *Ibid.*, XV, 87–89.

Mariannes (except Guam). Indisposition to offend the United States may perhaps be seen in this exception of Guam as well as in the failure to include Kusaie in the December agreement until it was learned that this island did not form a part of the Spanish-American peace regulations signed on December 10.[64] Thenceforth Germany felt justified in looking upon the arrangement with Spain as one which solely and exclusively concerned the contracting parties.

And yet Germany was willing to talk the matter over with the United States, and even went so far as to ask for official assurance of non-interference. This she received from John Hay, but the American Secretary of State took advantage of the occasion to inform Germany that her former protest in regard to Kusaie had caused displeasure in Washington. Hay then suggested that the United States might take the unowned Wake Island for a cable station, but expressed a doubt as to its adequacy for the purpose. In case it should prove inappropriate, Hay remarked that the United States would like to negotiate with Germany for one of the Marshall Islands (Gaspar Rico), for which she would be glad to grant Germany a coaling station on the Sulus.[65]

Holleben was advised to tell Hay, in response to these suggestions, that Wake Island had always been considered by Germany as a part of the Marshall Islands, but that Germany did not desire to press this point. Germany would quite willingly cede Wake or Gaspar Rico, or even Eniwetok, and hoped the United States would soon decide upon the island of the Sulu group which she preferred to transfer to Germany.[66]

Only one more conference between Hay and Holleben is dealt with in the published correspondence. It took place early in January, 1899, and was unsatisfactory to Germany. Hay's attitude was far less obliging than it had been formerly. He alluded again to Kusaie, or Strong Island, as he called it, remarking that it was the most appropriate place for an American cable station. He likewise intimated that Germany should be content with the mere lease of a coaling station in the Sulu archipelago, and spoke of the irritation that would arise in the Cabinet and Senate of the United States should these negotiations become known before the ratification of the Spanish-American peace treaty.[67]

Bülow thought that Hay was influenced by the storm of indigna-

[64] *Die Grosse Politik*, XV, 90-94.

[65] *Ibid.*, XV, 94-97.

[66] Bülow to Holleben, January 4 and 12, 1899, *ibid.*, XV, 97-98.

[67] Holleben to the Foreign Secretary, undated but received on January 15, 1899.

tion against Germany then passing over the United States, chiefly caused by the large meat-packing industries which resented the new German meat-inspection law.[68] In his comment to the Kaiser on this interview Bülow suggested that Germany should not allow herself to be driven to new concessions because of this rekindling spirit of animosity. America had already officially declared through the Paris Peace Commission that she had abandoned her Kusaie project in favor of Germany and that arrangements concerning the South Sea Islands now left to Spain were a purely Spanish-German affair.[69] There was no reason why Germany should reopen this question, nor should she condescend to enter upon negotiations for a lease of a coaling station on the Sulu archipelago in exchange for a lease to America of a coaling station on Kusaie when a Sulu island had already been adjudged to her in principle.[70]

Bülow was plainly piqued. Perhaps his attitude may be further explained by the rumor of a revolt of the natives in Ponape, said to have been instigated by American missionaries. Bülow feared that the United States might be persuaded by the Boston missionary station to interfere and thus get a permanent hold upon the island. He accordingly recommended that a German man-of-war be stationed in the Carolines until their future should be decided. The Emperor first gave his consent, but soon afterwards canceled the order because of the crisis threatened by the Fashoda incident and of anxiety to avoid a collision with the United States. He said that "it was now the task of diplomacy to avoid difficulties and misunderstandings with the United States so long as that was compatible with the dignity of the Empire." [71]

The negotiations respecting the South Sea Islands were then brought to a speedy and definite conclusion. On February 4, 1899, Germany agreed to pay Spain twenty-five million *pesetas* for the Caroline, the Pelew, and the Marianne Islands (except Guam). Spain also bound herself to allow Germany, in addition to these concessions, to have first option in case the Spanish government ever de-

---

[68] Keim, *op. cit.*, Ch. IV, discusses these commercial difficulties at some length. See also U. S. *For. Relations* (1896–1898), index.

[69] See Bülow to Holleben, December 28, 1898, *ibid.*, XV, 94–96.

[70] Bülow to Wilhelm II, January 15, 1899, *ibid.*, XV, 99–101.

[71] *Ibid.*, XV, 99–101, note.

This corresponds with Bülow's statement, made in 1914, that friction between the United States and Germany "reached its height in February, 1899, so that it seemed desirable strongly to advocate preparations for a better understanding between the two nations . . ." (*Imperial Germany* [New York, Dodd, Mead, 1914], p. 50).

cided to alienate Fernando Po.[72] The treaty was finally ratified in June, 1899—almost three months after the ratification of the agreement which concluded the Spanish-American War.[73] The United States had not acquired a cable station in the Carolines, but neither had Germany obtained a coaling station in the Sulus, which went to the United States along with the Philippines and Guam. Moreover, on January 17, 1899, an American man-of-war had seized Wake Island,[74] in spite of the German contention that it was in reality one of the Marshall group.

Conclusion

What generalizations may be made with respect to the attitude of the European Powers and especially of Germany in this second phase of the Spanish-American War? There is no doubt that Germany was more deeply interested than in the matter of Cuban mediation. The government revealed, however, neither an overweening eagerness to interfere nor a policy of adventurous aggressiveness. Neither the Filipino insurgents nor Spain herself could tempt it to take over the Philippines as a protectorate or in escrow. Nor does Germany appear to have sought to defeat American interests in the Philippines. It was a long time before the German diplomats or even the American statesmen themselves knew what these interests were, and plans for neutralization or division of the islands were dictated less by the wish to hinder the growth of the United States than by the desire—which seems to have been the primary motive of all of Germany's activities during the second phase of the Spanish-American War—to secure either a fair share of the Spanish spoils during the general distribution or compensation elsewhere. Aggressiveness here related as much to other Powers as to the United States. In fact Germany appears to have preferred, after the first of July, to reach her ends—which Andrew D. White more than once pronounced legitimate—in harmony with the United States and on the basis of the principle of "live and let live." The impartial historian will perhaps record the view that Germany was fully as "moderate" as the United States in the Pacific phase of this war with Spain. Of course it must be admitted that Germany's moderation was due in part to the coldness with which all projects for neutrali-

[72] *Die Grosse Politik,* XV, 102–103.

[73] *Ibid.,* XV, 104–105 and notes; French Ensor Chadwick, *The Relations of the United States and Spain* (New York, Scribner's, 1909), II, 427–473.

[74] John Bassett Moore, *Digest of International Law* (Washington, Government Printing Office, 1906), I, 555.

zation and distribution of the spoils were received by France, Russia, and Spain, and in part to a realization of the need of American friendship. Possibly Germany might have been more aggressive if international combinations and attitudes had been different, but here again one enters the realm of speculation; and, besides, it was an era characterized by lust for colonies on the part of all the Powers. Even Germany's secret colonial treaties with Spain lose something of their sinister aspect—if indeed this is not too strong a term—when it is borne in mind that they were not binding until after the conclusion of peace. And if Admiral Diederichs's conduct at Manila Bay was really offensive, it was out of harmony with the course pursued by his superiors at Berlin.

With reference to the entire war it must be concluded that official Germany, whatever their desires and aspirations, observed a neutrality which, in the words of Andrew D. White, was neither "cold nor grudging" but "all that could be desired." [75] The Kaiser and his diplomatic staff had monarchial interests to protect and colonial ambitions to realize, but they also saw the importance of avoiding the hostility of the United States.

It is proper to note also that the documents from the German archives do not justify a change of view with respect to the British attitude. It is a well-known fact that the British naval officer at Manila Bay (Captain Chichester) was friendly, that the Royal Family was sympathetic, that the press was generally favorable, that Colonial Secretary Joseph Chamberlain actually suggested an Anglo-American alliance in a speech made at Birmingham on May 13, 1898, and that Ambassador Hay believed that the United States "could have [had] the practical assistance of the British Navy," if this had been desired.[76] Except for the contention that Pauncefote took the initiative in an attempt to obtain joint condemnation of America's war upon Spain, the German documents tend to confirm the deep sympathy of Britain. After April 14, 1898, German officials observed this attitude on every hand; and even in regard to the Pauncefote incident itself they convey the impression that the ambassador acted with the intention of drawing the Continental Powers into an awkward position with reference to the United States.

As for Austria-Hungary, France, and Russia, it would seem that they played little more than a minor rôle. Germany agreed to the

[75] See his Leipzig speech of July 4, 1898, and his *Autobiography* (1907), II, 168.

[76] Reuter, *op. cit.*; R. B. Mowat, *The Diplomatic Relations of Great Britain and the United States* (1925), p. 280; and authorities cited by each.

joint mediatory note of April 6 largely to please Austria [77] and declined to participate in the proposed joint action of April 14 largely because Russia disapproved the step. Similarly, it appears that she abstained from pressing the neutralizing project on one occasion mainly because it was coldly received by France and Russia. Yet the documents make it clear that she was usually most concerned with the attitude of England and the United States.

[77] The London *Times* correspondent at Vienna in 1898 said in 1924 that the Austrian Ambassador to Rome was very hostile towards the United States. "With an acrimony rare in a man of his courteous temperament, he animadverted on the criminal shortsightedness of England in not opposing the designs of the United States. He assured me that the Emperor Francis Joseph, like the German Emperor, believed that the moment had come for the States of Europe jointly to make a stand against American high-handedness, and to bring the United States to reason. Indeed if England persisted in maintaining her foolish attitude, which was really encouraging the United States to flout Europe, she might find that Europe would turn against her. Germany, Austria-Hungary, France, and Russia would be ready to join in a European manifestation, and, if England would play her part, Italy might join too. Baron Pasetti [the Austro-Hungarian Ambassador to Rome] therefore urged me to represent to the British public the extreme expediency of concerted European action lest an opportunity be let slip that might never recur." (Quoted in Mowat, *op. cit.*, p. 281.)

CHAPTER XI

THE VENEZUELAN IMBROGLIO (1902–1903)

A WAR psychology and the hasty inferences of a contemporary press have given an erroneous interpretation of the Venezuelan crisis of 1902–1903. It is necessary to reconsider the whole matter if one desires to arrive at a correct understanding of what actually occurred.

Political Conditions in Venezuela in 1900; Grievances of the Powers

The opening of the twentieth century found Venezuela in a distressed and bankrupt condition. For several decades the country had been torn and impoverished by civil strife and political corruption. People and resources alike had been the prey of adventurers and rascals. The ruling class, consisting of only about six per cent of the population, not only had exploited the country and wasted its revenues, but had separated into hostile factions which impressed the lower classes into armies that fought for the opportunity of engaging in national plunder. Actuated sometimes by a sincere interest in the material advancement of the nation but more often by mere desire to increase the spoils, these politicians bargained concessions to foreigners who had entered Venezuela in search of trade or of such grants as corrupt officials could offer. These concessions tended to introduce an international element into the local disorders of the country.

From 1898 to 1902 conditions were worse than usual. Cipriano Castro, a cattle-man and bold *caudillo* of the western mountainous region, was carrying on a bloody civil war in order to secure the government and consolidate his power. Foreigners, who suffered along with Venezuelans, were very loath to submit their complaints to the exclusive jurisdiction of the Venezuelan government. Castro was a dictator who paid little respect either to the law or to the constitution. In fact he had not been in power long before he had "a majority of the members of the supreme court arrested, imprisoned, and finally removed from office for intimating that they would not decide a case in the manner desired by the Chief Executive." [1]

[1] Minister Francis B. Loomis to John Hay, February 22, 1901, in *Sen. Doc.* No. 413, 60 Cong., 1 Sess. (Ser. 5257), p. 332.

Instead of appealing to Castro for redress of their grievances, the nationals of several of the European states sought the aid of their home governments. By the closing days of the year 1902, Germany, England, and Italy were ready to undertake joint action for the purpose of obtaining satisfaction for the losses and injuries suffered by their subjects in Venezuela.

The claims whose immediate adjustment these Powers were now prepared to demand of Venezuela amounted to less than sixty-two million bolivars, or about twelve million dollars. Like most claims of this nature they fall into two categories; namely, those based upon contractual obligations of the Venezuelan government and those arising from financial losses and personal injuries suffered during the recent revolution. The most important of the German demands, for instance, related to interest seven years in arrears on Venezuelan bonds, the payment of dividends guaranteed by Venezuela on a German-built railroad, and indemnity for damages, injuries, forced loans, and inconveniences suffered during the civil war of 1898-1900. The claims of England and Italy were of the same general nature and differed only in detail. Moreover, it should be noted that similar claims were being asserted by citizens and subjects of the United States, France, Belgium, Mexico, Spain, Sweden and Norway, and the Netherlands.[2]

The imbroglio passed through three phases. The first lasted from December, 1901, when drastic action first began seriously to be considered, until December 17, 1902, when Germany, England, and Italy accepted limited arbitration in principle. The second phase —which was characterized by a long discussion over payment for claims withheld from arbitration, preferred consideration for the claims of the blockading Powers, and certain details of procedure— continued from December 18, 1902 to February 14, 1903, when all arrangements for adjudication of the claims were finally effected and the blockade was lifted. The third phase—of minor importance here— related to the final awards of the mixed commissions and The Hague Tribunal. The labor of these bodies was not completed until February, 1904.

The First Phase

In a survey of the Venezuelan affair two important facts must be kept in mind. First, negotiations for an Anglo-German alliance had been in progress since 1899, and although nothing had been ac-

---

[2] *Sen. Doc.* No. 316, 58 Cong., 2 Sess. (Ser. 4620), p. 480 ff.; *ibid.*, No. 119, 58 Cong., 3 Sess. (Ser. 4769), p. 757 ff.; *Foreign Relations* (1903), p. 871.

complished, an understanding may still have been considered remotely possible. Secondly, both England and Germany were eager to avoid giving offense to the United States; both thought of the United States as a possible ally, and each was determined not to allow the other to gain any advantage in this rivalry for American friendship.[3]

The first suggestion of a joint Anglo-German action against Venezuela appears to have come from the British Foreign Office on January 2, 1902.[4] Chancellor Bülow looked with favor upon the project, but the Kaiser, suspicious of England, declared that the suggestion was too vague. He also noted that England might take advantage of German proposals of joint action to arouse suspicion against Germany in the United States and thus destroy the effect of the contemplated visit of Prince Henry. "Not until after the expiration of Henry's mission," remarked the Kaiser.[5]

The question of coöperative coercion was accordingly not seriously considered until October, 1902. By the 12th of the following month the two Powers had virtually agreed upon a line of procedure, but on the next day the British government, acting without the knowledge of Germany, handed another ultimatum to Venezuela, the third in the past six months.[6] Apparently London was hesitating at the last moment to strike a bargain with Berlin. The answer of Venezuela proved unacceptable, however, and it was not long until the arrangement for joint action was completed. Each Power was to

---

[3] Since Italy's rôle was a minor one, it will receive little attention in this discussion. On Anglo-German relations at this period see *The Cambridge History of British Foreign Policy* (1925), III, 276 ff.

[4] *Die Grosse Politik*, XVII, 242, note. The British correspondence recently published does not confirm this view, but I have been informed by a reliable authority that documents exist in the Foreign Office of the British government which indicate that the suggestion of joint action originated with Lansdowne.

[5] Prince Henry's visit was designed to "win the Americans with manner and appearance, to convince them of the appreciation of His Majesty for the great and rapidly growing American people as well as of the usefulness of good relations between the Germans and the Americans, who are not separated by any political differences but are bound instead by numerous and weighty interests, ancient traditions, and ties of blood." The Prince was not to speak on his own initiative of affairs in Central and South America, and especially was he not to speak in detail of German designs in these Latin-American countries. If the Americans revealed anxiety with reference to German influence and possible German acquisitions in this part of the world Prince Henry was to treat the matter as an absurd phantom, refer to the many problems which Germany must solve elsewhere, and declare that Germany desired "peace throughout the Western Hemisphere and friendly relations with the United States." He was not, however, to make a free and formal explanation. (*Ibid.*, XVI, 243, note).

[6] *Ibid.*, XVII, 246–255; *Parliamentary Debates*, Fourth *Series* (1902), XCV, 1083–1095.

present Venezuela an ultimatum at the same moment, answer to which would be required in twenty-four hours. In case of an unfavorable reply, Venezuelan gunboats were to be seized, and then, if further action should become necessary, the ports of the country were to be blockaded. There was to be full and frank coöperation between Germany and England, and neither Power was to withdraw without the consent of the other.[7]

Affairs now moved rapidly toward a crisis. On December 7 the British and German ultimata were delivered to the Venezuelan government. Venezuela's response was unsatisfactory, and on the following day both legations withdrew from Caracas. On December 9 four Venezuelan gunboats were seized and three of them sunk. On December 11 Great Britain ordered the blockade of five Venezuelan ports and the mouths of the Orinoco. At about the same time Italy expressed a desire to participate in the action and offered to furnish two cruisers. The offer was eagerly accepted by the German government, which hoped that England and Italy might move into the foreground and thus divert any hostility which might be aroused in the United States against Germany.[8] Two days later a German and a British cruiser bombarded two forts at Puerto Cabello in retaliation for the seizure of a British steamer and an alleged insult to the British flag. On the same day Venezuela submitted through the United States an arbitration proposal. Soon afterwards the British and the German governments—the former on December 16 and the latter on December 17—agreed to arbitration in principle, reserving certain "first rank" claims. Thus Venezuela had asked for arbitration just four days after the allies began their coercive action and the allies had accepted a limited arbitration in principle just four days after Venezuela proposed it.[9] So ended the first phase.

Up to this point the United States had taken little part in the affair. The allies had kept Washington informed of their procedure, but formal protest had not been made. The American secretary of state had only remarked that "the United States Government, although they regretted that European powers should use force against Central and South American countries, could not object

---

[7] *Die Grosse Politik,* XVII, 255–258.

[8] The Kaiser commented thus on the despatch which informed him of Italy's desire to participate: "Approved. Italy may take part and the more ships England sends the better. Just so our action keeps to the rear and theirs comes into the foreground. We shall merely participate in the British programme. . . . We shall let our flag follow the lead of the British." (*Ibid.,* XVII, 260).

[9] *Sen. Doc.* No. 119, 58 Cong., 3 Sess. (Ser. 4769), pp. 637, *passim.*

to their taking steps to obtain redress for injuries suffered by their subjects, provided that no acquisition of territory was contemplated." [10] The United States had merely transmitted the Venezuelan arbitration proposal of December 13 without comment. Only with reference to a "pacific blockade," which Germany desired in order to avoid consulting the *Bundesrat,* was any objection raised. On this point the United States held the view that under international law there was no such thing as a pacific blockade. The British maritime lawyers agreed with the American contention, and Germany thereupon consented to a regular blockade.[11]

Before the Venezuelan entanglement had passed through this first phase, however, indications that American and British public opinion would have to be taken into consideration were not lacking. As early as December 12 Bülow had pointed out the desirability of avoiding every action which might give support to the impression commonly reported and widely circulated in both the English and the American press, that Germany was the initiator of the movement to coerce Venezuela. He said that most of the adverse criticism of Germany had been called forth by the sinking of the Venezuelan cruisers. He then remarked that this event had called anti-German agitation again to life and respectfully advised that due attention be given to the enlargement of Germany's military force.[12] On the following day Count Metternich, German ambassador in London, also called attention to press criticism, in England and elsewhere, of the gunboat episode and suggested the advisability of a published statement in justification of the act.[13]

During the next few days the tension in diplomatic circles became very decided. Metternich reported that Lord Lansdowne, British foreign secretary, was hesitant and uncertain, that King Edward viewed the joint action against Venezuela with disfavor, and that among political circles in England there was a widespread fear that the movement might lead to "coolness" with the United States.[14] From Holleben, the German ambassador in the United States, came a telegram stating that German-American and English-American financial circles in New York were speaking with anxiety about transactions in Venezuela; that the press, though hitherto reason-

[10] *Sen. Doc.* No. 119, 58 Cong., 3 Sess. (Ser. 4769), pp. 635–638. Germany had placed plans for a coercive project before the United States as early as December 11, 1901. (See *House Document* No. 1, Part I, 57 Cong., 1 Sess. (Ser. 4268), pp. 192–194.)

[11] *Foreign Relations* 1903, pp. 452, 254 ff.; *Die Grosse Politik,* XVII, 241, 242, 245, 237, 258; *British Documents on the Origins of the War,* II, 160–161.

[12] *Die Grosse Politik,* XVII, 258–260.

[13] *Ibid.,* XVII, 261–262.

[14] *Ibid.,* XVII, 262–263.

ably quiet and not unfriendly, was beginning to assume a sharper tone; that some held the view that England, lacking the support of Parliament, might break away from Germany and reach out a hand to the United States behind Germany's back; that certain well-informed merchants of Latin America were of the opinion that German trade would suffer; that, moreover, it was being urged that after the cannons had spoken and Germany had shown the world her ability and determination to support her just claims, it would be wise and create a good impression in all America if the Berlin government would accept the principle of arbitration. Holleben urged that this course could be followed without evil consequences, since Germany had already indicated a willingness to submit certain designated claims to mixed commissions.[15] "I believe," concluded Holleben, "that after all this suggestion may deserve some consideration." [16] At the same time Metternich sent another telegram which reported an interview with Lansdowne. During the interview the British foreign secretary had told Metternich that the cabinet favored arbitration, and that strong opposition to the joint action against Venezuela was developing both in Parliament and in the country at large. He had also called attention to signs that in the United States a storm of opposition was approaching, against which the Washington government would be powerless to proceed. Reflecting upon the situation, Metternich remarked that if the English government were supported by Parliament, the press, and public opinion, Germany might complacently look forward to further developments in the Venezuelan affair and not concern itself with "North American insolence." "But, alas," he continued, "this is not the case." He then concluded his telegram with the advice that the sooner Germany withdrew from the joint affair with England the better, and recommended arbitration. With such information and recommendations before it, the German government had agreed to the principle of limited arbitration in December, 1902.[17] Not official pressure exerted by Washington, but the state of public opinion in the United States and England, had been responsible for this concession.

The Second Phase

As matters approached the second stage, the United States revealed a disposition to take a more active part. On the same day

[15] This position had been taken in a telegram from Richthofen, of the German Foreign Office, to Metternich, dated February 14. (*Ibid.*, XVII, 260–261.)
[16] *Ibid.*, XVII, 264.
[17] *Ibid.*, XVII, 265–268. See also *British Documents*, II, 162.

that the German government agreed to limited arbitration, but after Germany already had reached this decision, the American ambassadors at London and Berlin, following out Hay's instructions, had repeated the Venezuelan proposal of arbitration "with strong commendation." [18] On the following day Secretary Hay talked over the situation with Count von Quadt, German *chargé* in Washington, and assured him that President Roosevelt as well as he himself reposed full trust in Germany so far as the Venezuelan affair was concerned. Moreover, Hay is reported to have declared also that the American government was firmly resolved not to interfere in any way. Nevertheless Hay at the same time expressed the view that because of the excited and nervous state of Congress and the public a speedy solution of the problem was most desirable.[19] A few days later the allied Powers, yielding to American opinion, requested Roosevelt to serve as arbiter—a step which was calculated to allay American apprehensions, but which, owing to the President's refusal to accept the offer, failed to bring the difficulties any nearer to a final settlement.[20] It was then decided to refer the question to The Hague.

Meanwhile the three allied Powers proceeded to establish a formal blockade of the Venezuelan ports (December 20, 1902).[21] Arrangements for payment of first-rank claims and the adjustment of the details of arbitration promised some difficulty, and the cruisers of the allies might therefore prove useful.

As the year drew to a close Germany and England presented detailed memoranda of their demands and concessions. First-rank claims—namely, German claims originating in the Venezuelan civil war of 1898–1900 and British claims based upon the imprisonment of British subjects and the seizure of British shipping—were strictly excluded. Venezuela would have to settle directly for these claims, which amounted to about £132,000, and begin payment at once. Even the other claims were to be withheld from a court of arbitration until the Venezuelan government admitted its responsibility in principle.[22]

In declining to serve as arbiter President Roosevelt had suggested

[18] *Sen. Doc.* No. 119, 58 Cong., 3 Sess., pp. 677, 679; *Foreign Relations* (1903), pp. 421, 424, 453, 792–798.

[19] *Die Grosse Politik*, XVII, 269.

[20] *Sen. Doc.* No. 119, 58 Cong., 3 Sess., pp. 684, 686–689; *Die Grosse Politik*, XVII, 270.

[21] *Sen. Doc.* No. 119, p. 685.

[22] *Ibid.*, pp. 272–275, 401–406, 687, *passim*. On December 29, Señor Luis Drago, Argentine minister of foreign affairs, attempted in vain to come to Venezuela's assistance with what has since become the rather famous Drago Doctrine. The United States refused to commit itself to the principle that armed force should not be employed in the collection of contractual obligations.

that a preliminary diplomatic conference be held in Washington for arranging the details of arbitration. This suggestion the allied Powers accepted, although Germany did so with some reluctance.[23] Herbert W. Bowen, minister of the United States in Venezuela, was chosen to represent the Caracas government in the conference. It was not until the latter part of January (1903) that formal preliminary negotiations began at Washington. Many difficulties were confronted and once more the people of the United States became impatient and irritated.

Soon after Bowen arrived in Washington to defend Venezuela's position, news of a ruthless German bombardment of Fort San Carlos was published in the American press. The public immediately lost its temper. "I hear indirectly," cabled Count von Quadt, "that Secretary Hay expressed himself very bitterly concerning our action. . . . At no time since the Venezuelan entanglement has feeling against us been so heated as now." [24] The British public likewise became hostile, and the British government prepared to beat a retreat. On January 23 Britain promised to return to Venezuela the boats which she had captured. Germany felt compelled to follow suit.[25] Four days later an agent of the British Foreign Office came to the German minister in London to plead for a curtailment of German demands for cash in payment for first-rank claims. Inasmuch as Britain had decided to be content with £5,500 instead of £66,000, would not Germany agree to a similar reduction? The refusal of Germany to consent to this arrangement would shake the British cabinet, immeasurably increase ill-humor toward Germany, and possibly seriously disturb the future relations of the two countries.[26] The next day Germany cabled acceptance of the reduction.[27]

The question as to whether the claims of the blockading Powers should have preferential treatment now took the center of the stage. Bowen insisted that all of the Powers should be placed on an equal footing. England was hesitant, and Germany appeared to be strongly opposed to such an arrangement. The Venezuelan affair had reached a most critical condition.

On January 28 King Edward had an interview with Count Metternich for the purpose of discussing the difficulty. The King expressed

[23] Die Grosse Politik, XVII, 270.

[24] Ibid., XVII, 274.

[25] Ibid., XVII, 275–276. Apparently the boats now held by Germany were merchant vessels. The gunboats had been sunk.

[26] Ibid., XVII, 278–279. Cf., likewise, Lansdowne, British foreign secretary, to Lascelles, the British ambassador in Berlin, Jan. 27, in British Documents II, 167.

[27] Die Grosse Politik, XVII, 279–280.

a strong desire to see the matter brought to an immediate conclusion. The Count replied that Germany entertained a similar desire but felt that she dare not come out of Venezuela with empty hands. He also complained that British reporters and journalists were largely responsible for the attitude of the American press toward the Venezuelan undertaking.[28]

On the same day Charlemagne Tower, ambassador of the United States at Berlin, reported a conversation of January 27 with the Kaiser, who complained of the recent attacks of the British newspapers. He "declared that the treatment of Germany in regard to the expedition against Venezuela was entirely unfair, because, so far from it being true that Germany had drawn England into this undertaking, the fact is that the expedition was planned in England before Germany knew anything about it. The Emperor said that during his last visit to England Lord Lansdowne had explained to him the difficulties which the British government had met with in attempting to enforce the claims of British subjects in Venezuela, and had told him that . . . the British government believed it to be necessary to adopt stronger measures. Lord Lansdowne thereupon invited the German Emperor to unite with Great Britain in enforcing by joint action the claims of Great Britain and Germany against Venezuela," and the Emperor had accepted the invitation.[29]

On January 31 Count Speck von Sternburg, who had just arrived at Washington on a special mission, reported a conference with President Roosevelt, during which the President remarked that the Venezuelan affair had begun highly to irritate public opinion both in America and in Europe, and expressed the ardent hope that it might soon be settled.[30] Three days later Sternburg cabled a nervous report to Berlin. He said nothing of an interview with Roosevelt, but declared that Germany was sacrificing what little sympathy she had left in the United States. He also noted that the Latin-American states were taking offense and that "Dewey's fleet had received secret orders to hold itself in readiness." He respectfully advised acceptance of Bowen's offer of 30 per cent of the customs receipts of

[28] *Die Grosse Politik,* XVII, 281–282. On Jan. 28 White telegraphed from London: "I urge daily great danger of explosion of American opinion if delay in raising blockade is prolonged, which this Government fully realizes and is making every effort to secure Germany's assent to raise it." (State Department MS.)

[29] State Department MS.

[30] *Die Grosse Politik,* XVII, 285. Consult also the telegram of Herbert, British minister in Washington, to Lansdowne, Jan. 31, 1903, in *British Documents,* II, 168.

La Guaira and Porto Cabello for three months in lieu of preferential treatment.[31]

Meanwhile the English government had made up its mind to submit the matter of preferential treatment to arbitration.[32] Germany, however, still held out, and Lord Lansdowne, being "a man of honor," was not inclined to break his agreement with Germany. The crisis confronting the British ministry was vividly described in a private despatch written by Metternich to Bülow on February 4. The King, the Queen, and the Prince of Wales were developing a strong aversion to the joint action against Venezuela. They regarded the Germans as mischief-makers, particularly since the bombardment of San Carlos. English public opinion, forgetting that British vessels had bombarded Porto Cabello not long before, sympathized with Castro. The ministry was beginning to defend its policy in public speeches. If Parliament should convene as scheduled, on February 17, and begin to ask questions regarding the originator of the Venezuelan project, the cabinet would be seriously endangered. If President Roosevelt should lose patience, submit to the advice of the yellow press, and demand the lifting of the blockade, the ministry would be overturned in a moment's time.[33]

The Kaiser noted on the margin of this report that the probable successor of the Balfour-Chamberlain-Lansdowne cabinet might be hostile to German interests. Evidently the time had come for Germany to retreat. Accordingly, on February 6, the ambassadors of the three allied Powers in Washington agreed to submit the question of preferential treatment to President Roosevelt as arbiter.[34] Germany had apparently consented to this compromise as early as February 4.[35] The question of security for the balance of Germany's "first-rank" claims—namely those not covered by the cash payment of £5,500—caused a few more days of argument and the exertion of further British pressure on Germany, but the difficulties were overcome by February 12.

---

[31] *Die Grosse Politik*, XVII, 285–286.

[32] *Ibid.*, XVII, 284–285; *Sen. Doc.* No. 119, p. 741.

[33] *Die Grosse Politik*, XVII, 288–289.

[34] *Ibid.*, XVII, 287; *Sen. Doc.* No. 119, pp. 742, 747.

[35] "Baron Sternburg is instructed to remain squarely in line with Sir Michael Herbert [British *chargé* in Washington]"—Bülow to Metternich, Feb. 4, 1903. "The English Ambassador has been instructed to submit the question of preferential treatment to the President for arbitration. The Italian Ambassador and I have acceded to his desire."—Sternburg to the German Foreign Secretary, Feb. 6, 1903. (*Die Grosse Politik*, XVII, 287.)

The Third Phase

The crisis had now passed. Roosevelt was no more willing to serve as arbiter in February than he had been in the previous December, but this was a merely a matter of detail. The question of preferential treatment of the blockading Powers could be submitted to The Hague. The imbroglio had reached the third phase. All claims except those of "first rank," which had already been arranged, were left to the decision of mixed commissions. It is interesting to note, as bearing upon the justice of the claims, that barely one-fifth of them were allowed by these mixed commissions. On February 22, 1904, a special court of The Hague handed down an unanimous decision in favor of preferential treatment for the blockading Powers;[36] and so passed the Venezuelan episode into history.

Roosevelt and the Kaiser

It remains to inquire what part President Roosevelt played in the settlement and whether Germany entertained ulterior territorial designs. At the outset it is well to be reminded once more of two important facts: (1) Anglo-German negotiations for a general alliance had virtually failed by the opening of 1903; (2) both England and Germany were to all appearances eager for the friendship of the United States, and each was determined not to permit the other to steal a march in the cultivation of American favor.

Roosevelt has given his own account of the action which he took in order to hasten the settlement of the Venezuelan imbroglio. His course in the matter had been set forth for the first time by William Roscoe Thayer in his *Life and Letters of John Hay*, published late in 1915. Thayer's narrative was based upon a personal interview with Roosevelt and its accuracy was immediately questioned. Thereupon Roosevelt wrote Thayer a letter setting forth his conduct in detail as follows:

". . . I speedily became convinced that Germany was the leader, and the really formidable party in the transaction; and that England was merely following Germany's lead in rather half-hearted fashion. . . . I also became convinced that Germany intended to seize some Venezuelan harbor and turn it into a strongly fortified place of arms, on the model of Kiauchau, with a view to exercising some degree of control over the future Isthmian Canal, and over South American affairs generally.

[36] *Sen. Doc.* No. 316, 58 Cong. 2 Sess. (Ser. 4620), pp. 260, 291, 480, 510, 641 871, 888, 916, 942, 954.

"For some time the usual methods of diplomatic intercourse were tried. Germany declined to agree to arbitrate the question at issue between her and Venezuela, and declined to say that she would not take possession of Venezuelan territory, merely saying that such possession would be 'temporary'—which might mean anything. I finally decided that no useful purpose would be served by further delay, and I took action accordingly. I assembled our battle fleet, under Admiral Dewey, near Porto Rico, for 'maneuvers,' with instructions that the fleet should be kept in hand and in fighting trim, and should be ready to sail at an hour's notice. . . . I told John Hay that I would now see the German Ambassador, Herr von Holleben, myself, and that I intended to bring matters to an early conclusion . . .

"I saw the Ambassador, and explained that in view of the presence of the German Squadron on the Venezuelan coast I could not permit longer delay in answering my request for an arbitration, and that I could not acquiesce in any seizure of Venezuelan territory. The Ambassador responded that his Government could not agree to arbitrate, and that there was no intention to take 'permanent' possession of Venezuelan territory. I answered that Kiauchau was not a 'permanent' possession of Germany's—that I understood that it was merely held by a ninety-nine years' lease; and that I did not intend to have another Kiauchau, held by similar tenure, on the approach to the Isthmian Canal. The Ambassador repeated that his government would not agree to arbitrate. I then asked him to inform his government that if no notification for arbitration came within a certain specified number of days I should be obliged to order Dewey to take his fleet to the Venezuelan coast and see that the German forces did not take possession of any territory. He expressed very grave concern, and asked me if I realized the serious consequences that would follow such action; consequences so serious to both countries that he dreaded to give them a name. I answered that I had thoroughly counted the cost before I decided on the step, and asked him to look at the map, as a glance would show him that there was no spot in the world where Germany in the event of a conflict with the United States would be at a greater disadvantage than in the Caribbean Sea.

"A few days later the Ambassador came to see me, talked pleasantly on several subjects, and rose to go. I asked him if he had any answer to make from his government to my request, and when he said no, I informed him that in such event it was useless to wait as long as I had intended, and that Dewey would be ordered to sail twenty-four hours in advance of the time I had set. He expressed deep apprehension, and said that his government would not arbitrate. However, less than twenty-four hours before the time I had appointed for cabling the order to Dewey, the Embassy notified me that his Imperial Majesty the German Emperor had directed him to request me to undertake the arbitration myself. I felt and publicly expressed, great gratification at this outcome, and great appreciation of the course the German Government had finally agreed to take. Later I received the consent of the German Government to have the arbitration undertaken by The Hague Tribunal, and not by me." [37]

In a speech delivered in Chicago on September 27, 1917, Roosevelt again referred to the Venezuelan affair. At that time he said that he gave the German ambassador the following ultimatum: " 'Tell your government that in ten days it must arbitrate the matter or I will send Dewey down there.' " "Thirty days before," Roosevelt added, "I had ordered Dewey to take our fleet into West Indian waters." The account then continues as follows:

"About a week later the ambassador called on me and talked about the weather and tennis, and when I asked about the Venezuelan answer, he admitted that he had not dared send the message to his country. He told me he knew I could not be serious in the matter.

"I then told him that instead of allowing the three days that remained for an answer I would order Dewey to sail in forty-eight hours . . .

"Inside of thirty-six hours he came back smiling and said he had received instructions from the German government to notify me that they would arbitrate . . ." [38]

That Roosevelt's account of what he did is not mere wartime propaganda or political bombast is strongly supported by a letter which he wrote to Henry White on August 14, 1906. Here he describes his method of procedure with the Kaiser as follows:

"My course with him during the last five years has been uniform. . . . I have always been most polite with him, have done my best to avoid our taking any attitude which could possibly give him legitimate offense, and have endeavored to show him that I was sincerely friendly to him and to Germany. Moreover, where I have forced him to give way I have been sedulously anxious to build a bridge of gold for him and to give him the satisfaction of feeling that his dignity and reputation in the face of the world were safe. In other words, where I have had to take part of the kernel from him, I have been anxious that he should have all the shell possible, and have that shell painted any way he wished. At the same time

[37] J. B. Bishop, *Life and Times of Theodore Roosevelt* (1920), I, 222–224.
[38] *The Daily News* (Chicago), September 27, 1917.

I have had to speak with express emphasis to him on more than one occasion; and on one occasion (that of Venezuela) have had to make a display of force and to convince him definitely that I would use the force if necessary." [39]

Roosevelt then entered into the details of his action. "At the time of the Venezuela business," he continued, "I saw the German Ambassador privately myself; told him to tell the Kaiser that I had put Dewey in charge of our fleet to maneuver in West Indian Waters; that the world at large should know this merely as a maneuver and we should strive in every way to appear simply as coöperating with the Germans; but that I regretted to say that the popular feeling was such that I should be obliged to interfere, by force if necessary, if the Germans took any action which looked like the acquisition of territory there or elsewhere along the Caribbean; that this was not in any way intended as a threat, but as the position on the part of the Government which the American people would demand, and that I wanted him to understand it before the two nations drifted into such a position that trouble might come. I do not know whether it was a case of *post hoc* or *propter hoc,* but immediately afterward the Kaiser made to me the proposition that I should arbitrate myself, which I finally got him to modify so that it was sent to The Hague." [40]

Such are Roosevelt's accounts of his action in the Venezuelan difficulty. Before passing final judgment on their veracity one would have to make a thorough investigation of British and German archives. A tentative conclusion, however, may be hazarded at this time. It would appear that Roosevelt did in fact attempt to exert pressure upon Germany, but in his later narratives of his procedure he confused dates and diplomats. He probably did not bring pressure to bear upon Holleben in the middle of December, 1902, but upon Sternburg during the last of January and the first of February, 1903. [41] If he actually took such a step his action may have hastened Germany's agreement to follow England's lead in submitting the question of preferential treatment to arbitration. Two factors appear to have been responsible for this concession: (1) the report of the con-

[39] Bishop, *op. cit.,* II, 270–271.

[40] Rhodes, *The McKinley and Roosevelt Administrations* (1922), pp. 251–252.

[41] It will be recalled that Germany had agreed to accept arbitration in principle just eight days after the allies began coercive action against Venezuela and only four days after Venezuela asked for arbitration. This period would appear too short for the events described by Roosevelt to transpire. Holleben ceased to function as ambassador about December 17. *Die Grosse Politik* contains only one letter of Holleben's concerning the Venezuelan affair—that of Dec. 16, 1902—and it makes no reference to Roosevelt or the U. S. government or Admiral Dewey.

centration of Dewey's fleet and the hostility of American public opinion, and (2) news of a cabinet crisis in England. It is impossible to say which was more influential. One thing, however, is certain: Germany was very desirous of avoiding any course which might promote an alliance between the United States and Great Britain. It should also be remembered that Roosevelt had knowledge of the state of British public opinion, of the anxieties of the British cabinet, and of the fact that the English government was prepared both to give way on the matter of preferential treatment and to urge Germany to grant a similar concession.[42] Under the circumstances he could afford to be bellicose, just as John Quincy Adams and James Monroe had dared "blow a blast on the republican trumpet, while sheltered behind the shield of England."

Germany's Motives

With reference to German territorial ambitions, it must be admitted that Roosevelt was unduly alarmed. Germany's policy of bidding against England for the friendship of the United States would not have permitted the seizure and permanent retention of Venezuelan territory unless England could have been induced to participate in such action and to enter into a general alliance with Germany. With England as a possible enemy, Germany must seek the friendship of the United States or at least avoid any action which would tend to promote Anglo-Saxon *rapprochement*. So far, no evidence has come to light to indicate that either Power entertained ulterior motives hostile to the Monroe Doctrine at any time during the common action against Venezuela. Although Germany had said something about "temporary occupation" of Venezuelan soil in December, 1901, and Lord Lansdowne had at first favored the seizure of Venezuelan custom houses,[43] nothing further than the capture of gunboats and the blockade of ports appears to have been entertained after coöperative coercion had once begun. On December 14, 1902, the German government declared to the United States that it had "no intention whatever . . . to proceed beyond a warlike blockade."[44] Two days later Metternich remarked to Lansdowne: "The American government knows full well that we do not wish to establish ourselves in Venezuela."[45] At the same time the British foreign

---

[42] See Andrew D. White's telegrams of January 26 and 28, 1903 (State Department MS.)

[43] *House Doc.* No. 1, Part I, 57 Cong., 1 Sess. (Ser. 4268), pp. 192-194; *Die Grosse Politik*, XVII, 254-255.

[44] *Foreign Relations* (1903), p. 421.

[45] *Die Grosse Politik*, XVII, 263.

secretary and the Prime Minister declared in Parliament that they had no intention of landing troops or seizing territory.[46] Moreover, as late as January 27, 1903, when Metternich and Lansdowne were discussing possible guarantees for the immediate payment of first-rank claims, the latter appeared to be very doubtful of the wisdom of any pledge which might involve the occupation of Venezuelan soil. Metternich reported the interview without expressing his own attitude on this specific point.[47] That Germany was not bent upon such territorial occupation, however, appears to be indicated by her willingness to scale down the demand for cash payment on the very next day.[48]

So far as the immediate Venezuelan problem was concerned, the sole motive of the German government seems to have been a desire to indemnify and protect German subjects and to convince all the states of Latin America of Germany's ability and inclination to defend these subjects wherever they might reside. Bülow argued in September, 1902, for instance, that "a severe policy toward Venezuela would now be desirable for the sake of our reputation in Central and South America and the protection of the large and growing German interests there." [49] Again, on November 3, Bülow urged that if the unjust treatment of Germans in Venezuela remained unavenged, German influence in Central and South America would "necessarily suffer injury." [50] This was evidently Germany's only motive and it appears to be sufficient to explain German action throughout the Venezuelan difficulty.

Of course this does not mean that Germany under more favorable circumstances would not have been eager to seize Venezuelan territory or domain in other parts of Latin America. It merely indicates that the international stage was not set for such an act in 1902–1903, just as it had not been set for the partition of the Philippines or the occupation of a naval base in Santo Domingo in 1898.

A few days after the final arbitration agreement had been reached, President Roosevelt and Speck von Sternburg took a long ride together. The President once more referred to the Venezuelan entanglement. Sternburg's despatch (February 19, 1903) [51] reporting Roosevelt's remarks and the Kaiser's marginal comments thereon throw

---

[46] *Parliamentary Debates* (Fourth Series), CXVI, 1920, 1489.

[47] *Die Grosse Politik*, XVII, 278. The British correspondence indicates that Count Metternich favored the landing of troops and the seizure of the custom houses (*British Documents*, II, 167. Lansdowne to Lascelles, Jan. 27, 1903.)

[48] *Ibid.*, XVII, 279–280.

[49] *Ibid.*, XVII, 245.

[50] *Ibid.*, XVII, 248.

[51] *Ibid.*, XVII, 291–292.

significant light upon Germany's Latin-American aspirations as well as upon Roosevelt's attitude regarding them. This document would seem to furnish a fitting conclusion to the present chapter. It is accordingly given in full. The footnotes are the Kaiser's reactions written upon the margin.

"In the course of a long ride which I had with the President yesterday [52] he discussed various pending questions. First he declared himself highly pleased over the outcome of the Venezuelan transactions, which had made the best impression imaginable here with reference to Germany. He had emphasized upon my arrival here the urgent necessity of the most rapid settlement of the Venezuelan question because public opinion was irritated to a high degree on account of the continued blockade. The sinking of the Venezuelan ships and the bombardment of the forts during the negotiations had aroused immediate sympathy here for Venezuela and produced a critical situation. The German warships of the blockade had seen their future enemy in the fleet of Admiral Dewey; [53] Dewey's sailors, on the other hand [54] had regarded the German ships as their next object of attack. It had been high time to make an end to these conditions. Then it had been the German ships, but in six weeks it might probably be the English.

"After the President had turned the conversation to the South American republics, he remarked: The best guaranty he saw for improving conditions there lay in the expansion of German influence [55] which had already gained so firm a foothold in southern Brazil. In the creation of an independent state of Germans in Brazil he saw the best solution of the South American question.[56] I felt a certain cooling of the President's sympathy for England.[57]

"Touching upon the Alaskan question the President said: In case the approaching negotiations should come to nothing we would without further delay proceed to mark out the boundary line claimed by us and insist upon its acceptance.[58]

"Speaking of the causes underlying the anti-German agitation in the United States, the President explained candidly that it had been provoked through the action of Admiral Diederichs in Manila. The

[52] How good it is when the German representative of His Majesty can ride out with the President. W. Approved.

[53] They never dreamed of it.

[54] Very foolish of them.

[55] right.

[56] right.

[57] good.

[58] Good luck be with him! Of course John Bull will be sure to let that happen.

American people had seen therein an insult to their national hero, Admiral Dewey.[59]

"I felt that the President does not place absolute confidence in Germany's assurances with regard to her respect for the Monroe Doctrine. I took occasion to assure him emphatically that Germany does not think of acquiring territory in South and Central America." [60]

This is an extremely important document and should be subjected to careful scrutiny. It shows that Roosevelt had been bringing pressure to bear upon Sternburg since his arrival in the United States (about January 30, 1903). It suggests that the President had his mind upon Dewey's fleet. It reveals his apprehensions in regard to Germany's possible designs of violating the Monroe Doctrine. It likewise reveals the Kaiser's genuine interest in Latin America as a field for German enterprise and settlement and his jubilation at the prospect of a serious disagreement between England and the United States. Lastly, it shows that during the early months of 1903 the Kaiser was not unwilling to give to the United States a formal pledge that Germany entertained no territorial ambitions in Latin America. In brief, the document appears to clinch the main points which have been insisted upon in this chapter. With reference to Roosevelt's statement regarding the advisability of the establishment of an independent (*unabhängigen*) German state in southern Brazil, it should be noted that the President probably meant a separate state within the Brazilian Republic, although he may not have considered an independent German state absolutely unconnected with the German Empire dangerous to the security of the United States.[61]

[59] ! !

[60] good.

[61] It is with pleasure that I refer the reader, at this point, to Howard C. Hill's, *Roosevelt and the Caribbean,* which comes from the University of Chicago Press while I am reading the proofs of the present work.

CHAPTER XII

THE PAN-HISPANIC MOVEMENT

THE last century has witnessed a gradual drawing together of Spain and her former colonies in the New World. The growing friendship has been largely the result of Spanish effort, or, more accurately, of the efforts of a fairly large, intelligent, and enthusiastic group of Spaniards who have labored and are laboring for what they conceive to be the welfare of their country and the interest of the Spanish race. Racial and cultural solidarity has been in fact the keynote of their propaganda. Prior to the opening of the present century they were motivated by the idea of rallying around this slogan the kindred nations oversea with the view of winning allies for a prospective struggle with the United States. More recently, other motives have been prominent.

The Early Movement

In the 'fifties of the last century, when the remnants of the Spanish empire in the New World, as well as the integrity of the newly-formed Latin nations, were being threatened by the Anglo-American filibusters, Spanish propaganda sought to play upon the note of racial solidarity in order to induce the Hispanic Americans to unite among themselves and with Spain for the purpose of stemming the tide of invasion. Newspapers were established, books were written, and even Spanish diplomats labored to this end. In Mexico City alone at least three newspapers were founded during this period with the avowed purpose of upholding the interests of the Spanish race in America—the *Eco de España,* the *Correo de España* and *El Español.* On January 7, 1852, the last of these declared that the United States had designs upon all of the Hispanic-American republics, and that the latter should pursue a policy of solidarity and alliance with Spain for purposes of mutual defense. On July 30 of the following year the *Eco de España* came out with an editorial calling attention to the consistently aggressive policy of the United States as a source of imminent danger to the Spanish race on this side of the Atlantic.

During the month of September, 1854, the *Correo de España* contained several tirades against the colossal invader of the North, which it compared to a Russia unrestrained by the balance of power.[1] But perhaps the climax of this propaganda was reached in a small book published in Cádiz by Don José Ferrer de Couto, who advised an alliance between Spain and Mexico for the purpose of repelling the Yankee invaders, saving Cuba and, eventually, the remainder of Hispanic America from absorption, and effecting a Hispanic renaissance throughout the world![2]

And there was some attempt to put this idea of solidarity into practice. Early in 1856 the Spanish minister at Washington held conferences with the diplomatic agents of the Hispanic countries resident in the United States for the purpose of discussing plans of union. A project was drawn up which proposed to bind the nations to the south of the Rio Grande not to consent to the abridgment of the independence or the infringement of the territorial integrity of any of the signatory Powers, but to treat the invader or offender of any member of the prospective alliance as a common enemy. No provision was inserted, at the time, that would include Spain in the union, but the action of the Spanish minister was approved and the Spanish secretary of state considered the matter of sufficient importance to communicate it to the captain-general of Cuba.[3]

Yet, while certain Spaniards were urging a *rapprochement* between Spain and Hispanic America, the Spanish government was slow to put aside the resentment caused by the Wars of Independence. Juan José Flores and the Spanish Queen dreamed of reconquering a portion of northwestern South America (1846–1847). Vigorous action was taken with reference to obligations and indemnities in Mexico (1856–62), Venezuela (just prior to 1861), and the Pacific States of South America (1865–66);[4] and recognition of the new republics was long delayed.

In Hispanic America, too, there existed, besides the bitterness which naturally arose from this Spanish stubbornness and these instances of aggression, certain factors which tended to stultify this racial propaganda. In the first place, Cuba and Porto Rico, still

[1] Incomplete files of these newspapers may be found in Bancroft Library, University of California.

[2] The second edition, the only one to which the writer has had access, was printed by *La Revista Médica*, 1859, 156 p.

[3] *The American Historical Review*, XII (1906), 94 *et seq.*

[4] Rafael Mariá Labra y Cadrana, *Orientación Americana de España* (Madrid, A. Alonzo, 1909), p. 100 *et seq.;* Anibal Maúrtua, *La Idea Pan-Americana y la Cuestión del Arbïtraje* (Lima, *La Industria*, 1901), p. 35 *et seq.*

under the Spanish yoke, appealed to the sympathy of their Latin sisters in the New World. On at least two occasions—namely, during the celebrated Panama congress of 1826 and while the Ten Years' War in Cuba was in progress (1868-1878)—the Hispanic-American republics entertained designs of snatching Spain's colonies from her grasp; and there was sympathy for Cuba until the last.[5] In the second place, there continued to exist a deep current of hatred toward Spain as an aftermath of the Wars of Independence, just as Anglophobia held sway in the United States for a century after the achievement of nationality.

The anti-Spanish propaganda deserves special notice, for it was participated in by many of the leading men of the country. The main thesis of a history of Hispanic America published in 1828 by Simón Rodríguez, the teacher of Bolívar, may be summed up in the assertion that in the fifteenth century Columbus discovered a New World in order to people it with slaves and vassals, but at the opening of the nineteenth century reason reclaimed it in order to found a society of free men obedient to their own laws.[6] Francisco Bilbao, the great Chilean writer, declared in his *American Gospel*[7] that the formula of Hispanic-American progress could be found in the expression "de-Spanishize yourselves" (*desespañolizarse*). The Peruvian author, Ricardo Palma, and the Chilean linguist, Valentín Letelier, were of the opinion that to accept a *rapprochement* with unprogressive Spain would be contrary to the very principles of American life.[8] Lastly, Domingo F. Sarmiento, the great South American statesman and educator, returning from a trip to Spain, declared that in three centuries there had not been introduced into the peninsula a single new industry save the manufacture of the sulphur match; that there was no national marine, few highways, no popular education, and no progress in the higher institutions of learning; that the arts of printing and engraving had decayed; that the market places remained as they had been described by Don Quixote; that the hatred for foreigners continued as strong as when the Jews and Arabs had been expelled; that, in short, America had nothing to gain from contact with Spain.[9]

[5] Labra. *op. et loc. cit.;* José León Suárez, *Carácter de la Revolución Americana* (Buenos Aires Juan Roldán, 1917), pp. 191-198.

[6] Suárez, *op. cit.,* p. 67.

[7] *El Evangelio Americano* (Buenos Aires, Soc. tip. Bonaerense, 1864).

[8] Fernando Ortiz, *La Reconquista de América* (Paris, Paul Ollendorff, 1910), pp. 76-77.

[9] Suárez, *op. cit.,* p. 21. See also Rafael Altamira y Crevea, *Mi Viaje á América* (Madrid, Victoriano Suárez, 1911), pp. 384-395.

These considerations make the absence of friendly relations between Spain and Hispanic America during the greater portion of the
last century a fact which will readily be understood. But it would
be a mistake to suppose that nothing was accomplished. Beginning
with the recognition of Mexico in 1836, Spain very slowly extended
this favor to the remaining Hispanic states of the New World, completing the process in the early 'nineties.[10] At the same time numerous
treaties relating to extradition, postal and telegraphic communications, literary, scientific, and artistic property, and commercial affairs, gave evidence of the abandonment of the policy of aloofness.
It was near the end of this period, also, that the Spaniards who were
interested in their kinsmen across the Atlantic founded the Ibero-
American Union, and by 1892 old grievances had been so far forgotten that the Hispanic-American states joined in the celebration of the
Fourth Centenary of the discovery of America.[11]

A Period of More Intense Effort (1895–1915)

This celebration, as was natural, gave considerable impetus to the
movement toward intimacy. And feasting and rejoicing had scarcely
ended when a renewed revolt in Cuba and war with the United States
furnished Spaniards further motive for *rapprochement* with Hispanic
America. The approach of hostilities with the Anglo-American republic caused patriots of the Iberian Peninsula to subject their country to a process of rigorous inspection and to cast about for possible
allies. When the inevitable came, Spain found herself without active
friends—unless Germany's demonstration entitled that country to
be considered such—and pathetically unprepared to meet the foe.
In a short time all was over, and the last vestige of a once glorious
empire in America had passed from Spanish control. The sense of
failure and loneliness which came to Spain could scarcely have been
more profound. The defeat was followed by a veritable flood of
literature dealing with the domestic and foreign problems of the
peninsula, and there was considerable uniformity as to what Spain's
international policy should be. Pan-Hispanism must be accepted as
one of the goals for the future, and in so far as it related to America
it was to be forged in part upon the anvil of Yankeephobia.[12]

[10] Labra, *op. cit.*, appendix, contains a list of these treaties with dates. See
also W. S. Robertson "The Recognition of the Spanish Colonies by the Mother-
land," in *The Hispanic American Historical Review*, I (1918), 70 *et seq.*

[11] Accounts of the juridical, the geographic, the literary, and the pedagogical
congresses held on this occasion were published in Madrid in 1892 and 1893.

[12] For a partial enumeration of the Spanish writers inspired by the prospect
of a war with the United States over Cuba and by the defeat of their father-

This anti-Yankee phase of the matter, scarcely to be detected in the more discreet and tactful writers, is clearly seen in such works as those of José F. Gómez and Ricardo Beltrán y Rózpide. The former was inspired by the prospect of war with the United States over Cuba. In his *Latin Solidarity* [13] he advocates a sort of *Zollverein* as the first step in the formation of a more important union; the pacification of Cuba; and a rapid *rapprochement* with the peoples of Spanish origin in America. The motives influencing Gómez are very evident in the following passage:

"If we know how to take advantage of the situation, our country may yet become the polar star of a Latin Confederation on this continent against the Saxon preponderance represented by this Anglo-American Colossus which we have opposite us, and we may advance firmly and serenely to a league of race, draw the former possessions to the mother country in the interest of all, and give potency, unity, and fire to the idea of solidarity among the people who pray, make laws, and speak in the beautiful language of Castile."

While recognizing the wealth and power of the United States, Gómez points out that financial and industrial disturbances and growing anarchism and jingoism are thorns in the side of the colossus. In view of these conditions, he contends that when fifty millions of Latin Americans join their European mother in a close league of race, there will be little need to fear the outcome of the struggle.

Beltrán y Rózpide wrote a two-volume history of the Hispano-American peoples in the twentieth century. The work is anti-Yankee from beginning to end. The whole American policy of the United States is painted in blackest terms and the Yankee peril is constantly held up before the Hispanic Americans with the view of persuading them to enter into a confederation. Rózpide expresses the hope that after such an organization has been formed, Spain and her kinsmen in the New World may enter into a profitable alliance which will give her the position of *"Presidencia de Honor"* in the great association . . . of the Hispanic-American people." [14]

Hostility to the United States is even more evident in writings of the journalists. In July, 1898, the *Correo Español* (Madrid) remarked: "When Spain has been driven from the continent she cre-

---

land in that war, see Ortiz, *op. cit.*, p. 99. From this group should not be omitted Angel Ganivet, Juan Valera, and Sánchez de Foca. See also Rafael Altamira, *España en América* (Valencia, Sempere y Companía, 1908), pp. 179-186.

[13] *La Solidaridad Latina en América* (Habana, "Los Guayabitos," 1897, pamphlet, 22 pp.).

[14] *Los Pueblos Hispanoamericanos en el Siglo XX* (Madrid, Imprenta del Patronato de Huerfanos de Administración Militar, 1907).

ated, the possessions of other nations still holding colonies there will soon be disposed of. The dreams of the North American politicians will be realized. Mexico, already mutilated by the amputation of Texas and California, will fall an easy prey. Venezuela will next fall under the talons of the American vulture. Brazil, Chile, Argentina, and the other South American republics would be succulent food . . . It is not only the Antilles that are threatened; the nations of Central and South America will also disappear before an . . . invasion more terrible than that of the Vandals and the Goths. . . . It is still possible to avoid the danger. The Spanish-Americans must, in union with the mother country, fight for their land, for their religion, and for their race." The *Correo* contended that there was a probability that England would participate in this conquest.[15]

This article was written under the fervor of a war psychosis, but it was little less vigorous than many which followed. Three years later, for instance, *España Moderna*[16] called upon Europe to "save us and the virgin South American continent from the barbaric Yankees"; and in 1910 the same journal called attention to the "Yankee Peril," pointing out that a part of Latin America was in danger of being "gobbled up," but expressing the hope that some of it might be saved by an alliance based upon "the traditions of race and the language of Castile."[17] During the same year Professor Vicente Gay, of the University of Valladolid, declared that Spain must rescue the Latin Americans from the intrigues of the United States. "We should insist upon the common blood of Spain and South America," said Gay, "and encourage trade and intercourse." "Spain is the Rome of the West and the fountain of its greatness. In Spain should be recognized the Pantheon of American heroes . . . It is necessary to bear this in mind if we would cultivate the Ibero-American spirit which must prove the salvation of Latin America."[18]

Thanks to the efforts of an able group who, under the name of "Americanists," have rallied around the ideal of Hispano-American friendship, the accelerated movement of the 'nineties has continued. From the beginning the program set forth by these so-called Americanists embraced three closely related phases: the racial and cultural, the economic, and the political. In approving the idea of calling a congress of all the Hispanic peoples at Madrid in November, 1900, the Spanish minister of state declared that the "social and economic

[15] As quoted in *The Literary Digest* XVII (July 23, 1898), 113.
[16] *Ibid.*, XXIII (July 13, 1901), 51. *Cf.* also XXI (July 28, 1900), 112.
[17] *Ibid.*, XL (April 30, 1910), 866–867.
[18] *Ibid.*, XLI (August 6, 1910), 198.

future" of his country depended to a large extent upon the growth of "those racial sympathies which Spain has in America"; and that now was an opportune time to cultivate the spiritual affections of the Hispanic-American peoples and to prepare for the inevitable contest for their markets. Again, the formal invitation sent to Mexico, which was probably typical, spoke of racial and cultural bonds, mutual economic interests, and the advisability of "a common action" which would result in the well-being of the world. Among the themes to be discussed at this assembly were: "means for the creation of a great current of public opinion which would lead the governments of Spain, Portugal, and the Ibero-American peoples to effect an intimate alliance;" the harmonization of the civil, penal and administrative laws of these countries; the unification of educational plans; the modification of commercial agreements; the improvement of communications; the establishment of international expositions; the creation of banks; and the study of the problem of migration.[19] These ideas, of course, were in harmony with those of the Americanist group who sponsored the congress.

The success of this congress encouraged the calling of others. In 1908 the Hispanic-American states took part in the celebration of the centenary of the Spanish movement for liberation from the Napoleonic yoke; [20] in 1910 a Hispanic-American congress was held in Barcelona; [21] in 1912 the centenary of the meeting of Cortes at Cádiz was celebrated by another Hispano-American Assembly; [22] in 1914 a Hispano-American Historical and Geographical Congress was held at Seville in order to commemorate the fourth centenary of the discovery of the Pacific ocean.[23]

Moreover, statesmen, merchants, and intellectuals have founded numerous organizations, which have occasionally received subsidies from the government, for the purpose of cementing relations of cordi-

[19] Probably one of the most convenient sources for a general survey of the correspondence connected with this conference as well as its program is the *Boletín Oficial de la Secretaría de Relaciones Exteriores de Mexico*, X (September, 1900), 269 *et seq*. For a more complete account, see *Congreso Social y Económico Hispano-americano, Madrid, 1900* (Madrid, Hernández, 1902).

[20] Labra, *América y España en el Centenario de 1908* (Madrid, Hernández, 1909).

[21] *The Hispanic American Historical Review*, IV (1921), 567.

[22] See the reports and bulletins of the various states of Hispanic America for the years 1912 and 1913.

[23] *The Hispanic American Historical Review*, IV (1921), 504, note. For the proceedings and reports of this congress see *Congreso de Historia y Geográfia Hispano-Americana de Seville de 1914, Actas y Memorias* (Madrid, Jaime Ratés, 1914).

ality with the Hispanic Americans. In fact some forty [24] of these institutions have been founded since the opening of the century, and many of them are organizations of considerable influence and dignity. Such, for instance, are the *Casa de América* and the center for the cultivation of Hispano-American intimacy in Barcelona; the Center of Americanist studies in Seville; the Hispanic-American Royal Academy of Arts and Sciences at Cádiz; and the Hispano-American Royal Academy, the Ibero-American Institute of Law, and the Center of Hispano-American Culture, all three of which are in Madrid. At the same time, some of the most important universities have created professorships devoted to the study and teaching of American history, law, and politics; and several journals and publishing houses have been established primarily for the purpose of distributing literature and information with reference to Hispanic America.[25]

Such organizations have carried their propaganda across the Atlantic. Spanish students have been encouraged to pursue their studies in Hispanic America, Hispanic-American students have been offered inducements to come to Spain, and professorial interchanges have been arranged; some of the leading Spanish Academies, as those of Languages, of Sciences, and of History, have established branches, correspondents, and interchanges in and with Hispanic America; [26] the some four million of Spanish immigrants in the Hispanic-American states have been organized with solicitous care as one of the best means of fostering friendly relations; and numerous expeditions for the purpose of carrying on propaganda have been undertaken.

The manner in which Spanish immigrants may cultivate the sentiment of racial solidarity is well illustrated by the celebration of the anniversary of the discovery of America by the Spanish Center at Caracas in 1918. On this occasion the orator, Manuel Díaz-Rodríguez, spoke in a fashion highly laudatory of Spain and urged more intimate relations with the mother country. He declared, *inter alia,* that the people of Venezuela had "committed the error of supposing that the revolution at the opening of the century had destroyed every bond connecting them with Spain and that their political destiny might be achieved by adopting and implanting the institutions of the United States or those of the radical period of the French revolu-

[24] Carlos Badía Malgrida, *El Factor Geográfico en la Política Sudamericana* (Madrid, Jaime Ratés, 1919), p. 101.

[25] Altamira, *Mi Viaje á América,* pp. 601–606; Labra, *Orientación americana de España, passim.*

[26] Labra, *Orientación americana de España, passim;* Ramón Orbea, *La Reconquista de América* (Madrid, V. Suárez [1905]), *passim.*

tion." He repeatedly lamented the fact that "guileless bachelors and unripe doctors," would-be-statesmen of the cloister, kept declaring that the Hispanic Americans must not resign themselves to the fate of being Spaniards in the New World and insisting that they imitate the United States, France, England, Germany, or some other large state, or else maintaining that they must not be Spaniards but Latins. "As if, disregarding Spain, we should be able to boast of being Latin! As if the . . . drop of Latin blood which circulates in our veins did not come to us through that Romanized Spain which made illustrious the annals of early Latinity with a goodly phalanx of moralists, poets, and emperors!" Away with such idea! The sooner these people give up this mistaken notion and strive to make themselves *Hispanic Americans*, the better; for they can never accomplish anything by seeking unnatural affiliations and trying to fasten upon themselves a civilization to which they are not adapted. Such was the burden of the orator's eloquence.

In conclusion, Díaz-Rodríguez counseled a tightening of the bonds of respect and love for the mother country and presented a vision of the day when there would spread from the Pyrenees across the Atlantic and from "Mexico to the polar limits of South America, with a glory that will [would]make the earth tremble, the announcement of a simultaneous and manifold renaissance of race." [27]

Of the expeditions sent out to America for the purpose of propaganda, that of the distinguished historian, Rafael Altamira y Crevea, who was dispatched as the agent of the University of Oviedo, deserves special mention because of its importance and because of the clear and eloquent statement of Pan-Hispanic ideals issued by this university while preparations were being made for the expedition. Altamira spent several months in Hispanic America where he visited the important intellectual centers of Argentina, Uruguay, Chile, Peru, Mexico, and Cuba, and aroused general interest and enthusiasm. The "Address to the Spaniards and Brothers of America" sent out by the Universary of Oviedo, contained the following interesting statement of the purpose of the expedition:

"On the noble eve of the Centenary of the Independence of America the University of Oviedo . . . desires that the affectionate voice of Spain pronounce a benediction upon her emancipated daughters; it desires to unite its song to the chorus sung by those peoples in commemoration of that memorable date when, eager for life, they went out from their paternal home (*dejarón los patrios lares*); it de-

[27] *Motivos de Meditación ante la Guerra y por Hispanoamericana Una* (Caracas, El Comercio, 1918, pamphlet, 24 pp.).

sires, above all, to bear to these puissant nationalities vigorous shoots of our spirit in order to plant them in these fertile lands bathed by the Gulf, enriched by the Plate, and shaded by the lofty Andes; it desires to send to America flames of our fire in order that our souls may be welded into one, and, the people who on both sides of the sea form the Great Iberia thus having been united, we shall be able to fulfil the high civilizing mission which destiny has confided to us." [28]

The Stimulus of the World War

This intensified Spanish interest in the Spaniards residing overseas was further stimulated by the World War. This great catastrophe seems to have stirred Spain as profoundly as the defeat of 1898. Spaniards were made to feel the loneliness of their situation, to doubt the efficacy of international law and agreements, and to consider the future of their nation in a world order where force was likely to be dominant for some time. Moreover, the war resulted in the improvement of Spain's commerce and finances [29] and at the same time gave such an impetus to her industries that the importance of Hispanic-American markets was appreciated as never before.

In 1916 considerable discussion of the proposed American policy of Spain was begun in the Spanish Senate. One senator demanded more favorable commercial treaties and careful direction of Spanish emigration to America; another believed that a customs union should be negotiated with the Hispanic-American states in order that Spain might secure the markets which had formerly been supplied by the nations of war-swept Europe; others demanded, in addition to these proposals, numerous reforms connected with steamship, postal, and telegraphic communications; and one of the members went so far as to advocate the establishment of an "Ibero-American Confederation." In response to these discussions the President of the Council of Ministers declared his conviction that the time had come to advance beyond the period of "romantic propaganda" and enter upon the "road of realities." [30]

Once more, too, able writers, for the lack of whom Spain has never suffered, put forth programs and abundant propaganda. Rafael

[28] Altamira, *Mi Viaje á América,* p. 11.

[29] For discussions of Spain's commercial and financial conditions, see U. S. Dept. of Commerce, *Special Agents Series, No. 202,* and the *Commerce Reports, 1917 et seq.*

[30] Altamira, *España y el Programa americanista* (Madrid, Editorial-América, [1917?]), p. 69 *et seq.*

María Labra y Cadrana, who for many years had been vitally interested in America, published numerous pamphlets and made vigorous lecture tours in Spain;[31] Altamira issued his *Spain and the Americanist Program;*[32] Frederico Rahola, prominently identified with the "Casa de America," a center of commercial information, formulated his *Americanist Post-War Program;*[33] and Edmundo González-Blanco included a discussion of what should be the American policy of Spain in a book dealing with Spain and the World War.[34]

Altamira's proposals differed from those of the earlier publications with which he had been identified in placing somewhat more emphasis upon the political and economic phases of the matter. He advocated such reform of the diplomatic and consular service as would insure a supply of able men for the American field; such a following-up of the emigrant as would insure his preservation as a force making for the perpetuation of Spanish culture and the achievement of Pan-Hispanism; such economic arrangements as would promote the growth of Hispano-American trade; the defense of the Spanish language in all its purity; the fullest and freest intellectual coöperation and interchange.[35] Such a program evinces considerable supplementation of his proposals at the opening of the century, when he took occasion to remark that the policy of the group of which he was a member might be summed up in the phrase "pedagogical politics."[36]

Rahola gives much more emphasis than Altamira to the commercial and political items of the program, although he does not neglect the intellectual and the cultural. He points out the commercial significance of the Yankee phrase, "America for the Americans," calls attention to the recent marvelous growth of the trade of the United States with Hispanic America, and urges that Spain collect and launch all her commercial forces while the United States is in the

[31] Among Labra's recent works, the most important bearing on this theme are his lecture read before the Atheneum of Madrid in October, 1915, entitled *Problema Hispanoamericana;* his *La Campaña americanista de D. Rafael M. de Labra en Galicia, Julio y Agosto 1916;* and his introduction to Rodrigo Zárate's, *España y América: Proyecciones y Problemas derivados de la Guerra* (Madrid, Casa Editorial Calleja, 1917).

[32] *Supra.*

[33] *Progama americanista post-guerra* (Barcelona, Casa de America, 1919).

[34] *Iberismo y Germanismo. España ante el Conflicto Europeo* (Valencia, Editorial Cervantes, 1917).

[35] *España y el Programa americanista,* p. 62 *et seq.*

[36] See Altamira's *Cuestiones hispano-americanas* (Madrid, E. R. Serra, 1900), *passim.*

midst of the war and its consequent readjustments. He expects the Ibero-American states to be the scene of a titanic commercial struggle in the near future, but in this struggle he believes Spain will be placed at an advantage because of her geographical position and ethnical affinities. Moreover, if any sort of international concert is to be hoped for, he believes that the mysterious force of racial and spiritual attraction ought to render possible a political union.

Writing in 1917, Gonzáles-Blanco expends a great deal of effort in order to show that the British and the Yankee peril should be met by Pan-Hispanism. He urges the denunciation and the abrogation of the treaty of Algeciras with the aim of recovering the Strait of Gibraltar, and the consolidation of the Iberian Peninsula by a federation with Portugal, in order to render the holding of that strait by another nation perilous in the future. When the geographical integrity of Spain is thus restored, the Hispanic-American states may be invited to enter what is destined to be the great "Iberian United States." Will they refuse to accept this invitation? "What overseas peoples whose sons have not lost the ethnical sentiment and the consciousness of that community of customs, of language and of civilization which perdures between Spain and Latin America, would reject this superb ideal, pledge of great destinies for the future? Who does not see that its realization is the only recourse of which the Ibero-American world can avail itself in order to oppose Yankee imperialism? . . . The immediate subjugation of Central and South America by the syndicates of North America is the future which awaits our brothers of the New Continent if there is not found in union a competent force for resistance." Moreover, when Pan-Iberianism has realized its ideal of unity, it may ally itself with Germany in order that *Iberismo* and *Germanismo* may wrest from the Anglo-Saxons "the palm of victory in the fight for the direction of humanity." [37]

Since the outbreak of the World War there have been published, also, works of a supposedly scholarly nature which reveal this same Pan-Hispanic aspiration of the Spaniards. Portions of two of these, at least, will be read with considerable interest in connection with the matter now under consideration. In 1917 Juan Ortega Rubio, an aged professor of the Central University at Madrid, issued the *magnum opus* which had cost him much labor, a three-volume *History of America*.[38] Two years later a student of a diplomatic and consular institute of Spain published under the auspices of the Royal

[37] González-Blanco, *op. cit.*, pp. 92–108. See also the severe volume of Luis Araquistain, *El Peligro yanqui*, published at Madrid in 1921.

[38] *Historia de América* (Madrid, Libería de los Sucerores de Hernando, 1917).

Academy of Jurisprudence and Legislation an excellent study entitled, *The Geographical Factor in the Politics of South America*.[39]

Some twenty-seven pages of the prologue of Ortega's ambitious work is given to a discussion of the American policy of Spain. Here the author declares that he has been moved to undertake the task while under the weight of age and infirmities, because he has felt that he would thus be rendering a service to Spain and also to her former colonies. He then sets forth his viewpoint. He begins with the affirmation:

"Our old and beloved Spain does not desire, nor is she able, nor ought she, to think of exercising any hegemony over the Ibero-American peoples. We desire, and we aspire to, only a fraternal communion. . . . Spaniards and Americans of the Iberian race, forgetting old grievances, should in the future think only of living the life of culture and of progress. . . . At the same time that we ask those sons of the republics of our race that they do not forget Spain and that they honor the memory of the discoverers and the colonizers of the Indies, we shall also declare to them that we are admirers of those brave heroes who proclaimed their independence and their liberty. In the accomplishment of such ends we believe that there is fulfilled an historical law that colonies when they reach a certain age, that is, a certain grade of civilization and culture, separate from the metropolis."

Ortega turns toward America because he has despaired of Europe: "We do not hope, nor do we desire, anything from the egoistic nations of Europe; we place all our confidence in the generous peoples of America." The end toward which he strives is both conciliatory and politic: "The work which we desire to realize is not only peaceful but also political, for we shall endeavor to foster the union of the Latin Republics with the mother country." And in accomplishing this twofold mission he desires to avoid striking the note of racial hatred and rivalry, but he nevertheless admits that he has at times sensed the Yankee peril and he cannot refrain from quoting a few Spanish authors who have taken a fling at the Colossus.[40]

The main contentions of the brilliant monograph of Badía are that there exists in Hispanic America strong supernational aspirations; that these are prevented from being realized by geographical absurdities in the present national boundaries, which furnish the motive for unnecessary squabbles regarding territory; that there are six geographical unities in Hispanic America—the *La Plata Confederation*,

[39] *Supra.*
[40] Prologue, pp. v–xxxii.

embracing the present republics of Argentina, Uruguay, Paraguay and a portion of Southern Bolivia; the *Confederation of the Pacific,* made up of the central portion of Bolivia, Chile, Peru, and southern Ecuador; the *Colombian Confederation,* composed of Colombia, most of Venezuela and the northern part of Ecuador; the *Brazilian Confederation* with the present territory of Brazil, plus the northern portion of Bolivia, the eastern sector of Ecuador, some districts in the south of Venezuela and the Antilles; and the *Mexican Confederation*—which when accepted in the political organization of the republics, will eliminate strife and pave the way to Hispanic-American harmony and solidarity; and that after their normal life has thus been restored these American states and Spain will find it natural and easy to form a society of nations, for, aside from the grandeur of such an organization of peoples of the same race and with similar culture and aspirations, the Yankee menace will constitute a powerful force impelling them in this direction.[41]

In view of this array of evidence—and it could be made more formidable if space permitted—there seems little room to doubt the existence in Spain of a strong desire for intimacy with Hispanic America.[42] The motives behind such a desire are racial and cultural as well as political and commercial, but the former seem to have been most emphasized. In writing of their aspiration Spaniards sometimes express, and probably more often feel, opposition to the United States, and the Yankee peril is therefore frequently held up before the Spaniards overseas.

Progress of Pan-Hispanism in Hispanic America

What progress has Pan-Hispanism made in Hispanic America since 1895, and what are its prospects for the future?

The revolt in Cuba and the so-called Spanish-American War furnished the people south of the Rio Grande an opportunity to express their sentiments toward the mother country before the enthusiasm aroused by the celebration of the Fourth Centenary of the discovery of America had died away. For instance, in the spring and summer of 1897 some of the leading newspapers of Mexico carried on a spirited discussion regarding what should be Mexico's attitude toward the prospective independence of Cuba. Francisco

[41] *El Factor Geográfico en la Política sudamericana,* pp. 3–135, 553 *et seq.*
[42] Other evidences of Spanish interest in a *rapprochement* with Hispanic America are revealed by the Second Congress of Hispano-American History and Geography, which met in Seville in May, 1921, as well as by the plans for a general Hispano-American Congress to be held in Spain in the near future.

Bulnes seems to have been one of the important champions of Cuban liberation, but he met with several able opponents, of whom Don Carlos de Olaguibel y Arista, Don Francisco G. Cosmés, and Trinidad Sánchez Santos may be taken as typical. Bulnes attacked Spain's colonial policy severely, defended the Cuban cause as analogous to that of Mexico in 1810, spoke disparagingly of the value of Spanish immigration to Hispanic-American republics, and gave evidence of a friendly disposition toward the United States. His opponents, first and last, defended the Spanish colonial régime and Spanish culture, declared that the Cuban separatist movement was similar to the "infamy of Texas" and not to the action of the Spanish colonies at the opening of the nineteenth century; that it would be a mistake for the Hispanic-American states which were trying to preserve the integrity of their national domain under the federalist system to champion the cause of separatism; that in case Cuba achieved its independence from Spain the island would not have the elements and the power to maintain such independence, but would fall, like Texas, into the clutches of the Yankees; and lastly, that Mexico, and the other Hispanic-American states for that matter, could ill afford to place obstacles in the way of the ever-increasing flow of Spanish immigrants which, "identified with us by all those bonds which attach a human group to the spirit and the characteristic tendencies of race," can alone "bring industry, prosperity, order and civilization to the deserts of our domain." [43]

This sympathy for Spain seems to have been somewhat general at the time, in spite of the widespread desire to see Cuba freed from Spanish control. The Chilean writer, Alberto del Solar, pronounced a terrible tirade against the rudeness, the grossness and the greed of the United States, and concluded his address with a hymn to Spain; [44] the young Argentinian statesman, Roque Sáenz Peña, expressed the fervent hope that the Spanish forces might be victorious; and numerous others revealed similar sentiments. [45]

The Hispano-American Congress which, at the instance of the *Unión-Iberoamericano,* convened in Madrid two years after the close of the war, gave further evidence of the growing feeling of

[43] A convenient compilation of the articles published in this connection was issued by Frederico de Pedro under the title, *La Independencia de Cuba en Relación con el Criterio americano y los Intereses de México* (Mexico, Avenida Juárez 624, 1897).

[44] *La Doctrina de Monroe y América latina* (Buenos Aires, J. Peuser, 1898).

[45] *Escritos y Discursos* (Buenos Aires, J. Peuser, 1914-15), I, p. 429 *et seq.* For brief mention of other champions of Spain see Altamira, *Cuestiones Hispano-americanas, passim.*

solidarity between Spain and her erstwhile colonies. This feeling was particularly noticeable during the inaugural session of the congress, when Don Justo Sierra, the distinguished Mexican author and statesman, speaking for the entire Hispanic-American delegation, delivered an address which breathed Pan-Hispanic sentiment from almost every sentence.[46]

The intellectuals of the countries south of the Rio Grande have continued to cultivate this attitude. Such important writers as Rubén Darío, José Santos Chocano, Gómez Jaime, Andrade Coello, Rufino Blanco-Fombona, José M. Vargas Vila, Eliseo Giberga, J. Francisco V. Silva and José León Suárez are champions of Pan-Hispanism in one form or another. There is, in fact, a considerable group of Hispanic-American idealists who express the conviction that the only means of saving their nationalities from deterioration and chaos within, and absorption from without, is a return to the law of their origin, their historical past, their maternal traditions, their primal racial heritage. In the opinion of this group the Hispanic-American nations are threatened with race deterioration and chaos within, hybridism, spiritual mystification, the disappearance of historical consciousness, in a phrase, denationalization and annihilation, unless they avail themselves of every opportunity to promote a vigorous revival of Hispanism in its fullest and most glorious sense.[47] The significance for Pan-Hispanism of this idea, if it should be generally accepted as a working hypothesis, needs no comment.

As revelations of Pan-Hispanic sentiment in the countries south of the Rio Grande, recent productions of two historians of the Argentine are particularly worthy of note. Late in 1916, or early in 1917, a distinguished professor of the University of Buenos Aires published a booklet[48] on the character of the Hispanic-American revolution, in which he contended, among other things, that it was unjust to blame Spain for not extending liberties to the colonies when despotism held sway in the peninsula, and for exploiting the riches of the New World when such exploitation accorded with the general colonial concept of the age; that Spain's treatment of the natives was not as cruel as it had been represented; that many Spaniards in Spain who were also seeking larger liberties sympathized with the colonials in their struggle for independence; that the real nature of the revolution can only be grasped when it is considered

[46] For an acount of this episode, see Ecuador, Ministerio de Relaciones Exteriores, *Informe* (1901), pp. 43–46.

[47] Carlos Badía Malgrida, *op. cit.*, p. 48 *et seq.*

[48] José Léon Suárez, *Carácter de la Revolución americana* (Buenos Aires, Juan Roldán, 1917).

as a *"crisis fatal* in favor of liberty and of human rights, which was produced as a consequence of the revolutions of the United States and of France at the end of the eighteenth century"—all of which seems to be well-founded; but the author makes it very clear that he is highly elated at being able to champion such a viewpoint and takes great pains to set forth the significance of his work for the Pan-Hispanic movement. In fact, the author's intense fervor for Spain is evident on almost every page; and what is more significant, his booklet seems to have aroused widespread interest and met with much commendation in all parts of Spanish America.[49]

Just as this booklet was going through its third edition, another Argentinian, J. F. V. Silva, published a much more radical work.[50] Silva went so far as to lament the separation of the Spanish colonies from the mother country, declaring that Hispanophobia and a slavish imitation of the United States has been the capital error of the Latins of the New World. He urged the formation of a vast empire including Portugal, Brazil, Spain and the Spanish-American Republics. The capital of this great organization was to be in Spain and full local autonomy was to be preserved for each of its parts. In support of his plan of union Silva held up the English, the German, and the North American perils, but he placed main emphasis upon the last of these. Nor were his ambitions confined merely to matters of defense. The new empire would have its *irredenta*. In Europe there would be Gibraltar and Morocco; in America, Porto Rico, the Falkland Islands, and the Panama Canal must be regained. The integrity of Mexico must be guaranteed. Yankee influence must be counteracted in Cuba, Santo Domingo, and Central America. Indeed, the new Hispanic nation should control both the Panama Canal and the Strait of Magellan, as well as the Caribbean area and all the islands adjacent to the Central and South American coasts!

This Hispanic friendliness of the intellectuals, and of a large group of the upper classes in general, has been revealed frequently by the enthusiastic receptions given to such Spanish scholars as Altamira and Adolfo Posada,[51] and such statesmen and financiers as Rahola and Cavestany. The Pan-Hispanic note was particularly prevalent in the numerous addresses given during the extended tour

[49] See appendix of the 1919 edition for evidence of the impression made by this work in Hispanic America and elsewhere.

[50] Francisco V. Silva, *Reparto de América Española y Pan-Hispanismo* (Madrid, Francisco Beltrán [1918], xv, 511 pp.).

[51] See Posada's *En América una Campaña* (Madrid, F. Beltrán, 1911); and *Para América desde España* (Paris, P. Ollendorff, 1910).

of Altamira already mentioned. The president of the University of La Plata declared that the unanimity of sentiment and opinion which had greeted Altamira lovingly as a friend and admiringly as a teacher was "nothing more than the mysterious and recondite salutation of blood to blood across an ocean which separates two hearths that once were one." He expressed his conviction, also, that the currents of natural *rapprochement* and cohesion would overcome the divergences caused by political vicissitudes and "reconstruct the primitive unity, the inherent affinity, the indestructible consubstantiality"; and closed his address with the prediction that the Spanish race "would be the arbiter in the future of a vast portion of human destiny." [52] The rector of the University of Chile hoped that there would be established across the Andes and the Atlantic "a great intercourse of merchandise and of ideas, of manufactured products and books, of things and men, of students and teachers"; for, whether "liberals or conservatives, Catholics or rationalists, the Hispanic Americans are not able to renounce either the traditions of Spain which constitute the foundation of our culture, or the rich Castilian language which serves us as the medium of appropriating all the treasures of classic antiquity and all the promises of the new spirit, and much less the warm blood . . . which stirs our hearts." [53] The speaker chosen by the "University Center" of Lima to express its sentiments to Altamira declared that both reason and racial attraction made for Pan-Hispanic solidarity, and that union with the peninsula could be predicted with mathematical certainty.[54] In Mexico the distinguished lawyer, Rodolfo Reyes, declared that the preservation of the characteristics of the mother race and relations of cordiality with Spain should be the Mexican ideal, and he asked the assistance of the thinkers of Spain in the solution of the problem of protecting Hispanic America from the disintegrating and absorbing influence of extraneous forces, the North American influence being one of the most dangerous of these.[55]

In Uruguay and in Cuba Pan-Hispanic expressions were hardly so numerous and emphatic. In the educational centers of the former republic there was evident some of the coldness and objectivity of the scientific attitude,[56] while in Cuba, as Altamira had possibly anticipated, he found himself somewhat on the defensive. And yet, his visit to this republic so recently emancipated from the Spanish

[52] Altamira, *Mi Viage a América*, pp. 125–139.
[53] *Ibid.*, pp. 254–261.
[54] *Ibid.*, pp. 315–322.
[55] *Ibid.*, pp. 319–383.
[56] *Ibid.*, pp. 231–249.

yoke did not meet with an entirely unfavorable response. Most conspicuous proof of this fact is found in the expressions coming from
the noted writer, Eliseo Giberga, from the head of the Institute of
Secondary Education, and from the veterans of Cuban independence.
It must be noted, however, that most of the documents which Altamira produces as evidence of the nature of the Cuban attitude toward his mission were inspired by the celebration given by the
Spanish colony of Cuba.[57]

More significant than this evidence of growing friendliness between
the intellectuals of Spain and Hispanic America are the accumulating
indications of increasing intimacy in official circles. In recent years
October 12 has been set apart as a national holiday in virtually all of
the Hispanic-American republics. This, however, is apparently not to
be taken as evidence of a growing desire to honor the great Italian
who, sailing under the Spanish flag, discovered America. Its significance lies rather in the fact that this great event is celebrated as
Fiesta de la Raza—Racial Day—and not Columbus Day. The Pan-
Hispanic note is universally sounded.[58] Moreover, one who takes the
trouble to search through the published correspondence exchanged
between Spain and the states of Hispanic America during recent
years will discover many documents expressing mutual admiration,
confidence and good will. This attitude appears to be quite general,
but space forbids the presentation of more than a few illustrations
from the official correspondence of Colombia, Venezuela, Mexico,
and the Argentine.

In his *Informe* for 1910 the Colombian Minister of Foreign Relations took occasion to remark that "Colombia, one of the American
countries which has shown itself most friendly to the mother country,
has been especially careful to cultivate with all cordiality and to make
day by day more intimate its relations with the noble Spanish people." The minister in charge of the same office remarked in 1919,
while lamenting the failure of the Spanish government to participate
in the celebration of the centenary of the Battle of Boyacá, that
this could in no way break the "bonds which unite us with the mother
country or extinguish racial affections." [59]

In 1903 the Venezuelan Minister of Foreign Affairs noted that his
government had participated in the celebration of the arrival of Don
Alfonso XIII at his majority and expressed gratitude to the Queen
Regent for the generous consideration she had given Venezuela.[60]

[57] Altamira, *Mi Viage a América,* pp. 401–492.
[58] *Current History,* Vol. XV (November, 1921), p. 363.
[59] Columbia, Ministerio de Relaciones Exteriores, *Informe* (1910), p. 91.
[60] Venezuela, Ministerio de Relaciones, *Informe* (1913), p. XV.

The dispatch by the government of Spain of a descendant of Don Pablo Morillo, the distinguished general who sought to put down the Venezuelan movement for independence, for the purpose of taking part in the celebration of the one-hundredth anniversary of the beginning of efforts looking toward emancipation, aroused marked enthusiasm in Venezuela. This act signified forgiveness and the forgetting of past injuries. Venezuela, accepting it in good faith, reciprocated. President Gómez and his government went so far as to lay the corner-stones of what were to be two monuments, one to Simón Bolívar and the other to Pablo Morillo, Count of Cartagena.[61] A year later, in receiving the new Spanish minister, the Venezuelan chief executive referred to these events, speaking of the love and esteem of his constituency for the mother country in the following terms:

"Señor Minister: You well know that there is ineradicable in the Venezuelan people the tradition of respect and endearment toward noble Spain, glorious creator of these American nationalities. . . .

"This tradition was exhibited in its highest relief on the occasion of the Centenary of our Independence, when by joining in these commemorative festivities, Spain gave added strength to the bond of blood and of the common glories of the race. And Venezuela knows how to appreciate these demonstrations of cordiality which respond perfectly to the intimate sentiments which here are guarded as the treasure of the Venezuelan hearth." [62]

Lastly, in 1913, another Spanish minister was received with the cordial assurance that he was coming into the midst of a people "who do not renounce their origin, but who see in the Mother Spain the glorious fountain of their life and are delighted with the spectacle of her resurrection under the reign of a great monarch." [63]

Mexico's response to the invitation to attend the Hispano-American Congress of 1900 was one of the most cordial of all those given by the American states.[64] In 1901 the Spanish minister to Mexico was assured that the fraternal sentiments of Spain toward Mexico were fully reciprocated "by the government and people of this Republic. Nor is it possible for less than this mutual and vehement sympathy to exist between two peoples united by tradition, . . . by

---

[61] *Idem, Boletín* (1911), p. 643 *et seq.*
[62] Venezuela, *Boletín* (1912), pp. 110–111.
[63] *Ibid.,* (1913), p. 196.
[64] Mexico, Secretaría de Relaciones Exteriores, *Boletín Oficial* (1900), p. 269, *passim.*

the blood which courses in their veins," and above all by a similar civilization.[65] The presence of the Spanish representative at the celebration of the centenary of Mexican independence elicited from President Díaz words of rejoicing at this indication of complete reconciliation between mother and daughter. He declared that had Spain been absent a painful void would have been felt, but with Spain present, the occasion possessed all that was necessary to render "unforgetable . . . the annals of a people who do not disdain their origin." [66]

The diplomatic correspondence between Spain and the Argentine Republic indicates that the two countries are on terms of complete and mutual cordiality. The minister sent by the Roca administration (1898–1904) to Spain was reminded that Argentinians "have the duty of maintaining, at all costs, intimacy with the mother country." [67] During this same administration certain expressions which gave offense to Spain were suppressed from the Argentinian national hymn.[68] A few years later the Argentine Minister of War gave an extremely fervent address on the occasion of the departure of the Spanish delegation which had been present at a magnificent horse show. In one of the most eloquent portions of his speech he sounded the Pan-Hispanic note in the following fashion:

"When you return to the old land of Iberia, say that if, in conformity to the universal law of life, the mature fruit has fallen from the branch that nurtures it, if the eaglet leaves its nest when its wings are able to sustain it, Spain should not consider lost the hive whose swarm populated America and which for a time she deemed lost, but which today is found again in the flourishing magnificence of her race and her genius. . . . Say that here we call ourselves Hispanic Americans; that if we receive all men fraternally, your race is ours and into its modernized mold we shall pour the human bronze which must form the determinate race of our people. Say that her Castilian language, sonorous and virile, which she gave us, will in the future be spoken from our lips so emphatically that no other language shall be able to sound above it. Say that here we shall work with enthusiasm, being anxiously desirous that the victories of peace, of prosperity, and of human improvement may succeed in placing our race in the lead of the world. Then Spain, the common mother of all these peoples, shall march triumphantly with an escort of children at her

---

[65] Mexico, Secretaría de Relaciones Exteriores, *Boletín Oficial* (1901), p. 260.
[66] *Ibid.*, (1910), pp. 292–293.
[67] *Labra, Orientación americana de España, passim.* See also Ramón Orbea, *La Reconquista de América.*
[68] León Suárez, *op. cit.*, pp. 69–70.

side and look with pride upon her issue in the new lands [across the Atlantic]." [69]

Special consideration given by Spain to the Argentine nation in the celebrations connected with its independence met with every token of fullest appreciation. The mother country's proposal to erect a monument to the Argentine nation evoked fervid expressions of friendship in the La Plata congress; [70] the visit of the Princess, Doña Isabel de Borbon, in 1910, was greeted with profound and sincere enthusiasm; the raising of the Spanish diplomatic representation in Buenos Aires to the category of an embassy in connection with the celebrations of 1916 was reciprocated by a similar step with reference to the Argentinian legation in Madrid, and all was accompanied by frequent and fervent protestations of admiration. [71]

The Future Significance of Pan-Hispanism

If words and international courtesies count for anything, surely the Hispano-American *rapprochement* has made much progress since the early days of the nineteenth century! In the field of the immediately practical no astonishing results have been achieved, although some progress has been registered. Arbitration treaties and various pacts relating to commercial, industrial and cultural matters have been signed, and there has been a growing tendency to refer matters of dispute between American states to the arbitration of the Spanish government. The movement of trade between Spain and the Hispanic-American countries will prove disappointing to those who are searching for this supposedly solid basis for intimacy. Spain's commerce with these states in 1907 was only half what it had been in 1897. This was due largely to the loss of Cuba. But no remarkable increase has been recorded since 1907. In 1913 Spain furnished only three and one-half per cent of the total commodities purchased by Hispanic America, while she purchased from it a still smaller portion of its exports. By 1918 these percentages had risen to about four and one-half and a little more than two and one-half, respectively, while in 1919 the relative percentages decreased, although the absolute bulk increased. [72]

[69] Quoted in Labra, *Orientación americana de España,* pp. 45–46.

[70] Argentina, Ministerio de Relaciones Exteriores y Culto, *Memoria* (1915–1916), pp. 215–217;—(1916–1917), *passim*. See also Joaquín V. González, *La Argentina y Sus Amigos* (Buenos Aires, J. Lajouane y Cía., 1919), p. 7 ff.

[71] Argentina, Ministerio de Relaciones Exteriores y Culto, *Memoria* (1915–1916), pp. 215–217;—(1916–1917), *passim*.

[72] Pan-American Union, *Bulletin,* January and November, 1919; May, 1921, *passim*. Data for 1920–1925 reveal no remarkable increase.

One's estimate of the importance of this Pan-Hispanic movement in Hispanic America will depend, however, upon one's theory as to the forces determining national policies and national action. Those who are convinced that economic considerations are the controlling element will be inclined to give it small weight. On the other hand, alarmists who expect the era of national combats to be superseded by titanic inter-racial struggles and those who give great weight to cultural and idealistic influences will take a very different view of the matter. It seems to me that the future of the movement will be conditioned largely by three factors: (1) the progress of liberalism and the continuance of economic prosperity in Spain; (2) the persistence of Yankeephobia among the Hispanic-American peoples; and (3) the prevalence in Hispanic America of that social philosophy which maintains that the social problems of these republics can be solved only by a revival of racial pride, a return to the culture and the ideals of the Spanish race. At any rate, one fact stands clear: the attitude of Spain toward the Latin-American policy of the United States has been, and continues to be, an obstacle to Pan-American harmony.

Of course the movement will also depend upon the amount of friction which develops among the Hispanic-American states. Hitherto their relations have been fairly pacific. The ideal of unity has always existed and many of their disputes have been settled without resort to hostilities. Yet several wars have occurred: one between Argentina and Brazil (1825–1828), another between Colombia and Peru (1828–1829), a third between Peru and Bolivia and Chile (1837–1839), a fourth between Paraguay and the other states of the Plate (1865–1870), a fifth between Chile and the Peru-Bolivian Alliance (1879–1883), to say nothing of minor outbreaks between Mexico and the states of Central America. Whether these disagreements will decrease or become more intense with increasing stability and prosperity time alone can reveal.[73]

[73] Alejandro Álvarez, *The Monroe Doctrine* (Washington, 1924), p. 12 ff.; Robertson, *History of the Latin-American Nations* (1925), *passim*.

CHAPTER XIII

ITALIAN TRADE AND IMMIGRANTS; THE JAPANESE FACTOR; RUMORS AND REALITIES

THE amount of capital invested by Italian nationals in the countries of Latin America is difficult to ascertain—perhaps it is only a few hundred million—, but one may speak more definitely in respect of Italian immigration and commerce. Italy's trade with Latin America was unimportant until after the close of the World War, and indeed—comparatively speaking—until 1923. In 1896 it had hardly reached thirty million dollars; it was about forty-six million in 1905 and some one hundred and fifty-four million in 1923.[1]

"The chief contribution of Italy to Latin America," as Professor Martin has well said, "has been the labor of her sons." "From the middle of the nineteenth century up to 1914," to continue quoting this authority, "an ever increasing stream of Italian immigration had found its way to South America, especially to Argentina and Brazil, amounting in the case of the former country to nearly two and a quarter millions and of the latter a million and a quarter. Through their energy and frugality many of these Italians have risen to opulence and their descendants have attained to some of the highest positions in political life."[2] Italian immigration has likewise been "pushing its way with decision into Mexico, Cuba, and Central America, as well as Peru, Bolivia, and Chile."[3] The years of the World War were marked by a large decrease in the number of arrivals, nor has the pre-war quota been reached by any means at the present writing (1927), but the stream continues nevertheless to be of some importance.[4] The Italian strain is to-day about seven per cent of Brazil's population and almost thirty per cent of that of Argentina.[5]

---

[1] *Cf.* United States Department of Commerce and Labor, Bureau of Statistics, *Statistical Abstract of Foreign Countries. Statistics of Foreign Commerce* (1909), *passim;* The Pan American Union, *Foreign Trade Series* (1924, 1925), commerce of the various Latin-American nations.

[2] Percy Alvin Martin, *Latin America and the World War,* (1925), p. 8.

[3] Robert F. Foerster, *The Italian Emigration of Our Times,* (1919), *passim.*

[4] International Labor Office, *Migration Movements,* 1920–1923, p. 16 ff.

[5] Foerster, *op. cit.,* p. 287 ff. See also his "The Italian Factor in the Race Stock of Argentina," in American Statistical Association, *Quarterly Publications* (1919), p. 347 ff.

The presence of this large alien Italian element—larger than that of any other country—has occasionally given rise to official demonstrations on the part of Italy in behalf of its nationals. Its international significance, as well as that of Latin-American citizens with Italian blood in their veins, was more emphatically revealed in 1914–1918 by the strong sympathy for Italy which showed itself in Argentina, Brazil, Peru, and Uruguay. It may possibly give further evidence of its importance in the future by a tendency toward a Pan-Latin *rapprochement*.

Possibly of far greater potential significance for world affairs, however, are the relations between Latin America and a certain nation of the Far East which began only recently to play an active part upon the international stage. At any rate the attention which it has attracted in the last two decades warrants a more extensive treatment of its attitude and rôle.

The Awakening of Japanese Interest

One day in 1892, while the Western Powers and Japan were still in the midst of difficulties arising from an attempt to revise their treaties with China, an agent of the Japanese government appeared in Mexico and conferred upon Porfirio Díaz an honorary membership in the Grand Order of the Chrysanthemum. Was this one of those historical events which are full of significance for the future? China and Latin America were then rapidly becoming spheres of great interest for the United States. Were they soon to become equally important to Japan? China has certainly become so, and during the last few years the Japanese have not been indifferent to the countries of Latin America.

The first treaty of amity and commerce between Japan and one of these countries was that signed with Mexico in 1888. It was followed by similar treaties with Peru, Brazil, Argentina, Chile, Colombia, Bolivia, and Ecuador, the last having been signed in 1918 and ratified in 1919.[6]

It is perhaps illustrative of the alertness of the Japanese government that such treaties should have been negotiated before commerce and intercourse with these countries became at all important. A nation with limited territorial possessions and a crowded and growing population must be farsighted and energetic in its search for markets and fields for the colonization of its surplus people. In 1907 Japan's trade with Latin America amounted only to about two million yen. Although it increased to more than seventy-one million by 1920, it

[6] *Receuil des traités et conventions conclus entre l-'empire japon et les puissances étrangères* (1920), *passim*.

fell off to about twenty-four million in 1922, and it has not experienced any marked change since that time. Argentina, Brazil, Chile, Peru, and Mexico are Japan's best Latin-American customers, but, so far, the trade movement between all of the Latin countries of America and Japan has never equalled two per cent of Japan's total trade.[7] Nor has any considerable progress been made in the matter of emigration. The first Japanese migrated to Latin America about 1897; very few came until 1907, and—despite frequent rumors during the last few years—there are probably less than 60,000 in all Hispanic America to-day (February, 1927).[8]

Thus it must be observed that as a land for surplus population and even in the matter of commerce itself Latin America's significance for Japan lies in the future. It may lie in the near future, however. For some time certain Japanese have looked upon this part of the world as a land of promise, and there are now indications that the Japanese are on the point of a more vigorous effort to avail themselves of the resources of this land.

As early as 1906 and 1907 the opportunities of Hispanic America became a live topic in the Japanese press. The discussion appears to have been led by the steamship companies and colonization enterprises and their business associates. The president of one of the shipping companies, the Toyo Kisen Kaisha, remarked through the columns of the Osaka *Shimpo:* "Our compatriots are boycotted in the United States, and they cannot go into Australia. With the exception of Korea and Manchuria, into what countries can the Japanese emigrate? It is necessary that they be sent to South America

---

[7] See Halleck A. Butts, "Trends in Japanese Trade," in U. S. Department of Commerce, Bureau of Foreign and Domestic Commerce, *Trade Information Bulletin,* No. 389 (1926) ; The Foreign Trade of Japan (Washington, Government Printing Office, 1922).

[8] This estimate is based upon an examination of all the materials on the subject in the Library of the Pan-American Union. The *Monthly Record of Migration* of the International Labor Office set the figure at 28, 141 for the total residing in Brazil in 1919 (No. 9, Feb., 1925, p. 353). The *West Coast Leader* (issue of June 29, 1926) stated that there were at that time 40,000 in Brazil. *The Brazilian American* (March 25, 1922) gave the following estimates:

Brazil	31,000	Argentina	2,000
Peru	6,000	Chile	400

The total in the rest of Hispanic America could not have been more than a few thousand at that time, and there has been no large migration since. Yet *cf.* Genaro Arbaiza, "Acute Japanese Problem in South America," in *Current History,* February, 1925, p. 735 ff., where the writer says the number of Japanese in Latin America is at least 100,000, and predicts a rapid increase in the near future.

where riches abound and labor is scarce." [9] At about the same time the Toyo *Keizai Shimpo* made this startling observation: "The government of Peru welcomes white workers and is not any too fond of yellow laborers, but business in this country is not sufficiently developed to appeal to white labor. It will therefore be obliged to depend upon Far Eastern immigrants. If the [Japanese] minister of foreign affairs and the Emigration Companies put forth all their efforts this country will become a second Hawaii," [10] Only a little less startling was the following statement from the Tokio *Keizai Zasshi*: "In Peru, as in most countries of South America, the governments are weak; they will accordingly never be able to refuse with any great energy to accept Japanese immigrants." [11] Other articles referred to Latin America as the great country of the future for the Japanese, the region holding out the fairest promises for a *Shin Nippon,* or new Japan. The discussion was characterized by all the ardor of a crusade.

Later Development

Nor has interest in the topic greatly diminished since 1907. In the summer of 1910, for instance, the president of another great steamship company wrote in the *Taiyo,* perhaps the most influential monthly in Tokyo: "Our population increases at the rate of 500,000 every year and the time will come before many years when we will be forced to find some new outlet for the surplus population. Some of the South American republics seem willing to receive our immigrants . . ." [12] A few years later a prominent Japanese journalist remarked with more fervor than tact: "The increase of population in this country has reached the breaking-point, and now that we are at the parting of the ways, is our Foreign Office right in keeping quiet? . . . We want to emigrate to South America and North America and the British colonies, first by peaceful means, if possible, and second by the force of the iron hand and the mailed fist, if our desire is resisted." [13] Let these stand as typical—although the last is a bit jingoistic—of the views entertained up to the entrance of Japan and the United States into the World War.

This struggle served only as a temporary distraction. The energetic move of the Japanese delegates in behalf of racial equality

[9] As quoted by Louis Aubert "Les Japonais, le Canada, et l' Amérique du Sud," in *La Revue de Paris,* Series 14, VI, 205.

[10] Quoted in *ibid.,* VI, 211.

[11] Quoted in *ibid., loc. cit.*

[12] Quoted in *Literary Digest,* XLI (June 2, 1910), 12.

[13] Kayohara Kozan, as quoted by Lyenaga, in *Japan's Real Attitude,* p. 37.

at the peace congress is well known. Their failure at that assembly naturally aroused bitterness in many quarters. The great nationalist organ of Tokyo, the *Kokumin*, probably expressed the view of the majority of the people of Japan when it remarked: "The Japanese who are confined to a narrow region in the Far East, together with the nine hundred million yellow population of the world, are at a loss to know why the vast regions of North and South America, Australia, and New Zealand, sparsely populated and rich in natural resources, should be set aside exclusively for the white population. They are quite unreasonable in considering that it is their special privilege to hold the regions for themselves with the notion that the strongest and quickest win. They are the most avaricious privileged classes of mankind. The present is the age in which equality and equal distribution is demanded instead of monopoly. We who are confronted with a great difficulty, with a crowded population, are extremely dissatisfied with the white people, who refuse to acknowledge the difficult position of Japan." [14]

During the last three years Japanese interest in Latin-American commerce and colonization projects has been greater than ever before. Business organizations have sent one mission after another, and the press has been filled with the subject. The *Japan Times and Mail* remarked on December 23, 1922, that it was "high time for Japan to establish a definite policy towards South America and conclude treaties, agreements, or secret pacts with the South American states . . . Opportunity never comes a second time, and we urge the government and business men of this country to seize this golden opportunity . . ." The Tokio *Yamiuri* declared that South America was a favorable field for Japanese emigrants and urged the government to encourage the movement by exchanging diplomatic representatives with the Vatican—a step which would be sure to please the Catholic countries of the New World.[15] Anti-Japanese agitation in California and the movement for exclusion which culminated in the immigration law of May 26, 1924, appear to have caused "a great boom in the idea of South America as a good place for the Japanese to go. Many articles appeared in "newspapers and magazines urging emigration to Brazil, Argentina, and Chile in particular." The Tokio *Yamato* said, "We are heartily in favor of Japanese emigration to South America."[16] Speaking of South America and Mexico, the *Japan Times Weekly* remarked: "Here are large regions which have much the same climatic conditions as are found in Japan; here are broad lands which

[14] As quoted in the *Japan Times and Mail,* December 2, 1922.
[15] As quoted in *Literary Digest,* LXXVI (March 24, 1923), 19.
[16] *Ibid.,* LXXVII (April 28, 1923), 20.

invite the agriculturist; here are growing industries which would like to employ Japanese workmen . . .; here are vast natural resources which beckon to Japanese capital." [17] The walls of the railway stations of Japan were hung with posters displaying maps of one or more of the Latin-American states and pointing out to the people the advantages of migration across the Pacific.[18]

Thus far largely the unofficial views of the Japanese. What of the government? For the last few years the press has been a powerful factor in Japan and the rise and fall of ministries, occurring with almost as much frequency as in countries of western Europe, clearly indicates a certain popular control.[19] Although much of government policy must naturally remain a secret, it may safely be asserted—as indeed we have already indicated—that successive ministries have been alive to the situation. The treaties which have been negotiated with the eight important states of Hispanic America are evidence of this. In every one of them Japanese commercial interests have been carefully safeguarded and great pains have been taken to place the Mikado's subjects on a plane of equality with the nationals of all the more highly civilized countries. Moreover, in spite of its financial difficulties the Japanese government has usually found it possible to subsidize steamship lines and emigration societies, as well as to bear the expense of official missions sent out to survey the field. The first important investigations were begun in 1905. The exclusion bill passed by the United States in May, 1924, appears to have spurred the government to a very special effort which resulted in a new treaty with Mexico (October 8, 1924) and the dispatch of a mission to Mexico and Central and South America for the purpose of studying Japanese emigration possibilities (August, 1925).[20]

Yet, despite all this interest, it must again be pointed out that the importance of Latin America to Japan lies in the future rather than in the present. Japanese trade with this region is still far from enormous and probably not more than 5000 emigrants left Japan for Latin America in 1924.[21] What fate awaits this commerce and this immigration in years to come depends upon several factors, but chiefly upon the official attitude of the United States, Latin America, and Japan.

Attitude of the Latin Americans

Until the present time the attitude of Latin America toward Japan

[17] March 29, 1924.
[18] Literary Digest, LXXXI (May 17, 1924), 22.
[19] See Kisaburo Kawabé, The Press and Politics in Japan.
[20] The Pan-American Union, Bulletin (1925), LIX, 503.
[21] The Japan Times and Mail, December 30, 1924.

and the Japanese has been for the most part friendly. Although certain indications of anti-Japanese feeling have from time to time become evident in Mexico, Argentina, and Brazil, none of the greater states of Latin America have yet seen fit to exclude the Nipponese by legal enactment. In five of the lesser states, however, exclusion has already been written upon the statute books. Costa Rica, by act of July 20, 1896, shuts out Asiatics and Gipsies; by the law of April 30, 1909, Guatemala excludes Asiatics in general; Paraguay has recently closed the door to persons of the yellow race; by decree of January 6, 1915, Uruguay provides for the exclusion of Asiatics whenever the immigration authorities see fit to reject them; Venezuela does not admit immigrants who are not of European race, but natives of the yellow race dwelling in the islands situated in the northern hemisphere may be admitted.[22] Over against these tendencies toward exclusion must be placed the some eight or nine treaties already mentioned, all of which place the Japanese upon a plane of equality with the nationals of all other progressive countries. Moreover, it must be noted that Japan is often viewed as an inspiring example for backward peoples who are trying to escape foreign tutelage and domination. Within the short space of seventy years Japan has risen from an inferior status to a place among the World Powers. This serves as an inspiration to the Latin-American states.

Indeed, in some quarters Japan is looked upon as a sort of godsend or ally. Perhaps there is a hint of this in the Peruvian poet Chocano's *Song of the Future.* There is much more than a hint in Manuel Ugarte's *Future of Latin America,* for here he says that a clash between the United States and Japan would have for the Latins of America "an enormous importance," freeing them from a smothering pressure and enabling them to order their own lives.[23] Soon after the Panama episode of 1903 certain Colombians spoke of the advantages of Japanese friendship and influence.[24] Writing in 1910, F. García Calderón noted that some of the writers of the Latin-American democracies entertained a "certain amount of confidence in the sympathies of Japan," perhaps even counting upon "an alliance with the Empire of the Rising Sun." President Huerta of Mexico probably desired such an alliance, and it is now definitely known that President Carranza actually entered into negotiations with this aim in view.[25] In like manner, a Japanese business delegation, returning in 1922

---

[22] Intenational Labor Office (Geneva), *Emigration and Immigration: Legislation and Treaties* (1922), p. 180 ff.

[23] *El Porvenir de la América Española* (ed. 1920), Ch. VIII.

[24] Aubert, *op. cit.,* p. 204.

[25] Hendrick, *Life and Letters of Walter H. Page,* III, Ch. XII.

from a tour of South America, called attention to the anti-American sentiment which had "arisen among politicians and other enlightened elements," who had realized that the policy of the United States was "more dangerous" than the policies of Japan and of Europe.[26] On the other hand, García Calderón probably states the view of many Latin Americans when he places Japan among the perils which confront these weak nationalities. He says that if Japan should emerge victorious from a war with the United States, "the Japanese would invade Western America and convert the Pacific into a vast closed sea, closed to foreign ambitions, . . . peopled by Japanese colonies." "The Japanese hegemony would not be a mere change of tutelage for the nations of America," Calderón adds. "In spite of essential differences the Latins oversea have certain common ties with the people of the States: a long-established religion, Christianity, and a coherent, European, occidental civilization. Perhaps there is some obscure fraternity between the Japanese and the American Indians,[27] between the yellow men of Nippon and the copper-coloured Quechuas, a disciplined and sober people. But the ruling class, the dominant type of Spanish origin, which imposes the civilization of the white man upon America, is hostile to the entire invading East . . . Powerful and traditional, the Japanese civilization would weigh too heavily upon the Latin democracies, mixed as they are . . . In the conflict between half-breed America and stoic Japan the former would lose both its autonomy and its traditions." [28]

Opposition of the United States.
Japan and Mexico

The attitude of the United States toward the growing influences of Japan in Hispanic America is in part a matter of conjecture. If it could be certain that the Japanese immigrants who enter these countries had no connection with the government of Tokyo, perhaps no serious objection would be raised. Any colonization that has the slightest suspicion of the official in its nature will be resented, however, as an encroachment upon the Monroe Doctrine. In 1912 the United States Senate by an overwhelming vote declared against Jap-

[26] *The Japan Times and Mail*, December 23, 1922.

[27] This is a point dwelt upon by certain writers both in Hispanic America and in Japan. (See *Literary Digest*, XLVIII [February 7, 1914], 252. Pooley, *Japan's Foreign Policies*, p. 130.)

[28] See his *Latin America* (ed. Miall), pp. 330-331.

anese acquisition of coaling stations or harbors in the Western Hemisphere.[29] It is probable that such a declaration met the approval of the American people. Henceforth it may be considered a part of the Monroe manifesto. For the rest, it must be noted that there is considerable Nipponophobia among the American people. And yet, since this is in large measure a contagion which has spread from the Pacific Coast, an abatement may be expected now that exclusion has become an established policy.

The United States has been, and perhaps will continue to be, most concerned with the relations between Japan and Mexico. The exact official procedure of the two governments has of course not been made public, but many rumors, fantastic or more or less plausible, have circulated in the press. A few facts have also come to light. There was a rumor that in 1910 or 1911 Díaz had entered into a secret agreement granting Japan a naval base on Mexican soil.[30] A letter written as late as February 7, 1916, by George C. Crothers, special agent of the State Department in Mexico, still gave a certain credence to the rumor. Crothers remarked that he would not be surprised to "hear that the Japs have landed and cached large quantities of arms and ammunition along the west coast of Mexico for the purpose of supplying the revolutionists with the understanding that their former agreement be upheld." [31] There were likewise interesting reports regarding the relations of Huerta and Villa with the Japanese. Late in December, 1913, Francisco de la Barra, a special agent of the Huerta government, was given an ovation by the people of Tokyo and cordially received by the Japanese court and government.[32] On the 22nd of the following January Hanihara, "the bright Secretary from the Japanese Foreign Office," turned up in Mexico City. He had come, as the wife of the American *chargé* believed, in order "to look into the conditions and, doubtless, the possibilities of the Japanese situation in Mexico." By the close of the month several officials of the Nippon government were being elaborately entertained. "The Japanese officers are being tremendously *fêted*," said Mrs. O'Shaughnessy, "fed by each and every department of the government, till I should think their abstemious 'little Marys' would rebel." On April 20 the Japanese minister appeared to be much ab-

[29] On the Magdalena Bay incident, see *Cong. Rec.*, 62 Cong., 2 Sess., XLVII, pp. 5659–5666, 10045, *passim*.

[30] Gulick, *Anti-Japanese War Stories*, pp. 80–81; Bell, *The Political Shame of Mexico*, p. 36.

[31] Fall of Committee, *Report*, I, 1777–1779.

[32] *Lit. Dig.*, XLVIII (February 14, 1914), 311–312.

sorbed in a plan for the arrangement of the Mexican problem. Certain diplomats who spoke of the matter informally at Mrs. O'Shaughnessy's tea, supposed that Japan would take the side of Mexico. The next day a mob gathered in sight of the American Legation. "Something about *vivan los Japoneses*" could be heard from the window.[33] In December, 1914, while Pancho Villa was in Mexico City, there was a Japanese vessel in Mexican waters. The commander of this vessel came to Mexico City to sound out Villa with reference to possible coöperation against the United States. According to Villa's report, the Japanese officer said that Japan had been preparing for war against the Yankees for three years and that their preparations would be completed in two more. Villa was at that time friendly toward the United States and did not hesitate to make this fact known. The commander of the Japanese vessel "seemed deeply disappointed." [34]

The little that is known and the much that is conjectured with regard to Japanese-Mexican relations between 1911 and 1916 do not serve to render the Zimmermann proposal of January 16, 1917, entirely absurd. It is now known that Carranza fell in at once with the scheme of a sort of triple alliance between Mexico, Germany, and Japan. Late in February, 1917, the Mexican chief had a conference with the Japanese Minister, which "lasted an hour and a half." The revelation of the Zimmermann note made delay seem advisable to Carranza. "The alliance," he said, "has been stultified by its 'premature publication' but would become necessary at a later period." [35] In July, 1919, however, important negotiations with Japan appeared to be under way, for on the 20th of the month the Mexican minister of foreign affairs wrote the Mexican minister in Madrid: "Aguilar [who has recently been connected with the Mexican Foreign Office] will advise you how the treaty with Japan is coming along and I remain convinced of the great advantage it will bring us for our national integrity." [36] Of course it must be noted that Japan publicly repudiated the Zimmermann project, just as the Japanese government, in deference to the United States, had asked a certain Mexican agent to postpone his visit to Tokyo in the summer of 1913; and the outcome

[33] Edith O' Shaughnessy, *A Diplomat's Wife in Mexico*, pp. 159, 168, 282–283, 289. When Manuel Ugarte was carrying out his propaganda in Mexico City in January–February, 1912, "some unknown person distributed . . . Japanese flags from a shop on the central avenue." (See *The Destiny of a Continent*, Rippy ed., p. 74.)

[34] George C. Crothers, in a report to the Secretary of State, dated February 5, 1915, and found in Fall Committee, *Report, loc. cit.*

[35] Hendrick, *op. et loc. cit.*

[36] Fall Committee, *Report*, II, 3364. I am assuming that this document is authentic. In view of its somewhat jingoist nature, however, this *Report* must be used with care.

of the negotiations of 1919 is unknown. Our main interest here lies in the possibilities of the situation. Certainly such an alliance would be viewed with uneasiness and disapprobation by the United States.

The Crux of the Matter

It appears just as certain that any exclusion tendencies which the Latin-American nations may display will be attributed by the Nipponese to the United States. Already this disposition has made itself evident, and Japanese, like Frenchmen, Spaniards, and Germans, are expressing uneasiness with respect to the possibilities locked up in the Monroe Doctrine. A few quotations will suffice to illustrate this phase of the matter. In 1910 an eminent Japanese geographer had the following to say: "There can be no doubt that the opening of the Panama Canal will bring about . . . fresh facilities for communication between Japan and the States of South America. But any sudden progress can hardly be expected either in our commercial or political intercourse with these States . . . because the United States, adhering to the Monroe Doctrine, is sure to intervene in any international affairs that may occur in any part of the American continent. . . . In the present condition of international politics the States in South America cannot enter suddenly into any close intercourse with Japan against the will of the United States. The first thing we have to do is therefore to endeavor to restore our bond of friendship with the United States to its former state . . ." [37] Speaking of the refusal of the Japanese government to receive Felix Díaz, special agent of the Huerta government, in the summer of 1913, the *Jiji-Shimpo*, the serious organ of a responsible group, declared that the Monroe Doctrine was crushing Premier Yamamoto. It expressed the view that the doctrine was being used to shut out the Japanese, not merely from California, but from Mexico and South America as well, and that Washington was resolved to exclude the Japanese from the entire Western Hemisphere, whatever the cost.[38] Fujisawa declared in a recent book that when Japanese immigration was on the point of prospering in Mexico, "America, putting in her oar, secretly gave Mexico a warning to the effect that it would bring danger to Mexico, and obliged the latter to expel the immigrants from the country." [39] In similar fashion Tokutomi, a member of the Japanese House of Peers and Japan's leading literary critic, remarked that the American public seemed inclined to apply exclusion not only to Mexico but "to all South America." "This means," declared Tokutomi, "that if

[37] As quoted in *The Oriental Economic Review*, I, 110.
[38] *Current Opinion*, LV, 316.
[39] *The Recent Aims and Political Development of Japan*, p. 163.

Japan should send her emigrants to South America on a large scale, the United States would have to see to it that they are expelled even if she has to resort to force of arms." [40] Even more recently the idle rumor that the question of Japanese exclusion was to be taken up in a Pan-American congress brought forth a serious lament from the Osaka *Mainishi*. "The proposed plan," remarked this journal, "is intended to extend the [Monroe] doctrine into the field of immigration, which means that the United States wants to have other American countries follow her immigration policy . . ." [41]

If this policy should really be pursued by the United States, much friction would be likely to occur. The seriousness of the ultimate outcome would of course depend upon the degree of coöperation which the Washington government could obtain in South America, the continuation of the exclusion policy in the British Empire, the vigor of American championship of the Open Door in the Far East, the pressure of Japanese population upon the means of subsistence, and the success of Japanese colonization projects in Siberia, Manchuria, and Mongolia. It might also depend in a measure upon the psychological factor of Japanese pride. What may well give rise to uneasiness is the fact that both the United States and Japan are likely to emphasize the Far East and Hispanic America at the same time. Synchronous rivalry in two vast regions by two of the Great Powers must prove a menace to world peace. If the United States could gradually relax its pressure in the Far East, the atmosphere might be cleared. It will certainly not be cleared if the United States should determine to stand for a closed door in the West, while she persistently champions an open door in the East.

[40] *Japanese-American Relations*, p. 105 ff.
[41] December 25, 1924.

CHAPTER XIV

PARTICIPATION OF THE LATIN-AMERICAN NATIONS IN EUROPEAN AFFAIRS

In general it probably may be said that the Latin-American nations have agreed with the United States in the policy of opposing European interference in the political affairs of the New World. There have been exceptions, as in the case of the Dominican Republic and Mexico, but here the invitations to intervene were extended to the European Powers by a minority in defiance of the national will. The Latin-American states have requested the mediation of Europe in their boundary disputes and they have revealed eagerness for European capital, trade, and cultural contacts, but perhaps not for political connections.

It cannot be said, however, that the Latin governments of the New World have had any such conscientious scruples against participation in European affairs as have characterized the United States. It is true that until recently they have not taken part in Old World politics, but this cannot be explained entirely by reference to isolation sentiment. They have been busy with their own problems; and, moreover, the governments of Europe had not evinced any disposition to invite their participation until the outbreak of the World War. Having recognized the independence of the new states at the opening of the last century, Europe had been content to permit them to linger "on the margin of international life."

Latin America at The Hague (1907)

They were not even invited to attend the first peace conference at The Hague, but—thanks largely to the influence of the United States —they were asked to send representatives to the assembly of 1907. They responded without hesitation, and their delegates revealed talents as superior as they were unexpected. Lacking material force to protect themselves, they had the appreciation of all weak states for any legal bulwarks which such a conference might erect.

On the whole, the attitude of the Latin-American delegations at this great assembly accorded with the most progressive ideas of the time. They voted unanimously for applying the Red Cross rules to warfare upon the sea and for the prohibition of the bombardment of undefended towns, villages, or buildings, as well as for giving merchant vessels "due warning and fair play at the opening of hostilities." With the exception of the representatives of the Dominican Republic, they unanimously favored "prohibiting the use of unanchored, automatic, submarine mines, unless constructed in such manner as to become harmless within one hour after their control had been lost," and they were unanimous in support of certain other limitations upon the employment of mines and torpedoes. All except Panama, which abstained from voting, backed the proposal to exempt from capture contraband of war found on neutral vessels, and all except Panama voted for more humane treatment of prisoners-of-war. The majority of these delegations also joined in a declaration against warfare in the air and the use of "dum-dum" bullets, but they were not in favor of the proposal to abolish the capture of private property in warfare upon the sea.

In the matter of arbitration they took a stand which recent developments have rendered most interesting. All but one of them (Haiti) supported a resolution accepting obligatory arbitration in "principle," and they unanimously approved a proposal, introduced by Peru, for voluntary arbitration; but a majority of them favored a Prize Court and a Court of Arbitral Justice only on condition that the judges should be chosen on the basis of the substantial equality of states. If one remembers this fact, the later attitude of Brazil and Argentina toward the League of Nations will more readily be understood.[1]

Latin America and the World War

"Of the twenty Latin-American republics, eight eventually declared war: Brazil, Cuba, Costa Rica, Guatemala, Haiti, Honduras, Nicaragua, and Panama. Five severed relations with Germany: Peru, Bolivia, Uruguay, Ecuador, and the Dominican Republic. Seven remained neutral: Argentina, Chile, Colombia, Mexico, Salvador, Venezuela, and Paraguay . . .

"Of the actual belligerents, only two, Brazil and Cuba, may be said to have taken anything like an active part in the war; while Argentina and Chile, both members of the group of the so-called A B C powers, carefully preserved a status of official neutrality. Mexico, the most important state north of the Isthmus, and next door neighbor to the United States, falls within the same category. In

[1] William I. Hull, "The United States and Latin America at The Hague," in *International Conciliation*, No. 44, July, 1911.

HISPANIC AMERICA,
1925

SPANISH-AMERICAN REPUBLICS

SPANISH-AMERICAN REPUBLICS—
FORMED SINCE 1828

UNITED STATES OF BRAZIL

other words, of the four countries of most consequence in the comity of Latin-American powers three studiously remained aloof from the struggle. It must also be conceded that the military contributions of the Latin-American belligerents to the common cause did little to tip the balance of victory in favor of the Allies. . . . The military and naval aid offered by Brazil and Cuba, owing in part to motives outside their control, was all but negligible. Of much greater weight to be sure, was the material assistance rendered the United States and the Allies. . . ." [2]

To this excellent summary quoted from the best authority on the attitude of the Latin-American nations toward the World War, only a few comments need be added. It should be noted, for instance, that some of the neutral states, like Mexico and Chile, furnished the Allies commodities most essential to the conduct of the war, such as petroleum and nitrates. It should be noted further that all except one of the belligerent states—namely, Brazil—are situated in the Caribbean area and, hence, were deeply affected by the influence of the United States.

More important, indeed, than the actual participation of these states in the war were the cross-currents of sentiment that were revealed and the prestige which the Latin Americans gained in world affairs. No longer can it be said of them that they linger "on the margin of international life."

The currents of opinion revealed during the war years from the Rio Grande to the Strait of Magellan served in a measure as a barometer that registered the results of the spirited rivalry which we have outlined in previous chapters. On the side of the Central Powers was the sympathy in some circles for Germany and, to some extent also, the sympathy for Spain. Counterbalancing this were the strong affinity for France and Italy and the economic influence of Great Britain and the United States, to say nothing of the appeal made by the idealism of Woodrow Wilson and perhaps also a certain pressure exerted by Washington in the Caribbean area. Nor should it be forgotten that Mexico's pro-Germanism and Colombia's neutrality were due in part to hostility toward the United States.

Latin America and the League of Nations

Although the rôle of the Latin-American nations in the World War was somewhat insignificant, their relation to this catastrophe nevertheless marked an important epoch in the history of the participation of these countries in European affairs. Henceforth their political con-

[2] P. A. Martin, *Latin America and the War* (1925), pp. 1-2.

nections with Europe are to be much closer. Thirteen of them were entitled to take part in the Versailles peace conference, and eleven of them actually signed the peace treaty, their procedure being subsequently ratified in every instance save one (Ecuador). Thus ten Latin-American states became charter members of the League of Nations. By the terms of the annex other states were invited to join, and soon afterwards all of the nations of Latin America save three—Mexico, which had not been invited; the Dominican Republic, whose national life had suffered a hiatus owing to the intervention of the United States; and Ecuador—voted their adhesion. Moreover, the Dominican Republic became a member in September, 1924, as soon as American military intervention was relaxed, so that all but two of the Latin states of America were listed as members on July 1, 1925, although, as will subsequently appear, the status of some of them was somewhat doubtful.

The Latin Americans have taken an active part in the work of the League of Nations. Two of them served as presidents of recent Assemblies: Augustín Edwards of Chile and Cosme de la Torriente y Peraza of Cuba; and two of them—Dominicio da Gama of Brazil and Alberto Guani of Uruguay—have been presidents of the Council. Two of the eleven judges of the Permanent Court of International Justice are from Latin America: Antonio Sánchez de Bustamente of Cuba and Epitacio da Silva Pessoa of Brazil, the latter having succeeded the distinguished Brazilian Ruy Barbosa. The Latin Americans are likewise represented on many of the standing committees of the League and there is a "Bureau in the League to deal with Latin-American affairs."

"The prominent positions to which the Latin-American republics and their citizens have been elected is evidence of the desire of other members to attach them strongly to the league. And some of the Latin Americans are saying that they have already been given more genuine recognition and accorded more actual power as fully coequal states in the League of Nations than they have received in their own Pan-American Union." [3] Perhaps their prominence has been due also in part to a sort of Latin solidarity, just as their adhesion in the first place was possibly caused in a measure by fear of the United States.

On several occasions the Latin-American delegates have become conspicuous in discussions relating to the League and its policies. Some of them caused a bit of a stir at the very outset by demanding a definition of the Monroe Doctrine which, at the insistence of the United States, was expressly mentioned in the Covenant. Very re-

[3] George H. Blakeslee, *The Recent Foreign Policy of the United States* (1925), pp. 174–175.

cently the position of Brazil on the admission of Germany brought the representatives of Portuguese America into the foreground. Between these two events several others transpired to remind the world that a new group of nations was actively participating in its international life.

As soon as the chief of the Honduran delegation, ex-President Policarpo Bonilla, learned of the move to demand recognition of the Monroe Doctrine in the League constitution he attempted to secure from the assembled Peace Conference a definition of the manifesto. In a communication which he presented to that body he said in part: "The Monroe Doctrine affects the Latin-American republics directly. As it has never been written into an international document, nor been expressly accepted by the nations of the Old Continent, nor of the New World; and as it has been defined and applied in different manners by presidents and other statesmen of the United States of America, I believe that it is necessary that in the pact about to be subscribed it should be defined with entire clearness, in such a way that it may be incorporated in the written international law."

The Honduran statesman then proposed the following amendment to the League Covenant: "This Doctrine, which the United States of America have maintained since the year 1823, when it was proclaimed by President Monroe, signifies that: All the republics of America have a right to independent existence; that no nation may acquire by conquest any part of the territory of any of these nations, nor interfere with its internal government or administration, nor do any other act to impair its autonomy or to wound its national dignity. It is not to hinder the 'Latin'-American countries from confederating or in other forms uniting themselves, seeking the best way to realize their destiny." [4]

When the League pact was finally framed, with Article XXX declaring that nothing in the Covenant should "be deemed to affect the validity of international engagements . . . such as the Monroe Doctrine," El Salvador evinced anxiety similar to that which had been revealed by the agent of Honduras. Secretary of State Lansing was called upon to define the Monroe Doctrine.

The affair proved to be merely a tempest in a teapot. Lansing took plenty of time—two months—to answer the request and then responded that the views of the United States with reference to the Doctrine could be found in the utterances of President Wilson; and the proposal of Bonillas was never seriously considered by the Peace Conference. Nevertheless, Honduras and El Salvador joined the

4 Martin, *op. cit.*, pp. 504–505, and authorities cited.

League. Their attitude regarding the Monroe Doctrine was merely a straw pointing the direction of the wind.[5]

Soon afterwards the Argentine delegation caused a brief disturbance by the submission of three proposals to the First Assembly of the League and a spectacular withdrawal when that body refused to consider them. The proposals were: (1) admission to the League of all sovereign states which should express a desire to join; (2) the adoption of the principle of equality in the election of members of the Council instead of giving the permanent tenure of five places to the great powers; (3) the establishment of a permanent court of international justice and acceptance of the principle of compulsory arbitration. The influential members of the League were not ready to accept any of these proposals, and least of all the first, which would have meant the admission of Germany. When a committee of the League reported against the consideration of any amendments to the Covenant at that time the Argentine representatives forthwith withdrew. Argentina has not participated in the work of the organization since that date, but there are indications that it will be only a matter of time until she will once more take part in its deliberations.[6]

Somewhat similar but not precisely analogous was the recent attitude of Brazil. In March, 1926, the League Assembly met in a call session to consider the admission of Germany. It was soon discovered that Brazil, Spain, and Poland had been engaging in a bit of secret diplomacy. They had agreed to vote in favor of admitting the German nation and granting it a permanent seat in the Council, provided they also were granted permanent seats, and apparently they had done this in spite of previous promises to support these concessions to Germany unconditionally. The Assembly could find no way around the difficulty and hence was forced to defer the question of admitting Germany until the following September.

Meanwhile a commission was appointed to work out a plan for the reconstruction of the Council. On September 3 this commission reported in favor of increasing the number of temporary members of the Council from six to nine. They were to be elected for a period of three years and were not to be re-eligible for three years after the expiration of their respective terms, but the Assembly could decide by a two-thirds majority to make certain exceptions. The purpose of this last provision "was to make it possible for Spain and Brazil to remain in the Council almost indefinitely, since presumably they could always secure the votes of the Latin-American delegates. By this means Spain and Brazil would in fact become permanent

[5] Martin, op. cit., p. 575.
[6] Ibid., pp. 554–564.

members of the Council, but would hold non-permanent seats. This solution had the merit of preserving the *status quo* as to the number of permanent seats in the Council and of satisfying the pride of the Powers demanding permanent membership in" that body. But the arrangement failed to meet the approval of Brazil and Spain and, when it became evident that Germany was going to be admitted and the new plan adopted in spite of their opposition, they announced their withdrawal from the League.[7]

In the settlement of difficulties between the nations of Latin America the League has as yet taken no part. Both Peru and Bolivia appealed to it for the revision of the Treaty of Ancón and the settlement of the Tacna-Arica dispute, but the Chilean delegation, with Sr. Augustín Edwards at its head, was opposed to the consideration of the question by the Assembly and a committee of jurists soon decided that the League had no authority to intervene. Early in 1921, when news reached Europe that Panama and Costa Rica, both members of the League, were at the point of war over a boundary dispute, the secretary-general of the League wired for information. Both states promptly replied, but before the League had time for further action Secretary of State Hughes interfered and the officials of the League beat "an almost indecorous" retreat.[8]

Thus it becomes evident that this great organization has not only failed to satisfy certain demands of the Latin-American states, but so far has been unable to assist in the promotion of peace in the Western Hemisphere. For these reasons, if for no other, it would seem that the ardor of the Latin Americans for the League is beginning to cool. Only one of the more influential nations of Hispanic America (Chile) continues to participate in its activities. Peru, Bolivia, and Costa Rica, as well as Argentina and Brazil, have withdrawn and Mexico and Ecuador, as already noted, have never belonged.

It must, in fact, be admitted that in their relation to the League the diplomats of Latin America have shown themselves to be not without ambition. They not only have demanded a permanent seat in the Council and acceptance on the basis of national equality, but they have urged that Spanish be considered as one of the official languages of the Assembly; they have sought to promote a sentiment of solidarity among the small nations; and they have often evinced the Pan-Hispanic spirit. Something of their attitude is revealed in a recent article written by a distinguished Peruvian who is one of

[7] *Cf.* Caleb Perry Patterson, in *The Southwestern Political and Social Science Quarterly,* VII (1925), 1 ff.

[8] Martin, *op. cit.,* p. 568.

the advisers of the League Institute of Intellectual Coöperation. Among other things the writer says: "The participation of the Latin-American people in the League of Nations has given it both strength and world significance . . . The enthusiasm manifested by the Latin-American nations towards the League is due to the fact that its principles were entirely in accordance with the idealistic traditions of Latin America. Besides this, participation in the League enhances the international significance of these countries." The writer then points out certain objections which the nations of Latin America have raised against the organization of the League and urges that its membership should be divided into ethnical and cultural groups which should be allowed freely to elect their representatives to the Council. He mentions eight possible groups and expresses the view that "every group should choose two representatives, except the Iberian group, which, on account of the number of nations involved, should choose four." [9]

[9] V. A. Belaúnde, in *Current History*, February, 1927, pp. 706–707.

CHAPTER XV

YANKEE HEGEMONY AND LATIN-AMERICAN SUSPICION

THE reader who has followed the narrative up to this point will perhaps not be surprised to learn that the United States is to-day politically and economically predominant in the New World. In recent years the European Powers have gradually come to recognize our paramount interest and have showed little disposition to run counter to our will in Latin America. In 1913 our share of Latin-American trade was greater than that of England and surpassed the total commerce of Germany and France combined. In 1925 it was considerably greater than that of all three of these European nations.

The investments of United States citizens in Latin America, comparatively small until the outbreak of the World War, had risen to more than four billion dollars by June, 1925—a sum almost as large as that of British subjects in 1913 and probably greater than the total of German and French nationals in 1925. And, what is more important, the investments of United States citizens are increasing and those of the Europeans are not.[1] In short, the United States and its citizens virtually dominate the economic and political life of the majority of the republics south of the Rio Grande.

There are several reasons for the present position of the United States. Its population, due largely to the tremendous inflow of immigrants, has increased more rapidly than that of the Latin-American nations. Its history has in general been characterized by order and growing unity, while the history of Latin America has evinced opposite characteristics. Lastly, the Europeans have been too jealous of one another, too involved in Continental turmoils, and too absorbed elsewhere, to defy the Monroe Doctrine, meet the economic competition of the United States, or prevent our growing ascendancy.

Caribbean Control

It is in the Caribbean that the expanding political and economic influence of the United States may most clearly be seen and only

---

[1] Even the investments of the British decreased some sixty million dollars between 1923 and 1925 (*Revista Económica*, XIV (1927), 300).

since 1898 have the most rapid strides been made. To-day we have two-thirds of the commerce and a virtual monopoly of the resources of this region. Let us briefly survey the countries in which the United States exercises a virtual control.

For many years the United States has been greatly interested in Cuba. In the early period its main concern was to prevent the island from falling into the hands of a strong European Power, but since 1848 there has existed considerable sentiment for its acquisition. The value which we once set upon this "Pearl of the Antilles" may be judged from the fact that in 1848 the Department of State offered Spain one hundred million dollars for it—a price far in excess of what we have paid for all of our territorial purchases combined. Since 1898 we have intervened in the island with military force on four occasions, and it has been a virtual protectorate of the United States since 1901. In 1895 the value of our trade with the island was a little less than sixty-six million dollars; in 1923 it amounted to more than five hundred and thirty-seven million. In 1898 our investments amounted to a paltry fifty million; in 1925 they were one thousand three hundred and sixty million, of which sum one hundred and ten million represented government loans. The United States has a navy base in the island, and the Cuban government can make no loan nor dispose of any territory without our consent. Our representative at Havana exercises great influence over the political and financial policies of the country and its "economic life is determined by absentee landlords and bankers living in the United States."

The government and citizens of the United States have been vitally interested in a canal route across Panama since 1846, and in 1903 we acquired this route largely as the result of a military intervention that prevented Colombia, of which Panama was a part, from suppressing a revolt. Since its birth in 1903 the Republic of Panama has been a virtual protectorate and we have intervened by armed force on four occasions. Since 1905 the value of our trade has increased from less than six to more than twenty-two million dollars, and in 1925 the investments of American citizens were estimated at twenty-two million, of which six million were in government loans. The United States has an agreement with the little nation which provides for the disbanding of the Panamanian army and the acquisition of any territory that may be necessary for the protection of the Canal. Our latest move has been the signing of a treaty which requires Panama to become our ally in any war that we may undertake against another Power.

The Dominican Republic has been a virtual protectorate of the United States since 1905 and American marines occupied the little country almost continuously from 1914 to 1924. In 1905 our Dominican trade was worth about six million dollars; in 1923 it had almost reached seventeen million. By 1925 citizens of the United States held government loans amounting to fifteen million dollars. Important revenues of the country are in the hands of a general receiver of customs appointed by the President of the United States. "Outside of the banking interests of the International Banking Corporation (National City Bank), with seven branches in the Republic and almost complete control over the financial life of the country, American companies are operating sugar mills, flour mills, and dye-extracting plants." [2]

The United States government and its citizens have been interested from time to time in Nicaragua ever since 1847 when they became rivals of the British for the control of a canal route which crosses its domain. Our marines have intervened six times since 1899, and we have exercised a virtual protectorate since 1912. In 1910 our exports and imports were worth three million dollars; in 1923 they were valued at more than nine million. In 1925 the investments of American citizens were estimated at sixteen million dollars and three million were in government loans. The finances of the country are in charge of a high commission of three persons—one appointed by the State Department, one by American bondholders, and one by Nicaragua—and an American collector has charge of the customs. Several thousand marines have recently been landed in the country to "protect" American interests and support Adolfo Díaz against a rival candidate for the presidency.

The United States has been more or less vitally concerned in the fate of Haiti since the opening of the last century when Napoleon Bonaparte threatened to make the country the capital of an American empire. Some two thousand marines were landed in the little republic in 1915 and since that time it has been a protectorate of the United States. Although the country was a part of the Spanish empire for two centuries, its people are mainly African and have been influenced more by French than by Spanish culture. The trade of the United States with the republic amounted to three million dollars in 1915 and to ten million in 1923. In 1925 our investments totaled twenty-three million dollars, of which seventeen million were in government loans. The revenues of the country are under the control of a high commissioner, a general receiver of customs, and a financial adviser, all Americans appointed by the president of Haiti on the nomination of the president of the United States.

[2] Robert W. Dunn, *American Foreign Investments* (1925), p. 133.

The United States has intervened with military force in Honduras five times since 1907. Our trade with the country was less than four million in 1910 and more than sixteen million in 1923; our investments totaled forty million dollars in 1925.

Military intervention by the Washington government occurred in Costa Rica in 1919. Our trade with the country was valued at six million in 1905 and more than nine million in 1923; our investments were worth somewhere between twenty and thirty million dollars in 1925, two million of this amount being in government loans.

Military or naval forces of the United States have occupied Mexico on numerous occasions since 1846, particularly the frontier regions. The occupation of Vera Cruz in 1914 was partially responsible for the overthrow of Huerta and the success of the Carranza revolution. Between 1895 and 1923 our Mexican trade increased from less than thirty-one to more than two hundred and forty-eight million dollars. Between 1899 and 1925 our investments increased from one hundred and eighty-five to about one thousand three hundred and eighteen million dollars. Of the latter sum about sixty million were in government loans. Diplomatic pressure has often been employed in support of our "vested interests," attempts to effect a change in the oil and land laws of the recent régime being a conspicuous example.

Here, then, are eight of the republics to the south whose destiny has been influenced by the military and diplomatic intervention of the United States. But this is still not the complete story of our control in the Caribbean. There is Salvador, whose trade with the United States has increased from a little over two million in 1905 to almost ten million in 1923, seventeen million dollars' worth of whose resources and government loans are owned in the United States, and whose customs are taken in by an American collector appointed by an American corporation with the approval of the Department of State. There is Guatemala where Americans own resources and enterprises valued at fifty million dollars and whose trade with the United States increased from less than six million in 1905 to more than seventeen million in 1923. Moreover, it should be added that the political life of all the Central American republics virtually has been dominated by the United States since 1907. At that time the Washington government, assisted by Mexico, helped these little republics to set up a Court of Justice.

In 1923 their representatives were invited to Washington where they were induced to sign treaties foregoing the "right of revolution." These treaties have been put forward as a partial justification for the recent landing of marines in Nicaragua, and they may serve as an excuse for further intervention in the future.

But the story of our expansion into the Caribbean area is still incomplete. The virtual control of the United States government does not extend beyond the countries already mentioned, but the economic influence of its citizens is very strong in Venezuela and Colombia, which may in a sense be denominated "Caribbean states."

American investments in the former country amounted to three million dollars in 1912 and to seventy-five million in 1925, while our trade increased from a little over ten millions in 1905 to more than twenty-four million in 1923. It should be recalled, also, that the United States served as a kind of protector of Venezuela in 1895 and in 1902-1903.

The growth of our interests ,in Colombia has been much more rapid. Our investments rose from two million in 1912 to eight-seven million in 1925; our trade from ten million in 1905 to sixty-four million in 1923. Recently a commission of American financial experts reorganized the fiscal system of Colombia and gave the government advice with reference to the expenditure of the twenty-five million which the United States had paid in compensation for the Canal Zone and in order to prepare the way for valuable oil concessions.

Economic Interests Beyond the Caribbean

Outside of the Caribbean area military and economic intervention by the United States government has not yet occurred, but our commerce and investments have undergone a speedy growth even here. American trade with the five republics of southern South America now amounts to about six hundred million dollars annually, while American investments were valued at one billion in 1925. These countries fall within the sphere marked off by the Monroe Doctrine, but internal stability and distance render the establishment of protectorates very unlikely in most of them at any time in the immediate future. Nevertheless, it is by no means inconceivable that the economic stake of the United States is rapidly moving toward a position of predominance and intervention in the nearer and more disorderly nations of Ecuador, Peru, and Bolivia.

The trend in the three last-named states may be indicated by reference to a few recent occurrences. Our commerce with Ecuador more than doubled between 1913 and 1923; our investments have reached thirty million; and a short time ago the Ecuadorian government employed an American financial adviser, perhaps to pave the way for a loan. In Peru, where the national government is headed by a dictator, American investments have increased very rapidly in the last few years. In 1925 they were valued at one hundred million dollars, some seven or eight million of which represented a government loan secured by revenues collected by an agent of an American company. Between 1910 and 1923 the United States' share of Peru's trade increased from twelve to thirty-two million. In Bolivia even more rapid strides have been made. Commerce with this republic has more than quadrupled in the last twelve years, and American investments have grown from ten million in 1912 to eighty million in 1925. Of this latter sum about thirty million dollars represent holdings in government loans, most of which have been negotiated recently by Bolivia's dictator-president upon very onerous terms. The main features of the twenty-four million loan contract of May 31, 1922, will amply illustrate this point. They were: "(1) the creation of a Permanent Fiscal Commission to supervise the Republic's finances, this Commission to consist of three members, of whom two were to be appointed on the recommendation of the Bankers, one of whose appointees was to be elected chairman of the Commission and a director of the Banco de la Nación Boliviana; (2) a pledge of all the securities of the Republic and practically all its revenues, as well as a railroad to be built with the proceeds of the loan, which railroad would be sold with a 99-year free and tax-free concession in case of default; and (3) the sale of $19,000,000 par value of Bonds at a purchase price of 92%, yielding interest at approximately 8.7% per annum." [3]

Yankeephobia

Such is our economic and political position in the Western Hemisphere and such the rapid movement by which it has been effected. The achievement has had its unpleasant aspects, however; and, among them, nothing has been more unpleasant than the growing irritation and suspicion which have been aroused in Latin America. Widespread fear and hatred have developed along with our hegemony. For the last twenty-five years Yankeephobia has been a rather prevalent malady south of the Rio Grande. It has been confined mainly to the literary men and the publicists, the university students and the radicals, but by no means exclusively to these classes. A few illustrations must suffice.

Professor Ford of Harvard University says: "In the writings of

[3] For the preceding paragraphs, see Dunn, *op. cit.*; W. R. Shepherd, in *Cong. Record*, 69 Cong., 2 Sess. (Jan. 20, 1927), p. 2051 ff.

more recent Spanish-American authors antipathy toward the United States presents itself in unmistakable terms, and is directed chiefly at what the authors are pleased to term our imperialism, our alleged desire to extend our territorial bounds and absorb the Spanish-American republics." [4] Doctor Goldberg sums up the attitude of the *literati* of Spanish America in the following language: "At best (always speaking generally) we are in their eyes as yet too engrossed in material ambitions to give attention to spiritual considerations; at worst we are the intriguing nation that despoiled Mexico of Texas and California, despoiled Spain of Cuba, despoiled Colombia of Panama, and who now, under the shield of the Monroe Doctrine and an alleged Pan-Americanism, cherish imperialistic designs upon the entire southern continent." [5]

Francisco García Calderón, the distinguished diplomat and writer of Peru, has a chapter on the "Yankee Peril" in his recent history of Latin America. Elsewhere he has written that the people of the disorderly and backward states of Latin America "prefer permanent revolution to order imposed from without; the sanguinary apprenticeship of autonomy . . . to the grandness and decadence of oppression . . ."—"They would choose anarchy, destruction even, rather than suffer the unlawful intrusion of any foreign power which ventures to interfere in the internal affairs of a free country." [6]

José Enrique Rodó, a Uruguayan poet much admired in Latin America and especially popular among the youth, sets forth a critical view of North American ideals mainly for the purpose of illustrating what the ideals of Latin Americans ought not to be. He says that we are materialistic, selfish, utilitarian; that we lack noble traditions, spiritual aspirations, the poetic instinct. Even our religion is merely an "auxiliary force of penal legislation which would abandon its past the day it should become possible to give to utilitarian morals the religious authority which John Stuart Mill was ambitious to give it." "The apex of its ethics is the ethics of Franklin," he says, referring to the United States. "A philosophy of conduct which ends in the mediocrity of honesty, in the utility of prudence, in whose bosom never surges holiness nor heroism, . . . it is no more than a fragile, dull creature when it endeavors to ascend the dizzy heights."

Rufino Blanco-Fombona, an able author and editor of Venezuela, began his career of "roistering antipathy" toward the United States

[4] *Main Currents in Spanish Literature* (New York, 1919), p. 273.
[5] *Studies in Spanish-American Literature* (New York, 1920), p. 95.
[6] For this and subsequent quotations, see Rippy, "Literary Yankeephobia in Hispanic America," *The Journal of International Relations*, XII (1922), 350 ff.

at the early age of eighteen. "The Yankees, the Yankees, these are
the enemies of our soul, of our civilization, of our character, of our
independence . . . the imitation of anything Yankeean, in whatever
line it may be, must be odious to us." With the spiritual unity of Hispanic America as his motto and opposition to the United States as
his program, he propounds his gospel wherever he goes. From his
editorial chair in Madrid he has been publishing for some time a
series of volumes calculated to promote Hispanic Americanism and
hostility toward the United States. In 1917 he gave a long list of
grievances against the North Americans. The people of South
America "detest them," he said, "for their fraudulent elections, for
their trusts, for their Tammany Hall, for their levity in feminine
customs, for the bad faith of their commerce, for their ridiculous,
palavering Roosevelt, for their shirt-sleeve diplomacy, for their university professors who write about the affairs of Hispanic America
with supine ignorance, for their blowing up of the *Maine,* for their
secession of Panama, for their supervision of the finances of Honduras, for their seizure of the custom-houses of Santo Domingo, for
the blood which they spilled and the independence which they nulli-
fied in Nicaragua, for the revolutions which they foment in Mexico
and their disembarkation at Vera Cruz, for their" trumped-up claims,
"for their malicious designs upon the Galápagos Islands of Ecuador
and the Chinchas of Peru, for their daily allegation that the statistics
of Argentina do not merit acceptance, for presuming to prevent
Brazil from fixing the price she desires upon her coffee, for the 'sand-
bagging' of Porto Rico, for the Platt amendment to the constitution
of Cuba, for having purposely converted their cables and periodicals
into a bureau for discrediting each and every one of the republics of
[Hispanic] America, for their aggressive imperialism, for all their
conduct with respect to [Hispanic] America, from the middle of last
century to the present."

Señor Carlos Pereyra, Mexican historian and diplomat, is another
prolific Yankeephobe, who exercises his pen upon such topics as the
Monroe Doctrine, Manifest Destiny, North American Imperialism,
the constitution of the United States as "an instrument for pluto-
cratic oppression," and the short-comings of George Washington. He
is ably supported by the Mexican radical Isidro Fabela, whose recent
volume entitled *The United States versus Liberty* is a severe attack
upon our imperialism.

The Nicaraguan poet, Rubén Darío, trembled at the spectre of an
English-speaking Hispanic America and composed an uncompli-
mentary *Ode to Roosevelt,* whose volcanic violence he considered
typical of Anglo-American aggression meditating an invasion "of

that ingenious America in whom glows indigenous blood," whose sons still pray to "Jesus Christ and speak Spanish." Salvador Merlos, another Central American, published a volume warning his countrymen against the Peril. "There is for the people of Latin America," he said, "a grave danger which no one ignores: Yankee Imperialism. This imperialism is somewhat like an infuriated sea which threatens to inundate our green fields and to extinguish the fire of our plutonic volcanoes; it is similar to a tempestuous wind which threatens to tumble down the great edifice of our republican institutions and bury beneath its ruins the heroic achievements and the name of the race . . ."

In far-off Argentina the United States has several bitter critics, and none more bitter than Manuel Ugarte. For more than twenty years this distinguished writer has been trying to arouse his compatriots to the Yankee menace. With this end in view, he has not only written numerous books and articles, but he has toured the Latin-American capitals on a campaign of propaganda. In a letter written to President-elect Woodrow Wilson in 1912 he stated the case of the nations south of the Rio Grande in the following emphatic manner:

"We desire that Cuba be freed from the painful weight of the Platt amendment; we desire that there should be granted to Nicaragua the ability to dispose of her soil, *leaving it to the people to depose those who govern them with the aid of a foreign army, if they deem it necessary;* we desire that the status of Porto Rico be settled in accord with the rights of humanity; we desire that the abominable injustice committed against Colombia be repaired so far as possible; we desire that Panama, which to-day suffers the consequences of a temporary displacement, be ceded the dignity of a nation; we desire that the pressure which is being exerted in the port of Guayaquil shall cease; we desire that the archipelago of Galápagos be respected; we desire that liberty be conceded to the heroic Filipinos; we desire that Mexico shall not always see suspended above her flag Damocles's sword of intervention: we desire that the disorders of Putomayo shall not serve as a pretext for diplomatic dexterities; we desire that the companies which commit abuses shall not be supported in their unjust demands; we desire that the republic of Santo Domingo be not suffocated by unjust oppression; we desire that the United States abstain from officiously intervening in the domestic politics of our countries, and that they discontinue the acquisition of ports and bays on the continent; we desire that measures of sanitation shall not serve to diminish the sovereignty of the nations of the Pacific; we ask, in short, that the star-spangled banner cease to be a symbol of oppression in the New World."

It is not necessary to continue with these illustrations. The citations here given are a bit extreme, but denunciations only a little less severe may be found in the works of scores of publicists, and in most of the newspapers and periodicals, whenever any crisis arises in inter-American relations. Enough has been presented to indicate the main causes of complaint. Whoever desires to pursue the matter further may find ample satisfaction in the bibliography presented in the English edition of Manuel Ugarte's *Destiny of a Continent* (1925), in the copious excerpts given by Juan Álvarez in his *Monroe Doctrine* (1923), or in any file of Latin-American periodicals for the last twenty-five years.

The sentiment of Yankeephobia, like all sentiments, is subject to ebb and flow. It has run both deep and broad since 1903, as already noted, but the springs of its origin must be sought far back in the mountains of the past. A brief sketch of its history will not be inappropriate at this point.

A great deal of bunkum as been written in this country about Pan-Americanism. As a matter of fact, an ardent desire for intimate relations with the United States has never existed among the majority of the political and intellectual leaders of Latin America. It has never existed at all save in such times of dire need as the independence period and the Maximilian era. Suspicion and jealousy of the United States showed itself even during the first quarter of the nineteenth century. Fear of the "Colossus" was expressed in Cuba as early as 1811 and by a Mexican diplomat before the close of the year 1822. It would be somewhat inaccurate to term the assembly which met at Panama in 1826 a Pan-American congress; for Simón Bolívar, who called the representatives of the American nations together, regretted that the United States had been invited and neither the Mexican President nor Bolívar thought that the Yankee nation should become a member of the American league. Both welcomed English representation as a check upon the United States, and the Mexican delegation sought to hasten the deliberations of the congress so that it might be adjourned before the Washington agents arrived.[7]

The annexation of Texas (1845), the Mexican War (1846–1848), and the raids of North American filibusters into Mexico, Cuba, and Central America (1850–1857) tended to increase these apprehensions until they were felt by the far-off mountain people of Bolivia.

[7] This view of the Panama Congress is based upon two illuminating papers read at the Ann Arbor meeting of the American Historical Association in December, 1925: R. F. Arragon, "Pan-Americanism versus Spanish-Americanism;" and Lewis Hanke, "The Attitude or Simon Bolívar toward the Participation of the United States in the Congress of Panama."

The danger of European intervention which revealed itself in so many instances during the 'sixties of last century assuaged but did not obliterate the fear of Yankee aggression, and Yankeephobia became more prevalent than ever during the decade and a half between 1897 and 1912. The defeat of Spain in 1898 alarmed a good many Latin Americans. They "saw in the triumph of 'Yankeeland' . . . the victory of the strong over the weak, of the lusty barbarian over the delicate and exquisite being." Roosevelt's procedure in Panama and his Big Stick policy in the Caribbean, Taft's so-called Dollar Diplomacy, and Lodge's Magdalena Bay Resolution caused a veritable epidemic of Yankeephobia to spread all over Latin America. Although President Wilson made an earnest attempt to check the malady, his inconsistencies in the Caribbean rendered anything like a complete cure impossible. The world policies as well as the Latin-American policies of subsequent administrations have served to aggravate rather than subdue the disease.[8]

Never have the Latin peoples of America been more bitter toward the United States than they are now. The recent procedure of the United States in reference to Mexico and Nicaragua, particularly the latter, has called forth almost unanimous condemnation. The newspapers of the Caribbean have expressed decided antipathy; students, labor organizations, and radicals throughout Latin America have been fervent in their denunciations. All this might have been expected, perhaps. But even the great dailies of Argentina, Brazil, and Chile have been severe in their comments. It is a condition which invites careful analysis based upon historical perspective.[9]

[8] For a fuller historical statement of the Latin-American attitude, see the Editor's Introduction to Ugarte, *The Destiny of a Continent* (1925).

[9] Where the Latin-American journals are not available, excerpts from them may be consulted in the New York *Times, The Christian Science Monitor, The Living Age,* and *The Literary Digest,* for the period extending from December 25 to January 25, 1926–1927.

CHAPTER XVI

CURRENT PROBLEMS IN INTER-AMERICAN RELATIONS
—CONCLUSION

AT the present time harmony in the Western Hemisphere is threatened by four specific difficulties and a general atmosphere of distrust and antipathy. Three of the specific problems concern the relations of the United States with nations of Latin America. The fourth not only affects the peace of the Latin countries of South America but, for historical reasons, involves the United States as well.

Tacna-Arica

In the evolution of the Tacna-Arica Question the United States has incurred a measure of responsibility as well as some degree of censure. Indeed, the problem might not have arisen in the first instance had it not been for the interposition of our diplomats. When, in 1879, a war broke out between Chile, Peru, and Bolivia over certain provinces bordering upon the Pacific coast, the United States was served in these regions by very incapable agents. Those who were there at the outset had been appointed as a reward for humble party loyalty, and those who came a little later were military officers who had to be cared for after the army of occupation had been withdrawn from the South. They were not only inexperienced, but they were exceedingly jealous of each other and prone to exceed their instructions. And matters were further complicated by three changes in the personnel of the State Department while the War of the Pacific (1879–1883) was in progress. More skilled European diplomacy stood ready to mediate, but on two occasions the United States frowned upon this proposal. It was a task which had to be confined to American diplomacy.

And American diplomacy lent a hand as inefficient as it was eager. The United States might have brought the struggle to a close in 1880 without serious injury to either combatant, had it not been for its bungling agents. Shortly afterwards our representative in Lima committed the crowning blunder of siding with Peru. He assured the Peruvian government that the United States would not permit Chile

254

to retain any conquered territory, and, in part as a result of this assurance, the Peruvians continued a losing fight only to find in the end that they had been depending upon an unauthorized promise. By the treaty of 1883 (ratified in 1884) Peru was forced to hand over one province to Chile and to surrender two more (Tacna and Arica) temporarily, their final disposition—in accordance with the suggestion of Major Logan, agent of the United States in Chile!— to be decided by a plebiscite ten years hence. Thus the eagerness of the United States to arbitrate and the inefficiency of its diplomacy had been responsible in a measure for creating the problem of the Pacific.

For one reason and another the plebiscite was not held at the scheduled time and the matter drifted along until hostilities between Chile and Peru threatened to break out just as President Wilson was departing for Europe to take part in the Versailles Peace Conference. A vigorous plea from the American president calmed the atmosphere, and five years later Wilson's successor was asked to decide whether, after thirty years, the plebiscite should still be held. The request was granted; a decision was handed down by President Coolidge in favor of a plebiscite, and the arbiter, contrary to precedent in such matters, undertook to assist in the execution of his decision. The outcome is well known. Two army officers of the United States were sent, one after the other, to help supervise the plebiscite, but the army officers came home, one after the other, and no plebiscite was held. The United States lost prestige and the ultimate solution of the problem was probably rendered more difficult.

The recent suggestion of Secretary of State Kellogg—that the disputed provinces be turned over to Bolivia in return for a compensation to be divided between Chile and Peru—has been accepted by Bolivia and by Chile, with reservations, but not by Peru. Whether the suggestion would have had a better reception had President Coolidge decided at the outset that the plebiscite was inadvisable, it is difficult to say. It seems clear, however, that neither the earlier nor the later participation of the United States has promoted harmony, and at present there is in Latin America a tendency both to criticise our methods and to question our motives. It has been suggested, for instance, that Kellogg's recent proposal was motivated by a selfish purpose. The enormous investments of citizens of the United States in Bolivia would be enhanced by Bolivia's acquisition of the disputed area, another Yankee loan would be necessary to pay for it, and the port of Arica, free or in the hands of Bolivia, would be an easy prize for the United States imperialists who have shown themselves so eager to strengthen their power in the Pacific Ocean! So the problem of Tacna-Arica continues after more than forty years to be one of the most vexing in inter-American relations, and the United States, even if it had been dominated by a vicious purpose, could scarcely have done more to disturb the harmony of South America, for it will probably be impossible to localize another war over Tacna-Arica.[1]

Recent Difficulties with Panama

Panama's recent rejection of the treaty of July 28, 1926, probably represents the culmination of a spirit of opposition to the United States which has been developing in this little republic for more than a decade. While Manuel Ugarte was making his tour of propaganda in 1912 the chief executive of this new nation was reported to have remarked: "The position of Panama grows constantly more difficult; my government cannot establish any real authority. I lack means for carrying out its decisions. I meet with difficulties even in arming the police properly, and they are frequently the victims of mysterious outrages. Persons come from the Canal Zone, assault my police agents, and return with impunity to North American territory. . . . If a political insurrection were to break out tomorrow, . . . I could not suppress it unless the United States authorized me to equip troops and transport them from one division of our territory to another."—"If you [Latin Americans] were only willing [to come to our support!]" "If we [Panamanians] had only known [what we now know we might have acted differently in 1903!]"[2]

Although Panama entered the war against Germany with "promptness and spontaneity" as soon as it received notice of the war declaration of the United States, friction arose four years later when the United States intervened in order to prevent Panama and Costa Rica—both members of the League of Nations—from submitting their boundary dispute to the League. Secretary of State Hughes contended that according to the Panama-Costa Rica treaty of 1915 these Powers had agreed to submit the difficulty to the mediation of the United States. The dispute was settled without the interposition of the League,[3] and Panama thought that the settlement was partial to Costa Rica. A riot which occurred on the isthmus while General

---

[1] This discussion of Tacna-Arica is based mainly upon Henry Clay Evans, *Chile and Its Relations with the United States* (1927), Chs. VIII and XIII. *Cf.* also Harry T. Collings, in *Current History*, March, 1927, p. 877 ff.; New York *Times*, January 17 to February 15, 1927.

[2] Manuel Ugarte, *The Destiny of a Continent* (1925, Rippy, ed.), pp. 146–147.

[3] League of Nations, *Minutes of the Council* (1921), pp. 42, 199, 201.

Pershing was on his way to Tacna and Arica revealed the sentiment of an offended people.[4]

The treaty of July 28 lays upon Panama the obligation of building certain roads, of considering "itself in a state of war in case of any war in which the United States should be a belligerent," and if the United States should consider it "necessary," the Panamanian government is required during such war to "turn over to" the Washington government "the control and operation of wireless and radio communication, aircraft, aviation centers and aerial navigation," as well as "the direction and control of all military operations in any part of the territory of the Republic of Panama." It also grants to the United States, among other things, "the right to expropriate privately owned lands" and "the use, occupation and control in perpetuity of Manzanillo Island . . . and Colon harbor."[5]

The League of Nations expressed the view that the terms of the pact were in conflict with Panama's obligations to that organization, and sharp opposition to the agreement developed in some circles of Panama. The municipal council of Colon condemned the treaty and called upon other municipalities to coöperate in the effort to persuade the national assembly to reject it. Groups opposing the pact declared tag days and distributed tags bearing the inscription: "The nation will force the rejection of a treaty, for the sake of a free Panama." An anonymous letter was sent to members of the National Assembly, threatening death to those who dared vote for the treaty.

There were several objections to the agreement. Some believed that the article requiring Panama to participate in any war in which the United States should become involved would bind that government to supply the United States with troops. It was even reported that peasants were fleeing to the hills to avoid conscription! Others objected to the road-building specifications, on the ground that they would involve an expenditure which the republic could not afford. There was likewise emphatic protest against the economic clauses of the treaty. It was alleged that the trade of Panama was being ruined by smugglers who were introducing goods through the zone and that the treaty failed to establish adequate safeguards against this evil. It was Panama's wish perpetually to close the Canal Zone to foreign trade, but the United States was willing to do so only for a period of twenty years, and even then with a proviso that the stipulation could be cancelled at a year's notice. It was contended that the treaty, as it now stands, would not only result in serious reduction of Panama's revenues, but also sound the death-knell of

[4] This from a reliable confidential source.
[5] C. W. Hackett, in *Current History*, February, 1927, p. 765.

the country's trade. The treaty was also severely criticised in Latin America and Europe.

As a result of the local opposition, the Panamanian assembly passed a resolution (January 26, 1927) indefinitely postponing further consideration of the agreement, and President Chiari expressed a determination to negotiate a pact more favorable to the interests of Panama.[6] Thus a new generation in the little republic at whose birth the United States so conspicuously officiated now reveals a disposition to move at cross purposes with its national godfather.

The Nicaraguan Muddle

In order to understand our present difficulties with Nicaragua it will be necessary to go back at least to the year 1909. At that time the country was under the rule of José Santos Zelaya, a dictator who was hostile to the United States and bent upon the establishment of a Central American Union by a policy of "blood and iron." A revolutionary movement "friendly to American interests" was soon set on foot, apparently with American support. Among the insurgent leaders were Juan J. Estrada, Adolfo Díaz, and Emiliano Chamorro. About two weeks after the revolt started, Zelaya very imprudently executed two American citizens who had joined his enemies and were trying to dynamite one of his troopships. The United States at once broke relations (December 1, 1909) and the dictator's enemies soon drove him from power. The way was then clear for a bit of Dollar Diplomacy. Thomas Dawson, who had had previous experience in the Dominican Republic and in Panama, was sent to Managua to negotiate. In a short time he had secured a pledge from the revolutionary leaders that they would undertake to settle outstanding claims and solicit the good offices of the United States in obtaining a loan. With this understanding and after Estrada had been duly and "unanimously" elected by a constituent assembly, the United States recognized him as the legitimate president of Nicaragua.

But Estrada soon found himself surrounded by almost insuperable difficulties. His course antagonized "practically all of the Central American republics" and "the natural sentiment of an overwhelming majority of Nicaraguans" was "antagonistic to the United States." Even some of the members of his cabinet were suspicious of the deal. Accordingly, it was not many weeks before he gave up the task and left the government in the hands of Vice-President Adolfo Díaz. From the summer of 1911 until near the close of the year 1923 Díaz and

[6] Hackett, in *Current History*, March, 1927, p. 920; *The Literary Digest*, March 12, 1927, p. 16.

two members of the Chamorro family were maintained in power, against the wishes of the population, by a detachment of American marines and the occasional appearance of American war vessels. Grateful for such support, these "statesmen" granted the United States more than the American Senate was willing to accept. On June 6, 1911, Díaz agreed to a convention providing for a loan of $15,000,-000 to Nicaragua, secured by the national customs receipts. This the Senate refused to ratify. Nevertheless, Díaz managed to secure smaller sums from American bankers in return for a pledge of the railways of the country, the control of the customs, and a permit for the establishment of a national bank. In 1913 another treaty was negotiated, which gave the United States the exclusive right to construct a canal across Nicaraguan territory, the privilege of establishing a naval base on the Gulf of Fonseca, and a ninety-nine-year lease on the Great Corn and the Little Corn Islands. It also contained provisions for an American protectorate under a kind of Platt Amendment. For all this the United States was to pay $3,000,000. After considerable delay the United States Senate accepted the canal and naval-base concessions, but rejected the "protector plan." Strategy diplomacy had been more successful than dollar diplomacy, but the two were closely allied.

In 1924 there occurred in Nicaragua one of the few fair elections in the annals of the country. It was held under a new law drafted by H. W. Dodds, an American expert. A coalition of the Conservative and Liberal parties named Carlos Solorzano as candidate for president and Juan B. Sacasa for vice-president. Emiliano Chamorro ran for the presidency on an independent ticket. The coalition candidates were elected by an overwhelming majority and the new president and vice-president took office on January 1, 1925. On August 3, following, the United States marines were withdrawn. A few weeks later the Chamorro-Díaz faction took the field and by the middle of November, 1926, Adolfo Díaz, erstwhile clerk of an American corporation and enemy of Zelaya and twice president of the republic, was once more in power. Just three days after his inauguration the United States extended recognition and before the close of the year our marines were again upon Nicaraguan soil.

The Coolidge administration has given various reasons for their return: the lives and property of American citizens were threatened; Nicaragua must be compelled to abide by the Central American treaties of 1923 which bind the nation to recognize only legitimate presidents; European Powers had called upon the United States to protect their nationals; and debarkation of marines was necessary in order to prevent Russian Bolshevism, sponsored by the Calles government of Mexico, from driving a Red wedge between the United States and the Panama Canal; the canal rights of the United States in Nicaragua had to be safeguarded—such were the motives gradually disclosed to a somewhat suspicious public. Critics of the administration arrived at other motives by inference. They alleged that the marines were landed not merely to protect but to promote the business interests of the United States. They are expecting more treaties providing for other loans and strategic concessions. Some even suspected that Coolidge and Kellogg were attempting to bluff Mexico into compliance with their demands or seeking a pretext for a break with the Calles government and the occupation of the oil zones. Meanwhile the President of the United States persists in his policy, augmenting the marines and multiplying the neutral zones in Nicaragua, and his supporters, writing in the most widely read journals of the nation, are coming boldly and profusely to his defense, while Britain strengthens his hand by sending a war vessel to the scene and concentrating attention upon the Monroe Doctrine, elastically interpreted.[7]

The Mexican Problem

The present Mexican tangle has three important aspects. One of them is legal; the other two involve considerations of equity, humanitarianism, and national policy.

Citizens of the United States have certain legal rights south of the Rio Grande. National sovereignty in Mexico is limited to the extent that it is not permitted to expropriate the legitimate property of foreigners without fair compensation. There are at least four respects in which the organic and statutory laws of Mexico affect the property rights of American citizens:

1. Foreigners are forbidden to own lands within certain maritime and frontier zones. Individuals and companies who possess such property must dispose of it within a limited period or become Mexican citizens. Individuals may continue to hold the lands until death, and their heirs have five years in which to dispose of them; corporations may remain in possession until their dissolution. In both in-

[7] U. S., *Foreign Relations* (1909–1916), index under "Nicaragua"; Foreign Policy Association, *Information Service*, Vol. II (1927), No. 24; Graham Stuart, *Latin America and the United States* (1922), p. 262 ff.; J. H. Latané, *The United States and Latin America* (1920), p. 280 ff.; *Current History*, January, February, and March, 1927 (articles by C. W. Hackett); New York *Times* and *United States Daily*, January 5 to February 5, 1927; *Cong. Record*, same period.

stances the value of the possessions will be reduced for the simple reason that the sale must be limited to Mexicans.

2. Aliens are not permitted to own more than fifty per cent of the stock of companies possessing agricultural lands in any part of the Mexican republic. Alien corporations must rid themselves of the excess within ten years; heirs must dispose of the excess stock which they inherit within five years. Once more the value of the holdings would be adversely affected because the market would be limited to Mexicans or non-American aliens.

3. The Mexican government is expropriating some of the lands of foreigners in carrying out its agrarian reforms. Since cash is not available, these lands are being purchased with 20-year bonds bearing interest at the rate of 5 per cent. Moreover, the properties so taken are valued as for purposes of taxation, plus 10 per cent. Hence the foreigner is being paid far less than the actual worth of his lands and, even then, not in cash but in bonds of uncertain value.

4. According to the recent organic and statutory laws of Mexico, ownership of the surface of the land does not include ownership of oil beneath the surface, as had been the case between 1884 and 1917. Those who, during this thirty-three-year period, acquired lands by title or the use of lands on long-term leases are placed into two classifications: (1) owners or lessees who paid extraordinarily high prices for their lands or who, prior to May 1, 1917, performed some positive act indicating that they expected to find petroleum, are compelled to exchange their titles or leases for a concession lasting fifty years, with the possibility of renewal; (2) owners or lessees who did not pay such a price or had not taken any positive step to develop oil prior to May 1, 1917, are to be given preferential consideration, but their titles and leases are not recognized. These provisions affect the status of the property of 380 companies and all but some 22 companies have accepted the laws. The titles of the conforming companies embrace 26,833,335 acres; the titles of the protesting corporations include 1,660,579 acres, or about 6 per cent of the entire area. But the non-conformers produced more than 75 per cent of the oil extracted from Mexico in 1926. Companies of the United States are conspicuous among those protesting. They own or hold under lease 87 per cent of the lands of the non-conforming group and produce (1926) about 58 per cent of Mexico's oil. The most important of the protesting companies of the United States are the old Doheny companies, the Sinclair corporations, and the Mellon interests.[8]

[8] On this section, consult C. W. Hackett, *The Mexican Revolution and the*

Thus it will be seen that American landowners and oil men are suffering, or are about to suffer, property losses in Mexico. In some instances the procedure of the Mexican government, if persisted in, may be tantamount to confiscation. So much for the legal phase of the problem.

What of its other aspects? From the standpoint of equity and human welfare the issue may be baldly stated as that of "vested interests" of foreigners versus, if not the birthright, then at least the reform program of a backward people. In the development of nations and groups, crises sometimes arise when there are more important considerations than legal rights of opulent individuals and companies. Confiscation is difficult to define in view of the wide exercise of police power by modern states. Considerations of equity and humanity as applied to *millions* of people may outweigh the legal rights, not infrequently acquired in the first instance by shady transactions, of a *few thousand* individuals whose existence and happiness would not be seriously threatened by the partial loss of these rights.

Only in the last decade or so have the interests and welfare of the Mexican masses been taken into consideration. Calles and his colleagues are endeavoring to carry out significant economic and social reforms in the interest of the entire nation.[9] During the régime of Díaz the wealth of Mexico passed into the hands of foreigners. These foreigners have conferred incidental and accidental benefits upon the Mexicans, but they have never considered this their main business. To-day aliens own much more of the natural resources and other wealth of Mexico than do the Mexicans themselves. Should legal barriers, erected often by corrupt and tyrannical rulers without the consent of the nation, be permitted to stand in the way of the ultimate recovery of the heritage of the Mexican masses?

Mexico's stability and prosperity in the future may depend upon the creation of numerous small, independent landowners and the return of the lands to the Indian villages. Mexico possesses arable lands in limited quantity, about one-fourth of its area being of this description. Americans and other foreigners own or control millons of acres of this land. If we should insist upon and obtain the right of permanently retaining all of our holdings, other foreigners would secure the same right under the most-favored-nation principle. Mexican landholders would then be left in an inferior position and this

United States (1926); *Cong. Rec.,* March 3, 1927, p. 5583; New York *Times* and New York *Sun,* March 1 and 2, 1927.

[9] For a convenient statement of these reforms, see Alva Taylor Good Will Commission, *Mexico 1926;* Moises Sáenz and Herbert I. Priestley, *Some Mexican Problems* (1926).

would lead to revolution and possibly to the defeat of the whole agrarian program.

Mexico's future prosperity will also depend upon the conservation of her fuel and water. The country has not yet reached the industrial stage. When it does, oil, gas, and water power will be needed. The Mexican nation is not using its petroleum. It is being consumed by foreigners; only about four or five per cent being used in Mexico. The United States burns most of it; Britain consumes nearly all of the rest.

Confronted with this clash, apparent or real, between the vested interests of our nationals and the Mexican reform movement, the United States government has employed all the resources of diplomacy in defense of the property rights of its citizens. Protests, remonstrances, even threats have been resorted to—and still Calles pursues his policies. Apparently President Coolidge has reconciled himself to the positive act doctrine in reference to the oil lands, as well as to the Mexican method of payment for lands expropriated in the process of restoring the community holdings to the Indian villages. Should he eventually accept Calles's whole program of reform?

Important questions of policy are involved. (1) Will the European nations and Japan insist upon interference in behalf of their subjects and violate the Monroe Doctrine in case the United States further recedes? It may be seriously doubted whether thy would run counter to our desires in the Western Hemisphere. Indeed, the European oil companies apparently have been more disposed than our own to conform to Mexican law.

(2) Can our government afford to allow Mexico to carry out measures injurious to our property interests—measures which may constitute at once a precedent and an incentive for similar procedure in other states of Latin America, where we have three billion dollars' worth of property at stake and Europeans and Asiatics are involved to an equal or greater amount? Before answering this question in the negative it would be advisable to consider what steps can be taken and where they might ultimately lead.

Withdrawal of recognition from Calles and the lifting of the embargo on the shipment of arms into Mexico, which have been much discussed in the press, would probably be more destructive to our interests than oil and land laws. It may well be doubted whether the revolt, or series of revolts, to which this policy would lead would result in the establishment of a government more friendly to our investors. The ability of such a government to maintain itself in power in the face of Mexican public sentiment is open to serious question.

If these steps should fail to bring Mexico to terms, or if Calles should have the ability to defy us and our non-recognition and maintain order, the next step in a more drastic policy would be armed coercion. Our property in Mexico is worth more than a billion dollars. Mexican legislation threatens only a small per cent of the total, but even if it all should ultimately be involved, it should be remembered that a billion is soon spent in war. Moreover, all Latin America is likely to be deeply offended by the coercion of Mexico. Such coercion would probably occasion injury to our economic and also our strategic interests in those countries. Would the logic of our policy then demand the application of similar drastic measures to them? If so, we should become involved in no end of trouble.

Lovers of harmony will doubtless hope that none of these unpleasant prospects confronts us. Mexico has indicated a willingness to arbitrate and the Senate of the United States has demanded arbitration. Perhaps this policy is more in accord with our national ideals, and it may prove just as profitable in the end. For will not the Mexican program of reform raise Mexican standards of living, create new tastes—even a demand for gasoline and other petroleum products, and Ford cars—augment land values, and increase the purchasing power of the Mexican people generally? If so, all of our relations will become more profitable and even our oil men and landowners, temporarily losers, will profit in the long run.

One of the most difficult problems of our age is that of dealing with situations which arise when *local* laws and movements involving a desire for political and social betterment conflict with vested foreign economic rights. Will the United States make any contribution to its solution? Or shall we permit our statesmen to function as Czars and Metternichs opposing for economic reasons the growing nationalism and liberalism of the twentieth century?

Such are some of the specific problems which are now confronted in inter-American relations. And back of them all is the sentiment of suspicion and antipathy to which reference has already been made. Until it is removed old problems will be difficult to solve and new perplexities will continue to arise.

Causes of Latin-American Suspicion and Hostility

This suspicion and antipathy is not wholly due to the aggressiveness which has characterized the energetic people of the United States. Not our acts alone, but the interpretation of these acts by Frenchmen, Spaniards, Germans, and at times also by Englishmen, together with the traditional attitude of suspicion south of the Rio

Grande, have been responsible for the apprehensions and hostility of the people of Latin America. In order to understand the anti-Yankee sentiment which has been so prevalent in the South it will be necessary to keep in mind racial and religious diversities and insurgent nationalism, as well as a certain exclusiveness and intolerance inherited from the Spanish régime. It will also be necessary to recall the hostile criticisms of the French and the Spanish—the intellectual leaders of Hispanic America—the propaganda of the Germans, and the severe comments which have sometimes come from the British press.

For Latin America's attitude toward us, then, we are not entirely to blame, but it cannot be said that our course has been faultless. We have been aggressive and sometimes haughty. It is in vain that we plead our innocence of imperialism. Our whole history gives the lie to such a plea, unless one wishes to quibble over the meaning of the term "imperialism!" The fact is that our boundaries are vastly more extensive than they were in 1783 and that most of our territory has been acquired at the expense of Spanish America. Nor can the historical fact that our control has been extending rapidly into the Caribbean successfully be controverted. A policy which has brought under our virtual domination some nine to twelve republics in a generation may differ from European imperialism in form but it is very near that imperialism in substance.

A benevolent argument has been advanced for our course, both for our earlier territorial and our later political and economic expansion. There is no imperialism without its benevolent argument! We have saved the people of the Caribbean from Europe and given them prosperity, order, sanitation, progress. But Europe naturally resents our presumption of superiority and refuses to believe in our sterling altruism; the Latin Americans are inclined to think that Europe, having suffered a change of heart since 1920, is a better friend than we; and we thus find ourselves in the embarrassing position of shielding the peoples to the south from a peril which they refuse to recognize and uplifting them against their will. We may enter the plea of benevolence, but neither Europeans nor Latin Americans are inclined to accept it. Our policy is benevolent in no eye but our own, and perhaps we are not the best judges of its nature.

Perils of Our Position

The dangers of our position are probably remote rather than immediate. There is nothing in the present state of affairs calculated to frighten the United States into a speedy change of policy. The influence of sentiment upon international trade is difficult to determine. Embargoes and non-intercourse acts are not unknown in history, but their general effectiveness is an uncertain quantity. The trade of the United States with Latin America has slightly diminished since the World War, but the decline may not have any connection with popular attitudes. Whatever may happen in the near future, no general disposition to put us on the black list has yet appeared. Popular hostility might conceivably affect the investment opportunities of United States citizens, particularly where so many of them depend upon government loans and concessions, but economic and political pressure, chicanery, military force, and the corruptibility of Latin-American politicians are effective weapons in defeating popular will in the backward states, at least temporarily. Our investments may confront greater peril in the progressive states where such tactics are not so readily employed.

If hard pressed, the Latins of America would be disposed to seek the aid of those European nations against whom we have talked of defending them. The attitude of the Europeans in face of such an appeal may be judged from what has been set forth in previous chapters. There are the Pan-Hispanic aspirations of Spain, the cultural affinity, the sentimental predisposition, economic rivalry, and melancholy rankling of France, the economic competition of England and Germany, and possibly Italy's interest in its trade and its millions of sons who have gone out to Brazil, Uruguay, and Argentina. All these powers would be vitally concerned, but, in view of complicated conditions in Europe and of their many interests elsewhere, it would probably be futile for the Latin Americans to rely upon their aid to counterbalance the expanding influence of the United States. Their support might be a possibility in the future, if ever Continental harmony should be reached in both the economic and the political spheres. Economic unity and a successful League of Nations might enable the Europeans to take the United States in hand. But this is only a distant prospect. Even the Latin-American nations, which at first evinced great enthusiasm for the League, have more recently lost something of their ardor. Argentina has withdrawn, Brazil has withdrawn, Peru, Bolivia, and Costa Rica have withdrawn. Ecuador and Mexico have never belonged.[10] The most populous of the Latin-American countries are therefore outside of the League, and the prospect of playing the United States against this organization is more remote than ever.

[10] *Current History* (February, 1927), p. 706.

Then there is the possibility of Japanese support which has not failed to enter the minds of certain Latin-American Yankeephobes, as we have already seen. But there is probably no occasion for immediate alarm even here. The Latin Americans are not devoid of fear of Japan, as is witnessed by García Calderón's chapter on the "Japanese Peril" (1910), by alarms confidentially expressed by Chilean diplomats (1916),[11] and, perhaps also, by the already-mentioned tendency toward Japanese exclusion on the part of some of the Spanish-American states. Nor would Japan lightly enter a league against the United States in the Western Hemisphere. Only under extreme provocation, such as a persistent attempt of the United States to oppose Japanese interests in the Far East while pursuing a policy of Japanese exclusion throughout the New World, would Japan be likely to consider seriously a combination of this sort.

Lastly, there is the possibility, though not the probability, of the formation of a Latin-American Union against the Colossus of the North. This is the dream of every Yankeephobe, many literary men, and some statesmen south of the United States. It is likewise the counsel of Frenchmen and Spaniards, and the ideal of unity has long been cherished by Latin-American heroes of the past. But in the way of its realization there have been, and are, almost insuperable obstacles. Many a Latin-American congress has been convened for the purpose of promoting unity, but few results have been forthcoming. Although many boundary disputes, which formally have been a fruitful cause of strife, have been disposed of, others still remain. The Tacna-Arica problem in particular—thanks in part to our bungling diplomacy of an earlier period and our ineffective diplomacy of the present—is still unsettled, and the attempt of the A B C powers to reach an armament agreement in 1923 proved a fiasco. Moreover, in view of the great disparity of progress and the varieties of race in these countries, such a league hardly seems practicable. There are turbulent and stable, backward and progressive, states. There are nations where the Indian element predominates, as in Mexico, Peru, Bolivia, and Paraguay; nations mostly mestizo, like Venezuela and Colombia; nations where the negro and negroid strains constitute the majority, such as in Haiti, Brazil, and the Dominican Republic; and republics predominantly white, as is the case with Argentina, Uruguay, and Chile. Race and class friction within these states themselves does not give fair promise of a larger international harmony and alliance.

[11] Seymour, *Intimate Papers of Colonial House* (1926), I, 227.

The Rôle of Public Opinion in the United States

Thus the means at hand for the immediate defense of the Indo-Hispanic peoples of America against the United States are scanty. A brilliant economist recently remarked: "The only protection against Yankee Imperialism which the Latin Americans have is public opinion in the United States, and I am not disposed to congratulate them on their protection." The first part of this statement is almost literally true, but with reference to the latter portion there appears to be some ground for disagreement. The stream separating divergent interests in the United States cuts deep and a potent current of idealism runs through the national conscience. The conflicting interests of rival groups and opposing ideals of policy have frequently held aggressive forces in check, and they will probably do so again.

Nothing could more strikingly illustrate this fact than our recent relations with Mexico and Nicaragua. The two countries are closely associated in American policy. The administration, pushed hard by the oil men and other interests, has been inclined to adopt drastic measures. Marines have been landed in Nicaragua for the alleged purpose of protecting American and European properties, defending a canal route, and counteracting Bolshevism and Mexican radicalism. Actually, the debarkation of American forces and the supply of arms to the troops of Adolfo Díaz, while withholding them from his opponents, has been tantamount to supporting this tool of American Big Business against Juan B. Sacasa, apparently an intelligent, high-minded liberal and an exponent of Nicaraguan nationalism. This procedure on the part of the Coolidge administration and the reasons advanced for it, together with the concentration of detachments of the navy at San Diego, California, and in the Caribbean, tended to provoke a crisis in our Mexican relations. The tendency of these acts and published statements was, in fact, to coerce the Calles government of Mexico, and encourage revolution in the neighboring country. Moreover, they might conceivably have led to an open break and the landing of marines in the oil zones.

But public sentiment in the United States began at once to reveal its strength. Almost all of the leading Southern newspapers and many of those of the West protested vigorously. Such great national journals as the New York *World* and the New York *Times* published editorial criticism of Coolidge and Kellogg and printed world opinion opposed to our policy. President William Green of the American Federation of Labor raised his voice against the idea that Mexican labor was Bolshevist. Churches and peace organizations mobilized their memberships speedily and effectively. Many democrats, par-

THE ZONES OF FRICTION IN
SOUTH AMERICA

1. THE GRAN CHACO.
2. TACNA-ARICA, TARAPACA, ANTOFOGASTA.
3. JUNCTION OF ECUADOR, COLOMBIA AND PERU
4, 5, 6. MINOR DISPUTED AREAS IN THE COL-
OMBIA–VENEZUELA FRONTIER

THERE IS ALSO A DISPUTE OVER THE BOUND-
ARY IN THE LA PLATA ESTUARY

ticularly in the South, criticised the administration for partisan and other reasons. Senator Heflin of Alabama showed that certain powerful elements of the Catholic Church favored a drastic Mexican policy, possibly with the view, as some alleged, of courting the favor of Alabama Klansmen. Senators Borah, La Follette, and Wheeler took a masterful stand in the Senate. Kellogg and Coolidge, Brisbane and Hearst, producers of oil, bananas, and mahogany, and the Knights of Columbus were held in check, and perhaps even routed. Arbitration of the Mexican issues was unanimously demanded by the Senate and this body may soon call for the withdrawal of the marines from Nicaragua. Latin-America's protection may prove efficacious in this instance. Conflicting groups and ideals are still a factor to be reckoned with in the United States.[12]

A Constructive Policy Needed

What is needed in inter-American relations, however, is a constructive policy. This hand-to-mouth restraint is not likely to get us anywhere and it may create grave dangers for the future. Are there any sources of pressure which may be depended upon to force our national government more definitely from the path of semi-imperialistic opportunism? Perhaps so. Never before in the history of the country has there been such eager interest in the foreign relations of the United States. Organizations for the study of foreign policy are springing up in every institution of learning and in every city which makes any pretense to culture. The people of the United States have not lost their deep sympathy for struggling peoples of whatever race or social status, nor have they lost that "decent respect for the opinions of mankind" which led them to declare their reasons for taking up arms in 1776. More or less remote economic and political dangers, which may arise from the procedure of the last generation in Latin America, and the value of Latin-American friendship in time of crisis (so definitely revealed during the recent World War) may not be sufficient to demand a change, but perhaps there is less reason to doubt the efficacy of democratic enthusiasm and a high regard for the good-will of the civilized world.

To willing statesmen the way which leads to Latin-American cordiality ought to be plain, although it is perhaps beset with difficulties.

[12] This view of recent Mexican and Nicaraguan relations is based upon the following sources: The New York *Times*, the New York *World*, *The Christian Science Monitor*, January 1 to 30, 1927; the Durham *Herald*, Greensboro *Daily News*, Raleigh *News and Observer*, and Nashville *Tennesseean* for the same period; *Congressional Record*, January 8 to 26, 1927.

Statesmen and publicists of the Latin South have frequently and clearly stated their demands.—They desire some assurance that we shall not use our wealth and power to exploit them; they desire to be called into council and allowed to participate in all matters which relate to American affairs; they desire to be consulted in the formulation of American policy toward non-American nations. To be more concrete in regard to the Western Hemisphere: they wish to be consulted in the establishment and administration of protectorates in the more turbulent and backward states; they are eager to have us declare that our national state will not back our masters of finance and captains of industry who are engaged in the conquest and development of the natural resources and finances of Latin America; they demand the right to regulate and control the development of their own national wealth. In brief, they would have us renounce our economic imperialism and Pan-Americanize the Monroe Doctrine.

Their readiness to respond to any concessions along these lines was demonstrated during the Wilson régime. He made the correction of Latin-American attitude one of the first concerns of his administration. Concerning the peoples to the south, he said: "They have had harder bargains driven with them in the matter of loans than any other peoples of the world. Interest has been exacted of them that was not exacted of anybody else, because the risk was said to be greater; and then securities were taken that destroyed the risk—an admirable arrangement for those who were forcing the terms." He did not propose to give any official countenance to this economic imperialism. Nor would the United States, under his administration, "seek one additional foot of territory by conquest." He even went so far as to offer to sign a mutual and reciprocal guaranty of the territorial integrity and national independence of the American states. Lastly, he took counsel of some of the Latin-American diplomats with reference to Mexico and became the champion of self-definition and the rights of small nations during the World War. In this way he gradually recovered the confidence of our southern neighbors. They proclaimed Wilson to be "the loftiest summit in the scenery of this dramatic hour of the world," and even a "Galilean" and "modern redeemer of humanity." There were some who did not appreciate his Mexican policy or his inconsistencies in the Caribbean. There were likewise a few, perhaps with imperialist ambitions of their own, who were unwilling to sign his Pan-American pact. But in general he was trusted and praised.[13]

[13] The sources supporting the assertions of this and the preceding paragraph are too numerous for citation here. See Ugarte, *The Destiny of a Continent*, Editorial Introduction and Bibliography.

The attitude of Hispanic-American leaders toward the policies of our more recent administrations constitutes just as clear a revelation of what they fear. The insistence of the United States Senate upon the incorporation of the Monroe Doctrine into the League Covenant alarmed them. Article X of this covenant guaranteed the territorial integrity and the national independence of the signatory powers. They maintained that such a guaranty was also the very essence of the Monroe Doctrine, rightly interpreted. The League of Nations would merely seek to extend this principle to the whole world. Then why should the Senate demand express mention of Monroe's manifesto in the League constitution? Men of Latin America feared that it was because the interest of the United States in the Latin-Americans did not end with this guaranty. Perhaps the Monroe Doctrine was designed to protect them from Europe in order that, in due time, they might be dominated and exploited by the United States. The failure of the United States to join the League tended to confirm this view. The "North Americans" refused to coöperate in the establishment of an international organization and they were preparing to seize the lion's share in the colossal nationalist scramble which was bound to follow if the League that they declined to enter failed to function.[14]

Similar in tendency were our procedure at the Santiago Congress (1923) and our more recent activities in the Caribbean. At Santiago, Chile, Latin-American diplomats attempted to discover the disposition and purposes of their Yankee neighbors. Would they object to a modification or definition of the Monroe Doctrine, a pledge not to encroach upon their southern neighbors, and such a reorganization of the Pan-American Union as would prevent it from resembling the British Colonial Office? An attempt to secure commitments on these issues was the leading feature of the assembly and the result was a disappointment to the Iberians of America. Minor changes in the organization of the Union were agreed upon, but the Washington delegates refused either to define or to Pan-Americanize the Monroe Doctrine and showed little interest in a proposal to establish an American League of Nations providing a pledge of territorial integrity and national independence for every American state.[15] So far as the policy of the United States was concerned, Wilson appeared indeed but a voice crying in the wilderness with no one to follow him.

[14] Ugarte, *op. cit.*, Editorial Introduction.
[15] New York *Times,* April 10 to May 12; Samuel Guy Inman, "Pan-American Conferences and their Results," in *The Southwestern Political Science Quarterly, IV* (1923), 239 ff.; J. Warshaw, "The Fifth Pan-American Congress," in *ibid.,* III, 323 ff.

And if our aggressiveness required more emphasis, this was given by the landing of marines in Nicaragua and the scolding of Mexico.

Thus the Latin Americans are demanding a modification in our policy. Should we satisfy them? Only the laborers, the common people, the churchmen, the idealists and democratic enthusiasts, and those who are sensitive to world opinion can decide this. Few of the large bankers and industrial *entepreneurs* are likely to insist upon a change. Can we afford to meet the demands of the Latin-American peoples? The question involves (1) the problem of the European attitude toward Latin America, (2) the safety of our investments, and (3) the political and economic capacity of certain of the little nations to the south.

Can we prevent Europe from intervening in Latin America without intervening ourselves? In view of present conditions across the Atlantic, it would seem so. If measures of prevention must be adopted, would it not be well to invite the coöperation of the more orderly sisters of the turbulent Latin-American states? This probably would tend to relieve our procedure of the suspicion of self-interest.

Should our "vested interests" be left largely to their own devices and told to shift for themselves? If such a policy deprived the Latin-American field of some of its attractions, perhaps the flow of capital could be turned to our own Far West and South without serious harm. Moreover, popular irritation in regions beyond the Rio Grande might render more energetic measures expensive and cause them to fail in the end. It is a fearful thing to attempt to suppress entire nations of people. At any rate, if the national government must protect these investors, should it not demand also the right to exercise a sort of supervision over their acts? [16]

If the more disorderly and backward nations of the Caribbean were left to themselves and the moral coöperation of the more advanced peoples of Europe and America, would they soon achieve order and progress? Or would it be better to force our views and tutelage upon them and occasionally even shoot the progressive and orderly spirit into them with machine guns?

All these are questions which the people of the United States should decide with proper care and caution. Meanwhile the little countries to the south ought to realize that the Great Powers of the world are very intolerant toward petty, chronic disorders in regions rich in the resources which these Powers so eagerly desire and that their pro-

---

[16] Hitherto the United States government has evinced only a slight disposition to supervise foreign loans. *Cf.* W. S. Culbertson, *International Economic Policies* (1925), pp. 373-374, 499.

grams of reform followed by their orgies of graft are likely to deprive them of the support of public opinion in the United States, their best means of defense until world conditions change. Moreover, both justice and prudence would seem to demand that Latin Americans read with due caution the bitter criticisms of Yankee policy which are often circulated by European journalists with the ulterior view of advancing their own interests at the expense of the United States and of Pan-American harmony.

INDEX

Aberdeen, Lord, 92-5.

Acadia, 6.

Adams, John, 13; John Quincy, 46, 53, 57, 70, 86, 196; Samuel, 28.

Africa, 1, 15, 115, 151.

Agents, British, 60, 61, 64, 66, 69, 71, 73, 92, 94, 96, 97, 99, 101; European, 14; French, 18; Napoleon's, 30, 36; Mexican, 68, 105; Texan, 92-3; United States, 38, 43, 60-1, 71, 100-1, 254.

Aggression, Anglo-American, 250; British, 115; French, 16, 126-41; United States, 70, 89, 111, 122, 132-3, 200, 264-5, 272.

Agreements, 173; United States and Spain, 17; Anglo-German, 176; Japanese-Mexican, 231.

Aguinaldo, 166.

Aix-la-Chapelle, Congress of, 42.

Alamán, Lucas, 69.

Alaska, 8, 47, 122, 198.

Alexander, Czar, 48-50.

Alfonso XIII, 218.

Algeciras, treaty of, 211.

All-deutsche Blätter, 147.

Alleghenies, 13, 15, 18.

Alliance, Anglo-American, 149, 180; Anglo-German, 168, 183-5, 188-9, 196; Britain and Latin America, 25; European, 49; Franco-Spanish, 17-18; German-Mexican, 154-5; Germany, Mexico and Japan, 232; Hispanic powers, 201; Neo-Holy, 37, 45-7, 54, 59, 86; possible Japanese, 229; quadruple, 31-3; Spain and former colonies, 62, 200; triple, 158.

Alliances, U. S. attitude toward, 12; entangling, 58, 63.

Allies, diplomatic, 42; Latin Americans as, 130; World War, 153, 237.

Altamira y Crevea, Rafael, 208, 210, 217.

Álvarez, Juan, 252.

Aleutian Islands, 8.

Ambitions, British, 15, 35, 65, 72-3, 173, 176; European, 19; German, 147, 170, 196, 198-9; Napoleon's, 36, 44; Portuguese, 1-9; Russian, 47; Spanish, 1-9, 10, 216-18; United States, 18, 56, 62, 72-3, 80, 85, 88, 140.

Amelia Island, 21.

America, early partition of, 1-9. *See* Central America. Also United States of America.

American Gospel, 202.

American Review of Reviews, 115.

American Post-War Program, 210.

Anglophobia, 202.

Anglo-Saxon relations, 10-23, 54-125, 196.

Antilles, The, 6, 127, 130, 205, 213.

Anti-Japanese feeling, 227-9.

Aranda, Count of, 13.

Arbiter, Roosevelt as, 188, 191-2.

Arbitration, Cuba, 156-63; Mexican issue, 269; League of Nations, 240; Spain and colonies, 221; Tacna-Arica, 254-5; Venezuela, 113, 121, 147, 183-8, 193-7; principle of, 236. *See* also Mediation.

Argentina, 58-9, 205, 208, 267; Germans in, 142, 148; Japan, 224, 227-8; Italians, 223-4, 266; League of Nations, 236, 240-1, 266; Pan-Hispanism, 213, 215, 218, 220-2; World War, 236; Yankeephobia, 251, 253.

Arica. *See* Tacna-Arica.

Armada, destruction of, 6.

Armenia, 119.

Arthuys, Pierre, 137-8.

Article X, of League of Nations Covenant, 239; XXX, 271.

Asia, 15, 115, 149.

Aspirations, 4. *See* Ambitions.

Assembly, of League of Nations, 238, 240-1.

275

A NOTE ON THE TYPE IN
WHICH THIS BOOK IS SET

The type in which this book has been set is based on the design of William Caslon (1692–1766), who brought the old-style letter to its highest perfection. While certain modifications have been introduced to meet changing printing conditions, the basic design of the Caslon letters has never been improved. The type selected for this book is a modern adaptation rather than an exact copy of the original Caslon.

SET UP, ELECTROTYPED AND PRINTED BY THE VAIL-BALLOU PRESS, INC., BINGHAMTON, N. Y. BOUND BY H. WOLFF ESTATE, NEW YORK · PAPER MANUFACTURED BY S. D. WARREN COMPANY, BOSTON, MASS., AND FURNISHED BY HENRY LINDENMEYR & SONS, NEW YORK.